Mediation, Remediation, and the Dynam

Mediation, Remediation, and the Dynamics of Cultural Memory

Edited by
Astrid Erll · Ann Rigney

in collaboration with
Laura Basu and Paulus Bijl

De Gruyter

This book first appeared as a hardback volume
in the De Gruyter series "Media and Cultural Memory"

ISBN 978-3-11-028396-9

Library of Congress Cataloging-in-Publication Data

A CIP catalog record for this book has been applied for at the Library of Congress.

Bibliographic information published by the Deutsche Nationalbibliothek

The Deutsche Nationalbibliothek lists this publication in the Deutsche
Nationalbibliografie; detailed bibliographic data are available in the Internet
at http://dnb.dnb.de.

© 2012 Walter de Gruyter GmbH & Co. KG, Berlin/Boston

Printing: Hubert & Co. GmbH & Co. KG, Göttingen

∞ Printed on acid-free paper

Printed in Germany

www.degruyter.com

Acknowledgements

This collection of essays emerged from a symposium on "Media and the Dynamics of Cultural Memory" held at the University of Giessen in September 2007. The symposium was hosted by the Giessen International Graduate Centre for the Study of Culture (GCSC) in collaboration with the research group "The Dynamics of Cultural Remembrance: An Intermedial Perspective" (Research Institute for History and Culture, Utrecht).

Many people were involved in making the symposium a worthwhile experience and in the publication of the present volume. Our heartfelt thanks go to Ansgar Nünning, director of the GCSC, for hosting this event; to Anna-Lena Flügel, Meike Hölscher and Jan Rupp, who took care of the organisation; to Paulus Bijl and Laura Basu for their highly valuable help in the editing and formatting of the text; to Sara B. Young for additional help in linguistic matters; and to Franziska Springstubbe for making the index. We gratefully acknowledge the financial assistance of the Netherlands Organisation for Scientific Research (NWO) and the Giessen International Graduate Centre for the Study of Culture, funded by the German federal government's Excellence Initiative.

Wuppertal and Utrecht, April 2009
Astrid Erll and Ann Rigney

Table of Contents

III. The Public Arena

Introduction:
Cultural Memory and its Dynamics

ASTRID ERLL and ANN RIGNEY

In his pioneering work *La mémoire collective* (1950), Maurice Halbwachs illustrated the social dimensions of individual memory by invoking the case of someone's first visit to London: the experience of the city, and hence the long-term memory of that experience, would be shaped by the various descriptions of the British capital that the visitor had heard beforehand from friends or read in books (53). This passage provides one of the few references in Halbwachs' work to the role of media in the formation of collective memory, his main emphasis being on the ways in which individual memory is moulded by the specifically social frameworks in which it operates. But his telling invocation of the influence of Dickens and other accounts of London on memories of the city is indicative of something that he himself did not discuss at great length, but of which he was apparently quite aware: the fact that "media" of all sorts—spoken language, letters, books, photos, films—also provide frameworks for shaping both experience and memory. They do so in at least two, interconnected ways: as instruments for sense-making, they mediate between the individual and the world; as agents of networking, they mediate between individuals and groups (see Schmidt).

Halbwachs himself may have paid only incidental attention to the role of media in memory-making. But it has recently become one of the central areas of attention in cultural memory studies. Indeed, the very concept of *cultural* memory is itself premised on the idea that memory can only become collective as part of a continuous process whereby memories are shared with the help of symbolic artefacts that mediate between individuals and, in the process, create communality across both space and time. The centrality of media to cultural memory is expressed in the title of the present series and this collection of essays pursues many of the issues already raised in earlier volumes. At the same time, however, it also marks a new step in this discussion by taking a fundamentally *dynamic* approach to the study both of cultural memory and of the media which shape it.

Initial discussions of cultural memory, especially those inspired by the work of Pierre Nora, tended to focus on those canonical "sites of memory" which provide relatively stable points of reference for individuals and communities recalling a shared past. As the field has advanced, however, one can note a shift towards understanding cultural memory in more dynamic terms: as an ongoing process of remembrance and forgetting in which individuals and groups continue to reconfigure their relationship to the past and hence reposition themselves in relation to established and emergent memory sites. As the word itself suggests, "remembering" is better seen as an active engagement with the past, as performative rather than as reproductive. It is as much a matter of acting out a relationship to the past from a particular point in the present as it is a matter of preserving and retrieving earlier stories. It follows from this that canonical "memory sites" themselves have a history and, although they represent in many ways the terminus ad quem of repeated acts of remembrance, they only continue to operate as such as long as people continue to re-invest in them and use them as a point of reference (Rigney, "Plenitude"). If stories about the past are no longer performed in talking, reading, viewing, or commemorative rituals, they ultimately die out in cultural terms, becoming obsolete or "inert" (Olick and Robbins). In the process, they may be replaced or "over-written" by new stories that speak more directly to latter-day concerns and are more relevant to latter-day identity formations (Irwin-Zarecka).

The rise, fall, and marginalization of stories as constitutive parts of the dynamics of remembering have thus emerged as key issues in memory studies. This turn towards memorial dynamics demands among other things new insight into the factors which allow certain collective memories to become hegemonic or, conversely, allow hitherto marginalized memories to gain prominence in the public arena. Fighting about memory is one way of keeping it alive and, as a number of recent studies has shown, the history of cultural memory is marked as much by crises and controversies running along social fault lines as it is by consensus and canon-building (Olick; Suleiman; Blanchard and Veyrat-Masson). It is the contention of this book, however, that the dynamics of cultural memory can only be fully understood if we take into account, not just the social factors at work, but also the "medial frameworks" of remembering (Erll 161) and the specifically medial processes through which memories come into the public arena and *become* collective. The basic point can be illustrated by referring to the role regularly played by novels or films in sparking public debates on historical topics that had hitherto been marginalized or forgotten (Assmann; Rigney, "Dynamics"). In such cases, particular media offerings become agenda-setters for collective remembrance and it is then through the inter-medial reiteration of the story across different platforms in the public arena (print, image, internet, commemorative rituals) that the topic takes root in the community.

It will be clear from all of this that media are more than merely passive and transparent conveyors of information. They play an active role in shaping our understanding of the past, in "mediating" between us (as readers, viewers, listeners) and past experiences, and hence in setting the agenda for future acts of remembrance within society. What may be less evident, but is something central to this collection, is the fact that media are themselves caught up in a dynamics of their own. Indeed, the shift from "sites" to "dynamics" within memory studies runs parallel to a larger shift of attention within cultural studies from products to processes, from a focus on discrete cultural artefacts to an interest in the way those artefacts circulate and interact with their environment. This shift of emphasis has led in particular to a new understanding of media as complex and dynamic systems rather than as a line-up of discrete and stable technologies. Media are always "emergent" rather than stable, and technologies for meaning-making and networking emerge in relation to each other and in interaction with each other (Wardrip-Fruin and Montfort; Lister et al.). Although we can speak of "photography" and "film", for example, as media with certain distinctive and stable characteristics, a closer look shows both photography and film to be constantly evolving in reaction to new technologies for recording information, but also to developments in the media landscape at large and to the ever-changing repertoire of sense-making tools available to us (the basic point can be illustrated by referring to the recent influence of video games and comic strips on the making of feature films).

In their seminal study *Remediation: Understanding New Media* (1999), David Jay Bolter and Richard Grusin have introduced the concept of "remediation" in order to draw attention to processes such as these and to describe "the formal logic by which new media refashion prior media forms" (273). What they observe is "the mediation of mediation". Not only in today's new media cultures, but at least since the Renaissance, media have continually been "commenting on, reproducing, and replacing each other, and this process is integral to media. Media need each other in order to function as media at all" (55).

Connected with this process is what Bolter and Grusin call the "double logic of remediation", its oscillation between immediacy and hypermediacy, transparency and opacity. "Our culture wants to multiply its media and erase all traces of mediation; ideally it wants to erase its media in the very act of multiplying them" (5). Hence the central paradox of remediation. On the one hand, the recycling of existent media is a way of strengthening the new medium's claim to immediacy, of offering an "experience of the real". On the other hand, remediation is an act of hypermediacy that, by multiplying media, potentially reminds the viewer of the presence of a medium and thus generates an "experience of the medium" (see 70f.).

The concept of remediation is highly pertinent to cultural memory studies. Just as there is no cultural memory prior to mediation there is no mediation without remediation: all representations of the past draw on available media technologies, on existent media products, on patterns of representation and medial aesthetics. In this sense, no historical document (from St. Paul's letters to the live footage of 9/11) and certainly no memorial monument (from the Vietnam Veteran's Wall to the Berlin Holocaust Memorial) is thinkable without earlier acts of mediation. In Grusin's words: "The logic of remediation insists that there was never a past prior to mediation; all mediations are remediations, in that mediation of the real is always a mediation of another mediation" (18).

The "double logic of remediation" is also visible in the dynamics of cultural memory. On the one hand, most memorial media strive for ever greater "immediacy". The goal is to provide a seemingly transparent window on the past, to make us forget the presence of the medium and instead present us with an "unmediated memory". On the other hand, this effect is usually achieved by the recycling and multiplication of media: internet platforms of remembrance such as www.YadVashem.org offer online photo archives, written testimonies and virtual museum tours, thus combining many different media to provide access to the past and occasions for remembrance. The relatively new TV-genre of "docufiction" tries to present viewers with a window to the past by combining documentary media with witness interviews and fictional re-enactments. Hollywood's war movies, such as *Saving Private Ryan* (1998) or *Flags of our Fathers* (2006) incorporate or emulate press photography and documentary footage, i.e. media which are commonly understood to have represented the "real thing/real past".

While "immediacy" creates the experience of the presence of the past, "hypermediacy", which reminds the viewer of the medium, points to the potential self-reflexivity of all memorial media. The paintings of Anselm Kiefer, for example, tend to multiply memorial media and rearrange them in heterogeneous spaces, thus pointing to the relevance, possibilities and limits of media for acts of remembrance. Similarly, a memory-reflexive movie such as Atom Egoyan's *Ararat* (2002) features a "film within the film", video footage, an art work, a photograph, oral stories—in short, a host of different media, all (insufficiently) referring to the Armenian genocide. *Ararat* thus prevents its viewers from becoming immersed in the past; it continuously keeps them on the surface of medial representations, thus creating an experience of the medium (rather than of the past) and drawing attention to the mediatedness of memory.

The *dynamics* of cultural memory—and this is another claim the present volume makes—is closely linked up with processes of *re*mediation. When we look at the emergence and "life" of memory sites, it becomes clear that these are based on repeated media representations, on a host of remediated versions of the past which "converge and coalesce" (Rigney, "Plenitude" 18) into a *lieu de mémoire*, which create, stabilize and consolidate, but then also critically reflect upon and renew these sites. Cultural memory relies on what Bolter and Grusin would call "repurposing", that is, taking a "property" (in our case a memory-matter) from one medium and re-using it in another (45). In this process, memorial media borrow from, incorporate, absorb, critique and refashion earlier memorial media. Virtually every site of memory can boast its genealogy of remediation, which is usually tied to the history of media evolution. The Trojan War and the French Revolution, Julius Caesar and Queen Victoria: such memory sites have been encoded and circulated in oral stories, handwritten manuscripts, print, painting, photography, film and the internet, with each of these media referring (either implicitly or explicitly) to earlier media and their technological and representational logics.

But these dynamics of remediation do not always take effect in cultural memory. Bolter and Grusin remind us of the fact that "no medium today, and certainly no single media event, seems to do its cultural work in isolation from other media, any more than it works in isolation from other social and economic forces" (15). In the case of cultural memory, it is—as Halbwachs famously claimed—the social frameworks which ultimately *make* the memory. It is the public arena which turns some remediations into relevant media versions of the past, while it ignores or censors others. This means that the dynamics of cultural memory has to be studied at the intersection of both social and medial processes.

*

The aim of this collection is to provide a bridge between the social dynamics of cultural memory and the dynamics specific to the ongoing emergence of new media practices. The collection is subdivided into three sections which are captioned with what we see as key components in the formation of cultural memory: *mediation*, *remediation*, and performance in *the public arena*. We certainly do not suggest that there is a clear-cut distinction between the three components; it is rather through their constant interplay that cultural memory is continuously being produced. However, the section headings indicate which of these processes our authors have stressed most. The essays in section one ("mediation") are concerned with the fundamental mediatedness of all cultural memories and highlight media-reflexivity in the domain of the arts (movies, novel) and of academic studies (trauma studies, new media theory). Section two ("remediation") offers examples of genealogies of remediation. It brings three influential sites of memory into focus and shows how they were constructed, altered and kept alive by repeated representations over time and a broad spectrum of different media. Section three ("the public arena") turns to the performance of memory in the public arena. The focus is on media producers and users and on the public occasions and discourses which turn a device for (re-)presenting the past into a medium of cultural memory proper. Here, mediation is linked to agenda-setting, iconisation and publicity.

The essays in the first section deal with mediation as an active shaping of information about the past using a variety of historically evolving technologies: writing, photography, film, digitisation. The different essays show the variety of modes of engagement with the past, from the literary writings of W. G. Sebald (Cooke, Crownshaw), through early photography and recent film (Bijl, Nungesser) to the new possibilities being provided by digital media (Hoskins). The individual essays demonstrate the impact particular technologies have on the way information is presented, but also the ways in which individual writers and artists manage to exploit the possibilities of their chosen medium in unpredictable ways; as "masters of the medium" they reflect on their medium even as they use it and hence continue to expand its possibilities. Thus Simon Cooke shows how W. G. Sebald used the traditional medium of the printed book in *The Rings of Saturn* (1995), but did so, using the model of travelogue, in such a way as to present cultural memories innovatively in a non-linear and yet interconnected form. Focussing on recent cinema, Verena Nungesser shows how the possibilities of fiction film are used in order to engage the viewer of *Memento* (2000) and *Eternal Sunshine of the Spotless Mind* (2004) in reflections on the instabilities of personal memory.

One of the most striking features of the different media offerings examined in the various essays here is the extent to which writers and artists, while themselves working on one medium, do so in order to reflect on others. Thus Nungesser shows how characters are filmed making photos, writing notes, and engaging in a range of non-filmic acts of remembrance. Turning again to Sebald, Richard Crownshaw focuses on the role of photography in the writer's struggles to find a way of talking about the traumas of twentieth-century history; he shows how photography is figured in

Sebald's novels as exemplifying the elusiveness and omnipresence of trauma. Moreover, the writer not only describes photos in words, but also includes photos and other images in the body of his novels. By combining texts and images in sometimes bewildering ways, and thus operating under the logic of hypermediacy, Sebald highlights the fact that our media landscape is thoroughly multimedial. In a highly self-reflexive way, he shows how meaning is produced not so much in one technology as in the interstices and interactions between different media, which are themselves constantly changing (thus combinations of word and image in novels have become much more common in the years since Sebald popularised the practice).

If such intermedial exchanges lead to the evolution of expressive practices, technological innovation can lead to more radical breaks and new departures. In his analysis of early photography in the Dutch East-Indies, Paulus Bijl shows how the technical possibilities offered by the new medium encouraged the colonial regime in the 1840s to attempt to appropriate the precolonial past in a new way by taking photos of all major monuments. The implementation of this plan led to unexpected results, however, as the strangely evocative photos led to unpredicted and unsettling perspectives on the past rather than to its definitive domination. That new technologies can offer both exciting new possibilities for cultural memory and provide a threat to certainties is also borne out by Andrew Hoskins' analysis of the impact of digitisation on memory practices. Digitisation allows us to store sublime amounts of information, he argues, but does so in a way that challenges traditional temporalities, the clear-cut distinction between past and present on which the very notion of collective memory is based. Since digitized information is highly instable, being regularly re-written and over-written, it is constantly eliding as well as producing memory. While Hoskins reveals the unprecedented challenges to memory at the present time, the other essays show that the current crisis of memory is not so much the first of its kind, although perhaps the most dramatic, but is rather the newest phase in the ongoing evolution of memorial media.

Where the focus of the first section was on processes relating to mediation, medial innovation, and media-reflexivity the second section deals with the phenomenon of remediation and its contribution to the creation of memory sites. The sites examined in the three essays give an idea of the national, intercultural and transcultural dimensions of modern *lieux de mémoire*. Astrid Erll writes about the "Indian Mutiny" of 1857, the famous uprising in Northern India against British rule, and its repercussions in British and Indian media cultures from the mid-nineteenth century to the present day. Remediations of the "Indian Mutiny", a memory site shared by colonizer and colonized, have become a platform for playing out cultural differences and intercultural conflicts. Laura Basu studies the remediation of "Ned Kelly", the Australian outlaw, who has become a highly contested national site of memory since his execution in 1880. David Wertheim's essay is on Anne Frank's diary, a truly transnational site of memory, which has been translated into many different languages and media ever since the papers of the diary were found in 1944.

The three essays in this section make different methodological and conceptual moves so as to attune the concept of remediation to the specific questions asked by cultural memory studies. Erll focuses on the interplay between "premediation" and "remediation" in the emergence of cultural memory, between what may be called the "prelife" and the "afterlife" of stories about the past. Premediation refers to the cognitive schemata and patterns of representation that are available in a given media culture (very much like the books, maps and conversations that Halbwachs mentally took with him to London), and which already preform the events that we later remember through remediation. Laura Basu introduces the concept of a "memory dispositif", drawing on the notion of "dispositif" as it was developed by Foucault and Deleuze. She understands the memory site as a "conglomeration of heterogeneous media texts, genres and technologies", the relationships between which determine the nature and function of a memory site at a given time. The case study of "Ned Kelly" highlights how the remediations of the site revolve around notions of truth and myth and how the battle for authority and veracity is enacted between the various media texts. Similar issues arise in David Wertheim's essay about remediation as a "moral obligation". The creation of different editions of Anne Frank's diary, of movies, theatre plays and documentaries is inextricably linked with the desire for immediacy and authenticity, with "the quest for the true Anne Frank". The memory site "Anne Frank" (like "Ned Kelly") is a case in point for the logic described by Bolter and Grusin, according to which our culture multiplies its media and at the same time tries to erase all traces of mediation. However, Wertheim makes clear that, even though remediation may not finally succeed in presenting a clear window on the "true" Anne Frank, it is only by remediation that the site has constantly renewed itself and the memory of Anne Frank has stayed alive.

All in all, the section on remediation is concerned with the ways in which the same story is recalled in new media at a later point in time and hence given a new lease of cultural life. With their reconstructions of genealogies of remediation the essays move along the axes of media history.

Remediation is thus viewed as a form of diachronic intermediality and cultural memory as a transmedial phenomenon, which is realized, over and over, by means of those media technologies that a community has at its disposal and to which it ascribes the potential of creating ever greater immediacy and memorial truth. This latter aspect, the fundamental embeddedness of all mediation and remediation in social constellations, is the main focus of the final section.

The essays brought together in "The Public Arena" address from various perspectives what we call the "social performance" of memory. By this we mean the ways in which particular memorial practices are taken up in the public sphere and hence become collective points of reference. This involves shifting analytic emphasis away from particular media products and how they remediate earlier products, towards the social actors and organisations which ensure that certain stories rather than others enjoy publicity and become salient; even more fundamentally, which ensure that certain topics rather than others are put on the society's commemorative "agenda". These agenda-setting organisations include media organisations such as the press and television, but also political and civic organisations with the power to orchestrate public attention for particular stories or issues in the form of official commemorations.

The latter certainly applies in the case of the jubilee celebrations marking the 50th anniversary of the coronation of Queen Victoria in 1897. In her detailed examination of this event, Meike Hölscher shows how the jubilee brought into play a whole range of media using different platforms (public spectacle, souvenir objects, music) which worked in tandem so as to produce an intense societal focus on the royal jubilee. She shows, moreover, how these media were mobilised both by commercial and civil powers, again working in tandem, so as to fabricate the sense of a media event that would in the future be remembered as a glorious moment in the history of the British Empire. That commemorations play a role in setting collective agendas in combination with media representations is brought out also in Maren Röger's essay, which examines the way in which the fate of the German refugees from Silesia at the end of the Second World War has been remembered in Germany and Poland since 1989. She shows how current-affairs magazines function as public platforms for initiating, relaying and re-interpreting public discussions on this highly contentious memory site, whose significance plays—like the jubilee, like the case of Ned Kelly—into the construction of present-day and future identities.

Where the essays by Hölscher and Röger focus on the interplay between media, memories, and national identities, the final two essays turn our attention to the role of media in creating an interface between different social frameworks of memory, including the familial and the religious. Focussing on several generations of Jewish families from Austria, Nicole Immler examines the impact of the governmental restitution policies on family remembrance of victimisation during the Second World War. She shows how the familial attitudes to restitution were shaped in significant ways by the public representation of restitution in newspapers and on television. Quoting at length from interviews with family members, she argues that the media helped turn the private acceptance of a modest material compensation for suffering into an act with public significance and hence private value. The intersection between public display and private value is also at the heart of the final essay by Jesseka Batteau which focuses on the remembrance of the religious past in the Netherlands. Analysing the work of two high-profile writers and its reception, she shows how novelists could play a central role in providing new re-alignments with the Christian heritage in a predominantly secular society. Thanks to the convergence of books, journalism, and television, moreover, the writers themselves have become icons of a particular relationship to the Christian heritage. In this media-reflexive way, the writers function as mediators for their fans as they individually and collectively reposition themselves in relation to the Christian past.

Together the essays make clear the fact that the ongoing production of cultural memory in and through the media is mixed up with the political and social forces which orchestrate memories. What we call the "dynamics of cultural memory" thus refers to a multimodal process, which involves complex interactions between medial, social (and ultimately also cognitive) phenomena. In order to understand it fully, we need close scrutiny of specific memorial configurations, of the kind which this volume hopes to offer.

References

Assmann, Aleida. *Der lange Schatten der Vergangenheit: Erinnerungskultur und Geschichtspolitik.* Munich: Beck, 2006.

Blanchard, Pascal, and Isabelle Veyrat-Masson, eds. *Les guerres de mémoires: La France et son histoire.* Paris: Découverte, 2008.

Bolter, Jay David, and Richard Grusin. *Remediation: Understanding New Media.* Cambridge: MIT Press, 1999.

Erll, Astrid. *Kollektives Gedächtnis und Erinnerungskulturen.* Stuttgart: Metzler, 2005.

Erll, Astrid and Ansgar Nünning, eds. *Cultural Memory Studies: An International and Interdisciplinary Handbook.* Berlin: de Gruyter, 2008.

Grusin, Richard. "Premediation." *Criticism* 46.1 (2004): 17-39.

Halbwachs, Maurice. *La mémoire collective.* 1950. Paris: Albin, 1997.

Irwin-Zarecka, Iwona. *Frames of Remembrance: The Dynamics of Collective Memory.* New Brunswick: Transaction, 1994.

Lister, Martin et al. *New Media: A Critical Introduction.* London: Routledge, 2003.

Nora, Pierre, ed. *Les lieux de mémoire.* 3 vols. 1984-92. Paris: Gallimard, 1997.

Olick, Jeffrey K., ed. *States of Memory: Continuities, Conflicts, and Transformations in National Retrospection.* Durham: Duke UP, 2003.

Olick, Jeffrey K., and Joyce Robbins. "Social Memory Studies: From 'Collective Memory' to the Historical Sociology of Mnemonic Practices." *Annual Review of Sociology* 24 (1998): 105-40.

Rigney, Ann. "Plenitude, Scarcity and the Circulation of Cultural Memory." *Journal of European Studies* 35.1 (2005): 209-26.

---. "The Dynamics of Remembrance: Texts between Monumentality and Morphing." Erll and Nünning 345-53.

Schmidt, Siegfried J. *Kalte Faszination: Medien, Kultur, Wissenschaft in der Mediengesellschaft.* Weilerswist: Velbrück, 2000.

Suleiman, Susan Rubin. *Crises of Memory and the Second World War.* Cambridge: Harvard UP, 2006.

Wardrip-Fruin, Noah, and Nick Montfort, eds. *The New Media Reader.* Cambridge: MIT Press, 2003.

I. Mediation

Cultural Memory on the Move in Contemporary Travel Writing: W. G. Sebald's *The Rings of Saturn*

SIMON COOKE

1. Introduction: The Paradox of a Place of Commemoration

In one of the mental digressions and associations that form much of the substance of the German émigré writer W. G. Sebald's *The Rings of Saturn*, ostensibly the travelogue of a walking tour of Suffolk in August 1992, the narrator describes his encounter with an historical event which has been mediated into (inter)cultural memory through sources as diverse as secondary school history textbooks, a London district and international train terminal, and pop hits by *The Kinks* and *Abba*: in connection with a critique of European colonialism, the narrator recalls a visit to Brussels, and describes how the "very definition of Belgian ugliness, in my eyes, has been the Lion Monument and the so-called historical memorial site of the Battle of Waterloo" (123). In Sebald's narrative, this "so-called historical memorial site"—depicted, ironically, with a modestly miniature pencil-drawn postcard—serves not one of the conceivable cultural memorial purposes envisaged by its patrons. Not only does the "definition of Belgian ugliness" already seem somewhat unlikely as the cultural memory intended in the construction; the memorial site turns out to be less an example of what Pierre Nora called *lieux de mémoire*—that is, "vestiges, the ultimate embodiments of a commemorative consciousness" (6)—and more of a *lieu d'amnésie*: "Why I went to Waterloo," the narrator continues, "I no longer know" (124). He does recall, however, his visit to the Waterloo Panorama, an enormous surround-mural of the eponymous Battle, in which the "horrific three-dimensional scene" is painted onto the inner wall of a "circus-like structure" (124), where his experience again seems out of keeping with any cultural memorial functions we might expect in such a reconstruction: "This then," he proposes, "is the representation of history. It requires a falsification of perspective. We, the survivors, see everything from above, see everything at once, and still we do not know how it was" (125). These reflections on two static models of cultural memory—one monumental, the other representational—lead the narrator to a sternly ironic series of questions about their relationship with our sense of the past: "Whatever became of the corpses and mortal remains? Are they buried under the memorial?" (125).

This is one of many instances in Sebald's work in which official or institutional storage sites for cultural memory—whether in the form of libraries, archives, or monuments—serve, literally as well as figuratively, as cover-ups of the past; either as instruments of wilful suppression in the name of the victor's view of history or as the result of indirect falsification through inevitable—even if unintentional—representational partial-sightedness or distortion. His efforts to engage with the past take as their uncertain foundation the premise, succinctly described by the novelist and travel writer Cees Nooteboom, that "the past becomes inaccessible at the very place where this same past is revealed"—a conundrum Nooteboom calls the "Paradox of a Place of Commemoration" (118). As even the example above illustrates, Sebald's means of overcoming or acknowledging this Paradox to recover the past—or perhaps, rather, to evoke it—is characterised and defined by its rejection of such static models—most obviously in his inter-medial weaving together of the textual and the visual, and through direct and self-reflexive discursive assessments of how different commemorative forms foster relationships with the past. The concerns of *The Rings of Saturn* thus resonate powerfully with what Astrid Erll and Ann Rigney have shown to be the most recent movements in cultural memory studies: that "the memories that are shared within generations and across different generations are the product of public acts of remembrance using a variety of media. Stories, both oral and written, images, museums, monuments: these all work together in creating and sustaining 'sites of memory'" (111). This is, indeed, a fitting description of the substance and preoccupations of Sebald's texts: his work sets cultural memory on the move[1], dislocating and reconfiguring embodiments of memory from their sites of origin and contexts, and focusing equally and self-reflexively on the processes by which they are recalled and reconfigured while *ex situ*.

That the process of re-mediating the Battle of Waterloo and its representations takes place, so to speak, in a walk around Suffolk, highlights the central point to be addressed in the following section of this article. Our sense of the distinction of Sebald's book derives in part from its dynamic relationship with that most directly dynamic of literary forms—the travel narrative—and our own cultural memory: the generic horizons of expectation that are confounded by his work. In some ways, the procedure governing Sebald's approach in *The Rings of Saturn* might be described as the result of transgressing, or even forgetting about, the defined generic model of the form he supposedly set out to write: a travel book. We can begin, then, by outlining some of the generic patterns of the genre, highlighting some features that are specifically relevant to cultural memory, as a way of casting in sharper relief the way Sebald's narrative relates to contemporary concerns in cultural memory studies.

2. Travel Writing and Cultural Memory

We might start with the observation that the practice of travel writing has intriguing implications for cultural memory. First, there is what Walter F. Veit has called the "cognitive necessity of comparison" (71): in any encounter with a new place (or text), our assessment implicitly involves an act of cultural recall, evoking and focusing the contents of cultural inheritance. Secondly, we might look to travel writing for a kind of pre-history of the issues of a mediated society, which are so pertinent to cultural memory studies (representing the equivalent in spatial form of the temporal mediation of vicarious memory). As Andrew Hoskins has put it, the three primary components of memory in society are "people" (with eyewitnesses as the primary source), "place" (attributed with special significance), and "mass media" (3); and the analysis is equally fitting for the travel narrative. The centrality of the claims of the first component—that of the witness—is emblematically evident in one of the touchstone texts for all subsequent travel narratives, Marco Polo's *Travels*, in which it is claimed that the "book will be a truthful one" about distant cultures for the "benefit of those who could not see them with their own eyes" (1). This "rhetorical attempt to claim authority as a direct observer" is so powerfully implicit that it can reasonably be identified as "the fundamental literary mechanism of legitimation in the genre of travel literature" (Elsner and Rubiés 3). Equally, and bound up with this, is the requirement that the traveller should have actually been there, at a certain place (it is place, rather than a specific event, that is defining of the genre). And lastly, corresponding to the component of media: the records of such journeys also foreground the issue of mediation, as such notoriously fabricated medieval accounts as those of John Mandeville already alert us to (in their tales of marvellous and monstrous creatures and customs, composed not of what has in fact been directly witnessed—as his contemporaries apparently believed—but from a compound of records and myths drawn from diverse accounts). Stephen Greenblatt's *Marvelous Possessions*, for example, shows with great subtlety how Mandeville's and other travellers' representations of cultural Others are entwined with formulations of the respective traveller's culture of origin. Simon Schama has shown, too, that our engagement with the natural environment is equally "loaded with complicating memories, myths and meanings ... Before it can be ever be a repose for the senses, landscape is the work of the mind" (7). The word *landscape* itself, Schama notes, is a translation of the Dutch *landschap* which, "like its Germanic root, *Landschaft*, signified a human occupation, indeed a jurisdiction, as much as anything that might be a pleasing object of depiction" (10).

The picture of the world created by exploration and discovery, then—whether carried out in the name of conquest, agriculture, trade, scientific inquiry or religious pilgrimage—is a kind of geographical equivalent of the mediated world of the past we access in terms of cultural memory. Since Edward Said's *Orientalism* (first published in 1978 and one of the foundational texts that introduced travel writing into scholarly debates, as well as an inaugural text for post-colonial studies), scholars of travel writing have been conscious of the degree to which this mediated aspect of travel accounts has meant that the "world" beyond one's direct experience is a product rather than an objective record, mediated by the ideological motivations and cultural precepts of the "witness" (the Orient was produced, rather than discovered, by the West). Mary Louise Pratt has done most to extend the Saidian analysis of the discipline of Oriental Studies to travel writing more generally, showing, in *Imperial Eyes* (1992), the degree to which the history of exploration recorded in travel writing contributed to the development of a "planetary consciousness" in the European psyche, a consciousness developed through mapping, the collection of samples (as in the case of the natural-historical taxonomist Linnaeus), and the pursuit and administration of knowledge as well as through economic and military colonial expansion (15-37). Pratt finds that the residue of this colonial history continues to find expression in the work of such well-known contemporary travel writers as Paul Theroux (217-21).

Colonialism is one of the back-histories haunting contemporary travel literature; the counterpart is found in the way in which the history of exploration as the foundation of travel has given way, as the world's "undiscovered" regions were explored, mapped, and mined for resources, in the twentieth century particularly, to a sense of surplus, the depletion and ultimately the (lamented) loss of new horizons. Paul Fussell's 1980 study of British literary travel between the wars is the prototype of that powerful engine of cultural memory, nostalgia, in terms of travel writing. An elegy

for what he calls the "last age" of travel, his book was pivotal in introducing the long-neglected and often disparaged genre of travel writing into
literary studies; but as it did so, it essentially pronounced the collection
complete. The book, "assuming" as it did "that travel is now impossible
and that tourism is all we have left" (41), by extension pronounced the
end of the possibility of genuine travel books. Voyages of discovery, we
might say, have given way here to what Michael Cronin has called (and
critiqued as) "discourses of exhaustion" (17). The idea itself is not exactly
new. Melville, for example, identified the fundamental issue with marvellous oratorical grandeur in 1851, in *Moby Dick*:

> Were this world an endless plain, and by sailing eastward we could for ever reach
> new distances, and discover sights more sweet and strange than any Cyclades or
> Islands of King Solomon, then there were promise in the voyage. But in pursuit
> of those far mysteries we dream of, or in tortured chase of that demon phantom
> that, some time or other, swims before all human hearts; while chasing such over
> this round globe, they either lead us on in barren mazes or midway leave us
> whelmed. (258)

Not an entirely new idea, but increasingly paradigmatic in the era of the
so-called global village. Of these two major directions from which travel
writing has been approached as a genre, then, the first (post-colonial)
stressed that the genre was potentially if not inherently immoral; the second (nostalgic) that it was now impossible (I am thinking of critical studies
of the literary form itself rather than the parallel adoption of metaphors of
travel in critical theory). Thus, in a recent book on *The Global Politics of
Travel Writing*, Debbie Lisle asks:

> How is contemporary travel writing coping with its embarrassing colonial past
> while also recognising there are no undiscovered places left to explore? Given
> this precarious position, can travelogues tell us anything relevant, let alone pro-
> vocative, about contemporary global life? (3)

Lisle's argument is centrally concerned with cultural memory, arguing that
even travel writing which does not openly "alleviate the anxieties created
by globalisation by recalling the assurances of Empire" and attempts a
"cosmopolitan vision" nevertheless "reproduces a dominant Western
tradition from which Western writers emerge to document other states,
cultures and peoples" (5; for other insightful, sceptical readings, see Holland and Huggan). While travel writing from the late twentieth century
certainly responds to these backgrounds and contexts in numerous other
ways, however, it is arguably precisely through a foregrounded self-

reflexive awareness of the degree to which the traveller's experience is filtered through cultural memory that the travel narrative has in fact become one of the most powerful literary forms through which such histories have been acknowledged and addressed and the colonial functions, after all, might be identified in other genres than the travel narrative, including the norms of the academic disciplines which, in many ways, travel writing transgresses. We must be careful, of course, not to overstate the novelty of contemporary examples of self-reflexivity: the Vicomte de Chateaubriand famously wrote of the way in which "[e]very man carries within him a world which is composed of all that he has seen and loved, and to which he constantly returns, even when he is travelling through, and thinks he is living in, some different world" (qtd. in Lévi-Strauss 52). Nevertheless, if this was, as recently as the eighteenth and nineteenth centuries, a kind of concession, for many travel writers today it is a primary focus (for an account of the increasing self-reflexivity of the travelogue, see Nünning). Similarly, the journey can operate as a vehicle for travelling not to New Worlds exactly, but for going back into history. Manfred Pfister has written authoritatively on the issue, showing that there is

> a general tendency in modernist and postmodernist travel writing to stage self-consciously what previous travel writers have tended to play down: the fact that travelling is always a travelling in traces, is always the pursuit of traces to be followed and read, and that the reading of these traces is more of an adventure than the travelling itself. (5)

Re-treading the footsteps of others, then, is one way of invoking and reinvigorating their memories: there is the sub-genre known as "footsteps", effectively coined by Richard Holmes's *Footsteps: Adventures of a Romantic Biographer*, published in 1985. Iain Sinclair's *Edge of the Orison: In the Traces of John Clare's 'Journey out of Essex'* (2005) is a fine example of how this mode can revivify such figures as the "mad poet" John Clare. Indeed, many writers whose work has emerged since the late 1970s—including Bruce Chatwin, Claudio Magris, and Predrag Matvejević, the later V. S. Naipaul and Cees Nooteboom, as well as W. G. Sebald—seem to turn to the travel narrative not only out of a concern for exploring and recounting unknown topographies and cultures, but equally, if not more notably, for the potential it offers, through providing a teleological structure, to weave together seemingly disparate and diachronic strands of personal experience and (inter)cultural heritage. Bruce Chatwin's restlessness as a traveller and his wide-ranging generic forms are in a sense the expression of his presiding obsession, the idea of a "Nomadic Alternative" to settled life, which was the subject of his ambitious, unpublished anthropological treatise (see

Shakespeare 215-65). As Claudio Magris describes his journey downriver in *The Danube*, it is not always clear whether he is travelling to each place on his itinerary on foot, or whether he is tracing his finger along a map and telling the stories of the writers and artists whose histories are attached to each place. Predrag Matvejević, in *Mediterranean: A Cultural Landscape*, attempts what Magris terms, in his introduction, a "Philology of the Sea" ("Introduction"), highlighting the way disparate histories cross paths in the Mediterranean, structuring his book into three sections: breviaries, maps, and glossaries. The technique is (again) not so much new, as a renewal of already existent forms (Darwin's insight into Alexander von Humboldt's travelogues—that they served as a "convenient vehicle for miscellaneous discussions" (qtd. in Nicolson xxvii)—might have been a response to any one of these authors). What is new (related, I think, to the capacity of the travelogue to accommodate heterogeneous and disparate cultural and generic forms) is that rather than being a marginal or even extra-literary form of writing, this "convenient vehicle" has now evidently become increasingly attractive to writers seeking specifically literary innovation. This contemporary salience, I think, is in part connected to the way in which the travelogue brings the writer—and us—up against the ghosts in its own generic closet: most importantly Empire, and relatedly the loss of undiscovered regions.

More pertinently still for our context, and perhaps even more profoundly, we could suggest that the sense of loss permeating contemporary travel narratives such as those cited above might be less a matter of nostalgia for a lost age of discovery (or at least, not always or only that), but rather nostalgia in the word's original sense, as coined by the Swiss doctor Johannes Hofer in 1688 as the term for what he identified as a medical condition: "the sad mood originating from the desire to return to one's native land" (qtd. in Boym 3). Nostalgia, as a longing for a lost homeland, fuses space and time in the experience of homelessness: the traveller's distance, spatial and temporal, from home; and exile and a sense of dislocation from an irrecoverable home has become one of the most powerful metaphors for modern memory, as Svetlana Boym and Peter Fritzsche have discussed so compellingly. In *Stranded in the Present*, Fritzsche argues that the Western conception of history was radically altered by the "sharp break between the past and the present" that was the French Revolution, which rendered the past "increasingly different, mysterious, and inaccessible" (7), and finds in the accounts of exiles such as the Vicomte de Chateaubriand (whose life and work figure prominently in an extended biographical portrait in *The Rings of Saturn*), that "[e]xile facilitated a view of the past as loss" (79). The travel writing of the contemporary period stresses not only that sense of personal dislocation that comes with absence from one's homeland, but also responds, by addressing the way the histories of many homelands intersect, to the historical worldview that Fritzsche identifies as developing as a result of the increased awareness of transnational history during and after the Revolution, that constituted a "dramatic reorganization of modern time and space, so that contemporaries felt themselves *contemporaries*, as occupants of a common time zone" (9-10). Sebald's writing, and particularly his most identifiable travelogue, *The Rings of Saturn*, can be seen as an apotheosis of these movements in contemporary travel writing.

3. The Dynamics of Cultural Memory in W. G. Sebald's *The Rings of Saturn*

In its opening lines, *The Rings of Saturn* announces itself inconspicuously as a travelogue: "In August 1992, when the dog days were drawing to an end, I set out to walk the county of Suffolk" (3). The German subtitle—"*eine englische Wallfahrt*"—additionally invites us to read the book as an example of one of the most evocative journeys regarding cultural memory: it is "an English pilgrimage". But the destination of the pilgrimage is not explicitly stated at the outset, and if it does have a Holy Land, it is between Yoxford and Harleston, where the narrator visits one Thomas Abrams to see his replica model of the Holy Temple of Jerusalem. The revision of the fundamental idea of place inherent in the pilgrimage is echoed here in a similarly radical revision of the generic model of the travelogue. Though the narrator does complete a walk (which a reader could follow) the teleology of the journey is skewed. The second chapter begins with a near-repetition of the opening line of the first: "It was on a grey overcast day in August 1992 ..." (29). And the principle of the "authority of the witness" (Elsner and Rubiés 3) is frequently dissented against: the fifth chapter, for example, is a reconstruction of the life of Roger Casement made because the narrator had fallen asleep during a documentary that was on television at a hotel he stayed in on his walk (it is an account, therefore, not of what he did witness, but specifically of what he did not).

Most appositely for our discussion, the path followed by the narrative weaves together seemingly unconnected and heterogeneous discourses, cultural artefacts, memories both personal and cultural historical, in what seems to be the performance of a kind of encyclopaedic imagination. One of the epigraphs to *The Rings of Saturn* prepares us for this: an entry from the Brockhaus Encyclopaedia, which gives an explanation of the constitution of the astronomical rings of Saturn as being "fragments of a former moon that was too close to the planet and was destroyed by its tidal effect", and provides a model for Sebald's approach. The contents page is a kind of bizarre Borgesian compendium of apparently unrelated fragments, references to names, events, cultural forms and miscellanea: the text itself, in drawing together Thomas Browne's skull, the natural history of the herring, the Chinese court train, Edward Fitzgerald's literary ventures, is a kind of museum, in which the narrator acts as a curator of cultural and personal history. Equally, if Sebald's narrative is in a sense a museum of cultural artefacts, rekindled by their association and defamiliarisation, it is also an echo-chamber for countless voices, both textually recorded and oral-historical. One of the striking features of Sebald's narratives is that many voices are subsumed into one holistic narrative without speech marks differentiating between the words of the narrator and those of his interlocutors and textually cited sources, and without any imitative change in tone. If we were to open a page at random, it would be hard to know if the narrating "I" was "Sebald" himself, or Thomas Browne, or the Vicomte de Chateaubriand, or a gardener the narrator happened to meet. All speak with the same archaic eloquence (the narrator supposedly "overhears" the nurses in Norwich hospital describing how the "Maltese, with a death-defying insouciance, drive neither on the left nor on the right but always on the shady side of the road" (18)). Indeed, the originality of his work stems in part from the remarkable degree to which his books include, often verbatim, the words of others, of acquaintances, writers, and interlocutors real as well as imagined. As Martin Swales has suggested, his work is the "summation of 200 years of European prose" in which *Herkunft* is all-pervasive: "It is the sedimentation of past living that produces present forms of being; it is a community of landscape cultivated, buildings inhabited, lives lived and stories told" (223).

Yet what is the organizing principle? Silke Horstkotte has noted (and statistically calculated) that only 15 per cent of the sub-headings in each chapter make reference to the itinerary of the walking tour itself. Twelve per cent are in reference to the destruction of the region; 18 per cent refer to (largely forgotten) genocides and catastrophes of history; but by far the greatest proportion of references (40 per cent by Horstkotte's reckoning) are intertextual and cultural references, suggesting that the main concern of the narrator is, in Hostkotte's words, a "texture of allusions to cultural history, to paintings (Rembrandt, Ruysdael) and to literary works (by Browne, Borges, Conrad, Goethe, Benjamin, Hoelderlin and others), as well as references to Sebald's other work" (30). While this may be statistically accurate and certainly an illuminating survey of Sebald's major concerns, we might also stress the point that the defining feature is not so much a quantifiable preoccupation as the manner in which potentially innumerable phenomena can be connected. Intriguingly, Horstkotte's taxonomy leaves fifteen per cent of the book unaccounted for, and perhaps it is the uncategorisable trivia and miscellanea that elude any account driven by systematic precepts that weigh most heavily in Sebald's work. One of the mainsprings behind his thinking is the question: "Across what distances in time do the elective affinities and correspondences connect?" (159). What seems clear is that with Sebald's method, whether following the mind in motion without censoring its associative leaps, or programmatically curating data in this manner, these affinities and correspondences are, in principle, limitless.

And controversially so. Since the German "Historian's Dispute" of the 1980s especially, the question of the relativisation of historical events after the Holocaust has been highly charged. Yet Sebald permits no compartmentalisation of even the trivial from the tragic (not to mention different orders of the tragic); and he is quietly but astonishingly provocative. Along the narrative thread of Sebald's prose, data are accumulated more than discursively compared; they are placed in proximity and "connected" by the narrative sequence, often associatively, but not sealed off in recognition that they are qualitatively different. This too, of course, occurs through the use of two media: word and image. Here is one such striking example: the narrator recalls an article which stood out from the "usual international items", concerning one Major George Wyndham le Strange, who left his entire fortune to his housekeeper. The introduction of the Major to us contains a subordinate clause mentioning that he had "served in the anti-tank regiment that liberated the camp at Bergen Belsen", before then returning to his estate in Suffolk. As we turn the page from the subordinate clause, a photograph apparently depicting Bergen Belsen takes up a two-page spread, before the sentence is picked up again as we move on to the idiosyncratic story about the Major's relationship with his housekeeper—the newspaper article of which is also pictured.

It has been suggested, for example by Mark McCulloh, that "to lump such qualitatively different data together" (65) may be ethically problematic. It is, however, a fundamental aspect of Sebald's ethical interpretation of cultural memory, as is startlingly evident in his frequent revision of what has been called, by Eviatar Zerubavel, the "most spectacular site of collective memory"—the calendar. Zerubavel suggests that the calendar of commemorative dates "encapsulates the conventional master narratives constructed by mnemonic communities from their history. By examining which historical events are commemorated on holidays, we can identify the most sacred periods in a group's collective past" (316). Yet Sebald's attention to the "so-called Calendar columns" suggests a line of thinking more akin to Jeffrey Olick's suggestion that "memory is never unitary, no matter how hard various powers strive to make it so. There are always subnarratives, transitional periods, and contests over dominance" ("Introduction" 7). The day on which the narrator "brings these notes to conclusion" is the 13th of April. The closing paragraph of the book takes this intersection to problematise the question of collective memory as a unitary history or consciousness, while simultaneously foregrounding the inextricability of the individual account from such instances of cultural memory: "It is Maundy Thursday, the feast day on which Christ's washing of the disciples' feet is remembered, and also the feast day of Saints Agathon, Carpus, Papylus and Hermengild. On this very day three hundred and ninety-seven years ago, Henry IV promulgated the Edict of Nantes"—and as the paragraph continues the anniversary value of the day becomes increasingly discomforting: it is the anniversary of the first performance of Handel's Messiah, but the Anti-Semitic League was also founded. And, finally, Maundy Thursday, the 13th of April 1995, was also the day on which the narrator's wife's father died. Sebald's sense of cultural memory here—or perhaps rather, his sense of the individual memory's path through culture—is deeply concerned with the question of travel that Susan Sontag pinpoints in "At the Same Time":

> To be a traveler—and novelists are often travelers—is to be constantly reminded of the simultaneity of what is going on in the world, your world and the very different world you have visited and from which you have returned 'home.'
>
> It is a beginning of a response to this painful awareness to say: it's a question of sympathy ... of the limits of the imagination. (228)

Sebald's travels, physical and mental, represent a striking embodiment of this "painful awareness". And, resident as an emigrant in England and deeply involved in the translation of his work from German into English, it is notable that he also made significant alterations according to the projected audience (or the culture) of his readership (so, for example, a house visited in Suffolk is pictured in the German, but not the English, version (Sebald, *Ringe* 287)). His inter-medial and interdisciplinary approach to cultural memory, and his focus on the dynamic movement between media (as well as between human beings), perhaps suggest that to awaken cultural memory it is necessary for the individuals within a culture to connect, through whatever idiosyncratic routes, the personal with the cultural or social, to lift it out of ritual or habit (which, of course, is etymologically linked to habitation, and thus opposed to the dynamics of travel). The digressive and coincidental means by which these journeys are made further elaborate this view: if what and how we remember is always a reflection of the preoccupations and requirements of the present and always concerns a projected future as well as the past (see Bal, Crewe and Spitzer) then the incidental and the circumstantial that play such an important role in Sebald's work might be read as following a less motivated (and, in a sense, despite the idiosyncrasy, more objective) route into cultural memory. Proust famously made chance encounters the foundation of his analysis of personal memory—the past comes alive only through involuntary memory, and cannot be intellectually engineered (an idea which has its first and most condensed explication in the opening paragraphs of "Contre Saint-Beuve"). Sebald can be said to shift the emphasis of Proust's involuntary memory into the domain of cultural memory: not the intensely personal memory of summer walks, or of our grandmother's love, but (just as emphatically) of a past that precedes our direct experience. Though our readings of either writer would be impoverished by a too clear-cut division in these terms, we can usefully observe that Sebald's memorial practices and forms represent a shift in emphasis towards vicarious memory, and an attendant stress on the role of re-mediation (in various and interacting medial forms). By setting cultural artefacts on the move, and recalling them in transit, placing them into new configurations according to personal and circumstantial contexts, he becomes something like the Proust of what Marianne Hirsch calls "postmemory", the seeker of an extended, involuntary—and imagined—memory.

4. Conclusion: The Onward Journey

As a travel narrative, or narrative that travels without heed of disciplinary or qualitative borders, *The Rings of Saturn* can be seen as an invitation to a way of remembering that might be described in terms of constellations of cultural memory. Artefacts, texts, and events that are formulated and reformulated through different media as embodiments of cultural memory are placed in new contexts and configurations with an ever-present sense of the possibility of what lies outside these parameters. Memory is cultural, for Sebald, inasmuch as the individual inner life is always a composite of stories heard and experiences inherited; but for culture to have a memory—rather than a hubris—it must attend too to the sense of the histories that it excludes, or that have not yet been discovered or set in motion. Indeed, Sebald too has already entered into a series of literary and artistic re-mediations as an example of what Ann Rigney has appositely termed "portable monuments" (Rigney). We might detect literary allusions in such works as John Banville's Booker-winning *The Sea* (2005), which has as its narrator an art historian engaged in a more personal journal, who shares the name by which Sebald was known to friends—Max; Zadie Smith's Orange Prize-winning *On Beauty* (2005), like *The Rings of Saturn*, contains a meditation on Rembrandt's "Anatomy Lesson" (298). More directly, the writer and academic Robert Macfarlane is engaged in an unconventional biography of Sebald, following in his footsteps by re-creating and re-recording the walks described (sometimes part-fictionally) in his works (Macfarlane). More unusually still, artists in other media have responded to his work, most notably in a multi-media exhibition, *Waterlog* (with an accompanying catalogue now published, see Bode) and a large-scale project orchestrated by the Institute of Cultural Inquiry in Los Angeles, *Searching for Sebald: Photography After W. G. Sebald* (Patt and Dillbohner). And so Sebald's work enters into that process of recycling, reformulation, transformation and adaptation that is explored so carefully throughout that work. His books invite us to do so, and suggest a mode of reading literature and history that attends to such journeys. But they invite us to do so by treading lightly, and with a sense of the paths not taken. It seems an at once fitting and strangely ironic memorial to this writer whose journeys were so digressive, then, and whose mental wanderings took cultural memory so persistently on the move, that the village council of his birthplace, Wertach in the Allgäu, has created a "walk" in his memory: "Der Sebald Weg".

References

Bal, Mieke, Jonathan Crewe, and Leo Spitzer, eds. *Acts of Memory: Cultural Recall in the Present*. Hanover: UP of New England, 1999.

Banville, John. *The Sea*. London: Picador, 2005.

Bode, Steven, et al, eds. *Waterlog: Journeys Around an Exhibition*. London: Film and Video Umbrella, 2007.

Boym, Svetlana. *The Future of Nostalgia*. New York: Basic Books, 2001.

Cronin, Michael. *Across the Lines: Travel, Language, Translation*. Cork: Cork UP, 2000.

Elsner, Jaś, and Joan-Pau Rubiés. "Introduction." *Voyages and Visions: Towards a Cultural History of Travel*. Eds. Jaś Elsner and Joan-Pau Rubiés. London: Reaktion, 1999. 1-56.

Erll, Astrid, and Ann Rigney. "Literature and the Production of Cultural Memory: Introduction." *European Journal of English Studies* 10.2 (2006): 111-15.

Ette, Ottmar. *Literature on the Move: Space and Dynamics of Bordercrossing Writings in Europe and America*. Trans. Katharina Vester. Amsterdam: Rodopi, 2003.

Fritzsche, Peter. *Stranded in the Present: Modern Time and the Melancholy of History*. Cambridge: Harvard UP, 2004.

Fussell, Paul. *Abroad: British Literary Travelling Between the Wars*. New York: Oxford UP, 1980.

Greenblatt, Stephen. *Marvelous Possessions: The Wonder of the New World*. 1991. Chicago: U of Chicago P, 1992.

Hirsch, Marianne. *Family Frames: Photography, Narrative and Postmemory*. Cambridge: Harvard UP, 1997.

Holland, Patrick, and Graham Huggan. *Tourists with Typewriters: Critical Reflections on Contemporary Travel Writing*. Ann Arbor: U of Michigan P, 1998.

Holmes, Richard. *Footsteps: Adventures of a Romantic Biographer*. 1985. London: Harper, 2005.

Horstkotte, Silke. "The Double Dynamics of Focalization in W. G. Sebald's *The Rings of Saturn*." *Narratology Beyond Literary Criticism: Mediality, Disciplinarity*. Ed. Jan Christoph Meister. Berlin: de Gruyter, 2005. 25-44.

Hoskins, Andrew. *Televising War: From Vietnam to Iraq*. London: Continuum, 2004.

Lévi-Strauss, Claude. *Tristes Tropiques*. 1955. Trans. John Weightman and Doreen Weightman. Harmondsworth: Penguin, 1976.

Lisle, Debbie. *The Global Politics of Contemporary Travel Writing*. Cambridge: Cambridge UP, 2006.

Macfarlane, Robert. "Afterglow, or Sebald the Walker." Bode 78-83.

Magris, Claudio. *Danube*. Trans. Patrick Creagh. London: Collins Harvill, 2001.

---. "Introduction: A Philology of the Sea." Matvejević 1-5.

Matvejević, Predrag. *Mediterranean: A Cultural Landscape*. Trans. Michael Henry Heim. Berkeley: U of California P, 1999.

McCulloh, Mark. *Understanding W. G. Sebald*. Columbia: U of South Carolina P, 2003.

Melville, Herman. *Moby-Dick, or, The Whale*. 1851. Harmondsworth: Penguin, 1992.

Nicolson, Malcolm. "Historical Introduction." *Personal Narrative of a Journey to the Equinoctial Regions of the New Continent.* By Alexander von Humboldt. Abr. and Trans. with an Introd. by Jason Wilson. London: Penguin, 1995. ix-xxxiv.

Nooteboom, Cees. "That Earlier War: The Memorial in Canberra." *Nomad's Hotel: Travels in Time and Space.* Trans. Ann Kelland. London: Vintage, 2007. 109-20.

Nora, Pierre, dir. *Conflicts and Divisions: Rethinking the French Past.* Ed. Lawrence D. Kritzman. Trans. Arthur Goldhammer. New York: Columbia UP, 1997. Vol. I of *Realms of Memory.* 3 vols. 1996-1998.

Nünning, Ansgar. "Zur mehrfachen Präfiguration / Prämediation der Wirklichkeitsdarstellung im Reisebericht: Grundzüge einer narratologischen Theorie, Typologie und Poetik der Reiseliteratur." *Points of Arrival: Travels in Time, Space and Self / Zielpunkte: Unterwegs in Zeit, Raum und Selbst.* Eds. Marion Gymnich et al. Tübingen: Francke, 2008. 11-32.

Olick, Jeffrey K. *States of Memory: Continuities, Conflicts, and Transformations in National Retrospection.* Durham: Duke UP, 2003.

---. "Introduction." Olick, *States* 1-16.

Patt, Lise, and Christel Dillbohner, eds. *Searching for Sebald: Photography After W. G. Sebald.* Los Angeles: Institute of Cultural Inquiry, 2007.

Pfister, Manfred. "Travellers and Traces: The Quest for One's Self in Eighteenth- to Twentieth-Century Travel Writing." *Life Writing: Autobiography, Biography, and Travel Writing in Contemporary Literature: Proceedings of a Symposium Held by the Department of American Culture and Literature Haliç University, Istanbul, 19-21 April 2006.* Ed. Koray Melikoğlu. Stuttgart: Ibidem, 2007. 1-14.

Polo, Marco. *The Travels of Marco Polo.* Introd. by Benjamin Colbert. Hertfordshire: Wordsworth, 1997.

Pratt, Mary Louise. *Imperial Eyes: Travel Writing and Transculturation.* London: Routledge, 1992.

Proust, Marcel. "Contre Saint-Beuve." *Marcel Proust on Art and Literature: 1896-1919.* Trans. Sylvia Townsend Warner. 2nd ed. New York: Carroll & Graf, 1997. 17-276.

Rigney, Ann. "Portable Monuments: Literature, Cultural Memory, and the Case of Jeanie Deans." *Poetics Today* 25.2 (2004): 361-96.

Said, Edward W. *Orientalism.* 1978. London: Penguin, 1995.

Shakespeare, Nicholas. *Bruce Chatwin: A Biography.* London: Harvill, 1999.

Schama, Simon. *Landscape and Memory.* 1995. London: Harper, 2004.

Sebald, W. G. *The Rings of Saturn.* 1998. Trans. Michael Hulse. London: Vintage, 2002.

---. *Die Ringe des Saturn: Eine englische Wallfahrt.* Frankfurt am Main: Eich-
   born, 1995.
"Der Sebald Weg: Erinnerungen an den Schriftsteller W. G. Sebald." *Wel-
   tach AllgäuInformation Website.* Touristinformation Wertach, n.d. Web.
   14.11.2008. <http://www.wertach.de/infos/infos/der-sebald-weg>.
Sinclair, Iain. *Edge of the Orison: In the Traces of John Clare's 'Journey Out of
   Essex'.* London: Hamish Hamilton, 2005.
Smith, Zadie. *On Beauty.* London: Hamish Hamilton, 2005.
Sontag, Susan. "At the Same Time: The Novelist and Moral Reasoning."
   At the Same Time: Essays and Speeches. Eds. Paolo Dilonardo and Anne
   Jump. London: Hamilton, 2007. 210-231.
Swales, Martin. "Theoretical Reflections on the Work of W. G. Sebald."
   W. G. Sebald: A Critical Companion. Eds. J. J. Long and Anne White-
   head. Edinburgh: Edinburgh UP, 2004. 23-30.
Veit, Walter F. "Voyages of Discovery and the Critique of European Civi-
   lization." *Travel Writing and Cultural Memory / Écriture du voyage et mé-
   moire culturelle.* Ed. Maria Alzira Seixo. Vol. 9 of the Proc. of the XVth
   Cong. of the Intl. Compar. Lit. Assoc. "Literature as Cultural Mem-
   ory", Leiden, 16-22 Aug. 1997. Textxet: Studies in Compar. Lit. 33.
   Eds. C. C. Barfoot and Theo D'Haen. Amsterdam: Rodopi, 2000. 57-
   82.
Zerubavel, Eviatar. "Calendars and History: A Comparative Study of the
   Social Organization of National Memory." Olick, *States* 315-37.

Notes

[1] The title phrase of this article alludes, and is indebted, to Ottmar Ette's
Literature on the Move (2003).

I Forgot to Remember (to Forget): Personal Memories in *Memento* (2000) and *Eternal Sunshine of the Spotless Mind* (2004)[1]

VERENA-SUSANNA NUNGESSER

Though memory has always been an important issue for narrative film, the interest of the film industry in remembering and forgetting has recently reached new levels of intensity, both in big-budget Hollywood productions and in avant-garde cinema (Althen; Johnston). To a certain extent this may be just a by-product of a more general preoccupation with memory at the present time. But the technical possibilities afforded by the medium of film have also played a role, by allowing film-makers to thematize memory not only in the stories they tell but in the very form in which they do so.

Like other media, film "exists in a relationship to contemporary discourses of memory and illustrates functions, processes, and problems of memory in the medium of fiction through [its] aesthetic forms" (Erll and Nünning 13). In order to demonstrate that film plays an integral part in the formation, transformation, and transmission of memory concepts I will introduce two productions that have challenged previous cinematic concepts concerning the acts of remembering and forgetting. Christopher Nolan's *Memento* and Michel Gondry's *Eternal Sunshine of the Spotless Mind*[2] are representative of a small body of films which have been dealing with the unreliability and incompleteness of what is brought to mind and with the fact that both remembering and forgetting are constructive processes.[3] By communicating memories and counter-memories as well as the loss of memories the films not only share the recollections of their protagonists, and their ways of evoking certain events of their past, with the audience; they also use the cinematic apparatus and visual language to (re)present and (re)shape our understanding of memory-constitution.

Very well aware, on the one hand, of the re-conceptualisations within neuroscience and memory research, and, on the other hand, of the role of the media and their input in the formation of memory discourse, *Memento* and *Eternal Sunshine* can be read as fictional realizations of scientific reconsiderations. In the following I would like to demonstrate how the two films develop the capacity to play with collective ideas of how we recollect and forget by granting us insights into the minds of individuals. Therefore,

my analysis of *Memento* and *Eternal Sunshine* aims at the forms and functions of "mediation" within the respective films: how does the processing
of "mediation" within each film communicate and circulate memorial acts
by individuals? What kind of film-specific narrative strategies are used to
depict the protagonists' acts of remembrance? Do the film-makers' practices point at traditional representations, or do they establish new accounts? What role do other media play within the cinematic narration?
How do *Memento* and *Eternal Sunshine* combine intramedial and intermedial
devices in their attempts to visualize amnesia or the deletion of past
events? And in which ways can the narrative film re-define or transform
what we understand by remembering and forgetting?

Memento's Leonard Shelby lost the ability to "make new memories", as
he puts it, when he and his late wife were attacked by burglars in their
house. This disorder goes back to a disturbed relation between episodic
and semantic memory (Baddeley 16). The problem with retrieving stored
and encoded memories turns everything from the immediate past back to
the night of his injury into a blank page. Physical harm and psychological
harm affect each other and make it impossible to lead a normal life. As a
consequence, Leonard cannot overcome the trauma, because it has altered
the patterns of his memory processing. Both the change and the vicious
circle are mediated by *Memento*'s content and form—a point we will come
back to within the discussion of the film.

As the story unfolds we learn that Leonard is searching for someone
he calls John G., a man Leonard wants to kill because he believes that he
has raped and murdered his wife. But the permanent brain damage Leonard suffered demands a well-organized system for everyday life, as well as
for the logging of all the information he has collected about the case of his
wife. Notes, hand-drawn maps, and Polaroid photographs with handwritten captions become substitutes for his lost ability to recollect. The copy
of the police file missing twelve pages, with some parts crossed out, and
many notes added is a further illustration of the fact that Leonard's memory consists of nothing but texts. He relies on photos to recognize the car
he drives, the motel he lives in, and the people around him. Apart from
these "cue-cards" making life possible the most impressive scenes are the
ones where we can see that Leonard is wearing his history and his identity
directly on his body. Tattoos with essential data about the case, about the
supposed murderer but also about Sammy Jankis, a man who—according
to Leonard—suffered from a disorder similar to his own, serve as reminders. In other words, Leonard has turned his body into his most precious
memorial site.

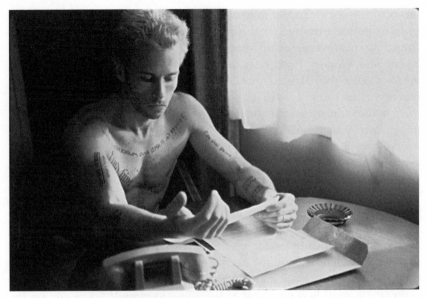

Figure 1: "Nothing but texts." Memento's tattooed hero (Guy Pearce) studying the police file.
Source: Deutsches Filminstitut – DIF / Deutsches Filmmuseum.

Michel Gondry's *Eternal Sunshine* recounts the story of Joel and Clementine. In a playful, sometimes even surrealistic, manner—a trademark of screenplays by Charlie Kaufman—we witness Joel's attempt to erase all memories of his former girlfriend. But as soon as the futuristic operation at the institute with the telling name Lacuna Inc. sets in, Joel regrets his decision. While Dr. Mierzwiak and his team are scanning and deleting his memories of Clementine, Joel tries to save them by re-contextualization. Inside his head he and Clementine become fugitives, who try to undo the current procedure by hiding their common experiences within memories that have nothing to do with their relationship. In keeping traces of memories at some other place Joel hopes to resist the procedure of elimination.

1. The Cinematic Mimesis of Memory

The term "mimesis of memory" (Basseler and Birke) describes both the ability of literature to (re)present memory and the narrative strategies depicting processes of individual remembering within works of fiction. The same categories—time, place, focalization, and reliability—that are essential for literary representations are also at hand to create a cinematic "mimesis of memory". In the following I want to demonstrate the spectrum of film-specific narrative strategies that mediate acts of remembering and forgetting. In my analysis of *Memento* and *Eternal Sunshine* I will show that Nolan and Gondry both refer back to traditional devices such as the voice-over or the flashback, and that they experiment with their films' narrative structures, as well as with the audience's reactions, to convey their heroes' disorientation that traces back to the continuous loss and uncertainty of their memories.

Memento and *Eternal Sunshine* make use of comparable film features. Both films open with an event close to the end of the story and in both films the time of the narrated action continually moves back and forth. One part of the narrative is linear, while the other is told in a fragmentary way, disclosing past events only layer by layer.

In *Memento* there are two story-lines displaying Leonard's attempt to come to terms with traumatic events in the past and their effects on his everyday life. The first three scenes introduce the film's structure: the documentary-esque black and white scenes running in chronological order show us Leonard in the present as he talks—to himself, to us and on the phone—in order to explain his situation. Past events are depicted in color and in sequences that take us backwards in time. To facilitate orientation for the viewer the end of the previous colored scene is shown. At the same time the repetitions offer us different viewpoints and alternative readings that already point at Leonard's unreliability. The falsifying narration which structures *Memento* becomes obvious when the two story-lines finally merge into an ellipsis.

Eternal Sunshine seemingly starts off as an ordinary "boy-meets-girl" story. Neither the viewer nor the protagonists sense that the first fifteen minutes do not show us the beginning of Joel's and Clementine's love-story, but a kind of re-enactment of events that took place two years before, when Joel and Clementine got romantically involved for the first time. After a wonderful and light-hearted opening the credits and a melancholy soundtrack set in. All of a sudden we see Joel crying while he is driving through the night, awaiting the deletion of his memories. Although *Eternal Sunshine* jumps to and fro as though to follow a chain of associations, one can differentiate between two major time-levels: what happened a few days before Valentine's day 2004 is related chronologically, while certain moments within the two-year relationship are told in single episodes; as they "are attacked in reverse-chronological order and as they are wiped we get to experience the recent ugly break-up scenes and to follow the disintegration of the affair in a manner similar at first to *Memento*'s reversal—until director Michel Gondry's visual ideas take hold

and the scenes become more like illustrations being erased figure by figure" (Johnston 17).

Innovation and creativity allow cinema not only to depict mnemonic
processes, film-makers also take the opportunity to negotiate the implications and consequences of memory-research within their works of fiction.
Recent developments in the field influence the cinematic "mimesis of
memory" in content and form and create films such as *Memento* and *Eternal Sunshine*. These examples highlight that the medium of film is predis-
posed to make acts of recollection and forgetting observable.

In order to build up structural analogies echoing modes of remembering Nolan and Gondry bring analeptic storytelling to perfection. In addition their innovative cinematography—among other things the interplay
of match-cuts and jump-cuts, or the way light and effects are used—sets
up visual allegories. The most impressive example is the opening sequence
of *Memento* which stands representatively for the whole film and its progressive narration: in the beginning there is a Polaroid image of a crime
scene. It fades away reversing its development. After it has become black,
we see how the hand holding it puts the photograph back into the camera.
At this point we realize that we are watching a film-scene running backwards. We see the picture disappearing into the camera. We see the photographer as he is taking the picture, returning the camera back underneath his jacket. We see blood streaming up a wall. We see glasses stained
with blood on the floor lying beside the dead man from the taken picture.
We see the death-bringing bullet on the floor hitting the man and returning into the barrel of the gun the photographer is holding. And then we
see and hear the victim screaming as he is being shot. At this point a hard
cut ends the scene and a new scene begins. Now the film is running forward and in black and white. The audience is confronted with an extreme
close-up of the killer's face. The following pan-shot shows a hotel room
as the man continues talking and wondering where he is.

Nolan takes the cinematic flashback, and thus *the* cinematic means to
depict an act of recollection, to extremes: firstly, because *Memento* opens
with a complete scene running in reverse order. Secondly, because the
film continues—though in a less radical manner—by telling half of the
story as an ongoing flashback taking us further and further into the past.
In contrast, the other half of the story is dominated by a "rhetoric of
memory" and proceeds in a linear manner. By filming the present in black
and white and the past in color Nolan inverts the viewer's expectations.
And he continues to play with film conventions, when he arranges acts of
remembrance according to the respective timeline they belong to. Consequently some embedded flashbacks are depicted in black and white—for

instance the Sammy-Jankis-story—, while others, such as the ones showing Leonard's wife or the attack, are in color.

2. Media as Objects (and Cues) of Memory

> A memento is an object which you keep because it reminds you
> of a person or a special occasion.
>
> ("Memento")

Look at your room: are there things you keep as a reminder? Are there
photos on your walls? Do you have a box where you store postcards or
letters? Do you listen to a particular song because it brings back a moment
of your life that is meaningful to you?

The urge to hold on to the past manifests itself in the form of memo-
rabilia, souvenirs, and media of remembrance serving us as substitutes or
triggers for memories. We want to maintain the ability to recall certain
moments of our lives. By preserving materializations of precious and faraway moments we hope to keep hold of them.

As referred to above, objects and media of remembrance also fulfill an
important role in cinematic narratives. They serve as agents enabling a
transfer from the film's past to the film's present (Shulman). While objects
and media of remembrance are present from the very beginning of *Memento* and *Eternal Sunshine*, their heroes' interaction with the objects as well
as the respective memories they belong to allow us a first insight. Although *Memento*'s protagonist clings to the objects that serve as surrogates
for his lost memory, he destroys and manipulates them and thus moves
further and further away from his (imagined) past. In contrast to this *Eternal Sunshine*'s Joel suffers from the loss of experiences that he has ordered
himself. The re-emergence of moments with Clementine triggered by
objects initiates a melancholic longing that opens out into productivity,
while Leonard's ongoing quarrelling leads to ceaseless destruction. Thus it
is telling that *Memento* opens with the close-up of a Polaroid image which
has the function of reminding Leonard of a deed he has committed—an
act of killing he would otherwise forget, which is symbolized by the fading
or reverse-developing of the photo. The opening of *Eternal Sunshine* presents a totally different attitude: we see Joel searching his diary for missing
entries. Two years of his life have been ripped out of the notebook as they
were ripped out of his mind a short time before. The young man is not
only speechless, his fragility and vulnerability become highly visible.

In order to demonstrate the crucial role of objects in the process of
"mediation" of memories I would like to recall two comparable episodes

in the films where certain items serve as both keepers and "triggers" of memory. To identify the memories he wants to have eliminated *Eternal Sunshine*'s hero is asked to bring everything he associates with his ex-girlfriend to Lacuna Inc. To enable Dr. Mierzwiak and his team to "empty [his] life of Clementine" (0:27+) Joel empties his home and puts everything that reminds him of Clementine into two huge bin liners.

Before the technical procedure can take place, Joel has to give a long description of all his thoughts and feelings about his time with Clementine. As he concentrates on the possessions he brought to Lacuna Inc. a scan of his brain and its mechanisms signifies the regions where the respective experiences are kept. Based on this scan an elimination of the memory traces and their "emotional core" (0:30), as Dr. Mierzwiak calls it, can be initiated. A machine locates the memories and erases them systematically according to the "map of Clementine" (0:27) that was made before. Every item that has been shown, either as Joel searches his flat or during his sitting at Lacuna Inc., will reappear throughout the attempt to erase Clementine from his mind. Some serve as triggers for certain moments, some just come into view, but all of them fulfill their function as mediators of memories.

The fact that objects have the capacity to preserve both their mnemonic and their emotional impact is also displayed in *Memento*. For a long time Leonard kept his wife's belongings to maintain the ability to remember her and the traumatic event. In order to re-assure himself of her existence and the attack Leonard re-enacts the final minutes before the crime with a call-girl playing the role of his wife. But after an unsatisfying attempt to call back the past, Leonard decides to leave this ritual behind. He realizes that the nostalgic celebration of intimacy with his beloved and the idealized love he preserves to give meaning to his life keep him from making progress. One night he leaves for a cemetery, where he burns his wife's possessions. As he puts her favorite novel, her hair-brush, and other items into the fire, memories come to his mind. A flashback in warm and bright light depicts moments of the couple's past, but surprisingly it shows Leonard and his wife in a discussion. Again *Memento* plays with the expectations of viewers anticipating a scene of bliss and harmony. Instead, form and content deviate from each other.

Figure 2: Burning and burying his memories. Leonard at the cemetery. Source: Deutsches Filminstitut - DIF / Deutsches Filmmuseum.

As Leonard watches the mementos burn he puts his dilemma in simple words: "I probably tried this before. Probably I burned truckloads of your stuff. I can't remember to forget you!" (0:54).[4] The ambivalence of the situation is accentuated by the symbolism of fire, which connotes both remembering and forgetting. According to Assmann fire represents a revitalizing force that has the power to bring back the past. By referring back to Plato Assmann tells us about the symbolism of the spark (36). It represents a sudden insight that goes back to a latent memory and thus stands for the chance to re-awaken what seemed to be forgotten. At the same time fire can destroy everything and erase what may remind some-one of something. These two aspects come together when we see Leonard as he burns and buries his memories. He finally decides to leave the last moments he can actually remember to their natural process of fading in-stead of conserving them. But the procedure also initiates another—possibly final—re-awakening of the past.[5]

A further reason for Leonard's decision to depart from the scene is that it also represents the guilt from which he suffers because he woke up too late to prevent the crime and the loss of his existence. But above all, some recollections of moments with his late wife indicate the second trauma that Leonard constantly suppresses by assuming that his wife was killed by the burglars' assault. A symptom of this repression is the misremembering and partial wrong re-telling of the Sammy-Jankis-case that unfolds as the film progresses. We find out that the real Sammy Jankis did not suffer from short-term memory loss. Instead Leonard turns out to be the one responsible for the death of his diabetic wife. She survived the attack but confronted with an amnesiac husband she desperately tested him by repeatedly asking for the insulin-injection—until she died of a lethal overdose. Although he already killed the second intruder over a year ago Leonard continues to hunt one John G. after another and finally kills John Gamill, the undercover policeman who helped him to find the original attacker.

By constantly making up his own truth *Memento*'s protagonist reminds us of the creative and "constructive nature of autobiographical remembering" and "the fact that our sense of continuous identity is a fiction, the primary fiction of all self-narration" (Eakin 93). The constant re-telling of the Sammy-Jankis-case illustrates the extent to which narrative "constructs the durable properties of a character, what one could call his narrative identity, by constructing the kind of dynamic identity found in the plot which creates the character's identity" (Ricœur, "Narrative" 195).

The fact that the Sammy-Jankis-story turns out to be a fictionalized version of Leonard's own case both qualifies and emphasizes the function of the series of flashbacks. As a whole the sequence of flashbacks serves as a counter memory; a fact that is articulated by police-officer John Gamill. According to Gamill, the wrong-telling of the Sammy-Jankis-case, the elimination of the pages within the police file, the manipulation of information, as well as the ongoing killings help Leonard to "create a puzzle [he] could never solve" (1:41). All facts that point to the truth are destroyed by Leonard, whose life would be senseless if he were to accept that he and no one else has killed his wife and that there is no one left to hunt. Instead Leonard lies to himself and lives, as Gamill puts it, "in a dream", and for "a dead wife to pine for. A sense of purpose to [his] life. A romantic quest" that he would not end even if he (Gamill) was not "in the picture" (1:42).[6]

Monologues and dialogues dominated by a "rhetoric of memory" are important devices within fictions of memory. As in earlier works of literature, Leonard's self-reflections, guiding him and us through the story, demonstrate the constructive process of all remembering, which is "borrowed from narrative understanding, by which we attempt to discover and not simply to impose from outside *the narrative identity which constitutes us*" (Ricœur, "Life" 32). But instead of establishing coherence the disturbing "stream of consciousness" reveals a mental labyrinth in which Leonard is trapped. And the longer the film continues the more hints at Leonard's unreliability come to the fore. Within the series of flashbacks showing Sammy Jankis, Nolan plants an important clue. After the death of his wife Sammy is shown in a mental institution. But for an instant the man sitting in the chair switches from Sammy to Leonard and back again. This visualisation of John Gamill's calling Leonard's task and his current existence into question backs up the viewer's growing doubts.

Leonard turns out to be a storied self with an unstable identity that is based on unreliable self-narration. Whenever Leonard returns to the story that helps him understand his situation and that should help others come to terms with his state of mind, memory disorder, narrative disorder, and identity disorder come together. On the one hand, Leonard hopes to overcome his personal trauma by repeated acts of communication, on the other hand, the re-telling has initiated an ongoing process of moving further and further away from the actual truth.

3. Moments of Instability

As these scenes have already demonstrated, *Memento* and *Eternal Sunshine* show an extreme awareness of memory discourse. Traditional memory concepts are combined with recent insights. This dialogue enables the establishment of a film-specific "mimesis of memory" that re-invents the (re-)presentation of remembering and, equally, installs new possibilities for depicting processes of forgetting. In order to demonstrate the fictionalization of memory research I would like to refer to a number of ideas that are dealt with in *Memento* and *Eternal Sunshine*.

In film as in real life "memories become manifest through . . . personal assemblage[s]" (Shulman). These medial objects and the experiences to which they are connected build up a "personal archive". Traditional theories of memory assumed for a long time that memories are like volumes stored in a library. This notion is dealt with in *Memento*, where objects become actual placeholders for memories. In contrast to that *Eternal Sunshine* embodies a conclusion scientists have come to in recent years. By stressing the dynamic and procedural aspect they foreground the insight that memories get rewritten and hence re-established whenever they are activated (Roth and Prinz 375).

Different assumptions concerning the memory process are brought across by the films' structures and narrations: the disintegration of Joel's experiences with Clementine may dramatize the act of forgetting by speeding it up. Apart from that, Gondry's equivalents for mental pictures and the visualisation of the procedure in progress take insights from neuroscience into account. The chase inside Joel's head, which fictionalizes his attempt to stop the initiated program, impressively visualizes the mechanism of memory processing: past experiences fall to pieces, details disappear, locations switch, and faces fade away— memories are wiped out in a continuous and systematic manner. While Joel and Clementine, inside Joel's world of memories, move from one experience to another to keep at least one precious moment of their time together, the viewer witnesses what has been carelessly deleted by Clementine before.

Figure 3: *Eternal Sunshine of the Spotless Mind*'s Joel and Clementine at Montauk Beach, where they first met each other. Source: Deutsches Filminstitut - DIF / Deutsches Filmmuseum.

The strength of *Eternal Sunshine*'s storytelling lies in its narrative strategy. Bad memories of fights and discussions at the end of their relationship give way to beautiful experiences and events that let us fall in love with the couple as they are falling in love with each other. Joel, who is supposed to be unconscious during the elimination, perceives everything in a dream-like state. As he is watching one memory after the other being erased, he realizes that it was a mistake to hire Lacuna Inc. As he is reliving one of the most beautiful memories—the night at the frozen Charles River[7]—, he desperately tries to call off the operation.

In order to convey how irritating and far-reaching the process of elimination is *Eternal Sunshine* turns to visual and sound effects: cross-fadings, pan-shots, swish pans, jump shots, as well as overlapping editing

sketch the instability of time and space. What also contributes to the estrangement effect is the asynchronous soundtrack: monologues and dialogues fall together, alienating articulation and strange noises; hall effects
and increasingly staccato music bring across the chaos in Joel's head,
where past and present blend. Within a dense montage of memories that
marks the film's climax all these narrative strategies are combined. Joel's
striving to keep certain moments of his time with Clementine leads to a
continuous rushing from one event to another and finally to a reminis-
cence of his talk with Dr. Mierzwiak. After witnessing a number of emotionally loaded situations as they are taken from him, his mind takes him
to the inventor of the memory-erasing technology. But it is impossible to
cancel the procedure. The sound of the deleting computer recurs and the
scenes get darker and darker. Only one artificial spotlight remains. It follows Joel, wherever he runs. On the one hand this spotlight stresses his
status as a fugitive, on the other it symbolizes both the hope Joel clings to
and the fear that his venture might fail.[8] Clementine's suggestion to "hide
somewhere, where [they] don't belong" (0:57) re-situates them in events
of Joel's childhood or youth. But no matter how beautiful, shocking, or
humiliating the episodes were, Joel can only delay the erasure.

To raise our awareness of the limited capacity of an amnesiac mind as
well as of the "making, revision and distortion of memory" (Thomas 205)
Memento also draws on recent insights from neuroscience and cognitive
psychology. The character Leonard Shelby is the screen incarnation of the
consolidated findings that memories are deconstructed and reconstructed
every time that they are recalled. And Leonard equally reminds us of the
fact that memories continually move away from reality (Schuhmacher). To
evoke the constant feeling of déjà vu and confusion that Leonard under-
goes *Memento*'s narrative structure externalizes what happens inside Leonard's head: every time his short-term memory collapses, we witness him
re-establishing it. Left with nothing except the basic points of reference he
has created (for) himself, we are set into his situation. The narrative structure as well as the combination of over-the-shoulder-shots and subjective
camera forces us into Leonard's way of perceiving his world. Moreover,
Leonard's state of isolation is conveyed by the setting—a contemporary
American city- and landscape that has nothing memorable about it. The
impersonal, alienating environment and atmosphere mirror Leonard's
problem of constant disorientation. "[S]tripped of any cultural specificity
and historical marking" (Little 77) his context is as faceless and anonymous as Leonard himself. With the loss of the ability to remember he
equally lacks personality. The trauma makes him exist outside time and
space. It has created a gap between the person Leonard once was—before

the incident—and the person he became afterwards. The only thing he is made of, the only thing that keeps him going is a purpose that turns out to be as constructed as the narration telling us about it.

The relevance of memories for identity constitution is also stressed in *Eternal Sunshine*, for instance when Clementine feels as if she is disappearing and disintegrating after the procedure has taken place. Although she is not aware of the deletion at Lacuna Inc. she feels totally scared, confused and lost. Instead of enabling her to move on, the procedure puts Clementine into a situation she cannot explain. Repeatedly she utters the feeling of falling to pieces: "I'm lost, I'm scared I feel like I'm disappearing. My skin's coming off. . . . Nothing makes any sense to me" (0:47). Joel experiences this feeling as well: when he finds out that Clementine's new boyfriend Patrick, who works at Lacuna Inc., recycles his "relationship-archive" to make her like him, Joel articulates anger and frustration: "He's stealing my identity. He stole my stuff. He's seducing my girlfriend with my words and my things" (0:54). Even though Joel got erased from Clementine's mind, certain emotions can still be triggered. By using particular words or objects that seem to preserve their meaning, it is possible to recall the emotional core of autobiographical events.

We automatically dislike characters like Patrick, who oversteps boundaries by laying his hands on someone else's belongings and memories. *Eternal Sunshine* however grants the viewer satisfaction and punishes those who get hold of precious memories.[9] On the contrary *Memento*'s protagonist seems to get away with the constant manipulation of his own recollections and the consequences it has for himself and others. But because we have accompanied Leonard in his daily struggle throughout the film and because we have witnessed him holding on to meaningful moments which help him to carry on, the revelation at the end affects us in a particular way. His closing statement "We all need memories to remind us who we are. I'm not different" (1:45) is not forgiving. Instead, it leaves the viewer with a disappointment that goes hand in hand with another declaration Leonard is wearing directly on his body—a warning that seems to have become his credo: "Memory is Treachery."

4. Conclusion

Memento and *Eternal Sunshine* reflect the shift away from static models of memory to more dynamic ones. As Nolan and Gondry tell us their stories in a complex and elliptic way, we are constantly made aware of the constructive process of remembering which never literally repeats a past activity or event. We experience the relativity of truth and we are reminded of the importance of memories for our identity and personality. This can be exemplified by a leitmotif within the films. Repeatedly, the protagonists' handwriting serves as an important means to assure them of their past and their selves. Joel, who is used to writing down everything that matters to him, is shocked when he sees that two years of his life are no longer incorporated in his diary. For Leonard, his handwriting is even more essential. It helps him to organize his investigation and gives him all the information he needs to get through his everyday life. On the other hand, Leonard's blind trust in his tattoos, captions and notes (0:10), standing in for his memory, leads to the deletion of meaningful details and the manipulation of facts and consequently to misremembering.

As the films depict individual acts of remembering and forgetting they both modify and confirm our everyday understanding of memory. The multi-layered structure, the skilful emplotment, and the intramedial and intermedial devices that are employed to mediate the dynamics of recollection, display the directors' consolidated knowledge of cognitive and psychological insights and their awareness of how to arrange them for their audiences. The films not only underline the variety involved with a media-specific "mimesis of memory"; by following and deviating from the way narrative film displays acts of remembrance and forgetting *Memento* and *Eternal Sunshine* call to mind how our notions of memory are influenced by medial representation. Devices such as the voice-over or the flashback traditionally used to depict processes of recollection are modified through the utilization of visual and sound effects. But apart from conveying the heroes' irritation and helplessness concerning amnesia or the disintegration of memories the use of certain devices and the modification of others also serve a second purpose. The strategy of fragmentation helps the directors to bring to mind the dynamics and instability of memory and thereby the fragility of the protagonists' self.[10] The innovative narrative structure thus puts the viewer in a comparable situation—particularly by withholding the information *Memento*'s amnesiac narrator lacks or by allowing us to experience what will be missed by *Eternal Sunshine*'s heartbroken protagonist. Thus Leonard Shelby's venture to recapture his lost memories and Joel Barish's endeavour to save recollections that are about to be eliminated (re-)present and illuminate our notion of memory.

Figure 4: "Row, row, row your boat gently down the stream Merrily, merrily merrily ..." Singing a song transports Joel and Clementine to a corresponding moment of his childhood. Source: Deutsches Filminstitut - DIF / Deutsches Filmmuseum.

References

Althen, Michael. "In Hollywoods Spiegelkabinett: 'Vergiss mein nicht'." *Frankfurter Allgemeine Zeitung* 19 May 2004: 38.

Assmann, Aleida. "Zur Metaphorik der Erinnerung." *Gedächtnisbilder: Vergessen und Erinnern in der Gegenwartskunst.* Ed. Kai-Uwe Hemken. Leipzig: Reclam, 1996: 16-45.

Baddeley, Alan D. "The Psychology of Memory." *Handbook of Memory Disorders.* Ed. Alan D. Baddeley, Barbara A. Wilson and Fraser N. Watts. Chichester: Wiley, 1995. 3-25.

Basseler, Michael, and Dorothee Birke. "Mimesis des Erinnerns." *Gedächtniskonzepte der Literaturwissenschaft: Theoretische Grundlegungen und Anwendungsperspektiven.* Ed. Astrid Erll and Ansgar Nünning. Berlin: de Gruyter, 2005. 123-147.

Eakin, Paul John. *How Our Lives Become Stories: Making Selves.* Ithaca: Cornell UP, 1999.

Erll, Astrid and Ansgar Nünning. "Concepts and Methods for the Study of Literature and/as Cultural Memory." Ed. Ansgar Nünning, Marion

Gymnich, and Roy Sommer. *Literature and Memory: Theoretical Paradigms - Genres - Functions.* Tübingen: Francke, 2006. 11-28.

Eternal Sunshine of the Spotless Mind. Screenplay by Charlie Kaufman. Dir. Michel Gondry. Perf. Jim Carrey and Kate Winslet. Constantin Film, 2004. DVD.

Holland, Norman N. "Unity Identity Text Self." *Publications of the Modern Language Association of America* 90.5 (1975): 813-22.

Johnston, Sheila. "I Forgot to Remember to Forget." *Sight and Sound* 14.5 (2004): 14-19.

Little, William G. "Surviving *Memento.*" *Narrative* 13.1 (2005): 67-83.

Memento. Screenplay by Christopher Nolan. Dir. Christopher Nolan. Perf. Guy Pearce. 2000. Columbia Tristar, 2001. DVD.

"Memento." *Collins Cobuild English Dictionary.* Ed. John Sinclair. London: Harper Collins, 1995.

Perthes, Nicolas, and Jens Ruchatz, eds. *Gedächtnis und Erinnerung: ein interdisziplinäres Lexikon.* Reinbek bei Hamburg: Rowohlt, 2001.

Pope, Alexander. *Selected Poetry & Prose.* Ed. with an introd. by William K. Wimsatt. 2nd ed. New York: Holt, Rinehart and Winston, 1972.

Ricœur, Paul. "Life in Quest of Narrative." Transl. David Wood. Wood 20-33.

---. "Narrative Identity." Transl. David Wood. Wood 188-199.

Roth, Gerhard, and Wolfgang Prinz, eds. *Kopf-Arbeit: Gehirnfunktionen und kognitive Leistungen.* Heidelberg: Spektrum Akademischer Verlag, 1996.

Schuhmacher, Andrea. "Das Betrogene Ich." *Zeit Online.* Die Zeit, May 2005. Web. 29 Oct. 2008.

Shulman, Frederika. "The Objects of Memory: Collecting *Eternal Sunshine.*" *Philament: an Online Journal of the Arts and Culture* 5 (2004): n. pag. Web. 29 Oct. 2008.

Sperb, Jason. "Internal *Sunshine*: Illuminating Being-Memory in *Eternal Sunshine of the Spotless Mind.*" *Kritikos: An International and Interdisciplinary Journal of Postmodern Cultural Sound, Text, and Image* 2 (2005): n. pag. Web. 29 Oct. 2008.

Thomas, Peter. "Victimage and Violence: *Memento* and Trauma Theory." *Screen* 44.2 (2003): 200-07.

Wood, David, ed. *On Paul Ricœur: Narrative and Interpretation.* London: Routledge, 1991.

Notes

[1] I want to thank the Deutsche Filmititut - DIF e.V. / Deutsches Filmmuseum in Frankfurt am Main for providing the images for this article.

[2] *Eternal Sunshine of the Spotless Mind* owes its title to Alexander Pope's poem "Eloïsa to Abelard" (1717). It is quoted by the character Mary Svevo, who collects famous aphorisms about the act of forgetting:

> How happy is the blameless Vestal's lot
> The world forgetting, by the world forgot:
> Eternal sunshine of the spotless mind!
> Each prayer accepted, and each wish resigned. (207-10)

[3] Following forerunners like Welles, Kurosawa, Bergmann, Godard, Resnais, and Marker, a number of films have promoted a cinematic memory-discourse in recent years. These include *The English Patient* (USA 1996), *Lost Highway* (USA 1997), *Irréversible* (France 2002), *Finding Nemo* (USA 2003), *2046* (China, Hongkong, France 2004), *The Final Cut* (USA 2004), *50 First Dates* (USA 2004), *The Butterfly Effect* (USA 2004), *The Jason Bourne-Trilogy* (USA 2002-2007).

[4] The analogy between Joel's and Leonard's situations becomes visible and audible in this scene.

[5] To eliminate the information about the murder he has committed, Leonard burns the Polaroid picture police-officer John Gamill shows him to prove that there is no one left to track down.

[6] The fact that Leonard's wife remains nameless throughout the whole film also signifies her status as a "blank page" onto which Leonard can project all his hopes and wishes.

[7] Water in all aggregate states plays an important role in Joel's memories (e.g. the episode that is situated on a rainy afternoon of his childhood, or the one where baby-Joel is taking a bath). Like fire, the ambivalent symbolism of the element of water also transmits the interplay of remembering and forgetting (Assmann 33).

[8] For an elaborate analysis of the spotlight's function, see Sperb.

[9] Dr. Mierzwiak loses his wife and Lacuna Inc., his secretary Mary finds out that she is a victim of the technology she promoted, and Clementine breaks up with Patrick.

[10] "*Unity* is to *text* as *identity* is to *self*. . . . *Identity* is the *unity* I find in a *self* if I look at it as though it were a *text*" (Holland 815).

Old, Eternal, and Future Light
in the Dutch East Indies:
Colonial Photographs and the History of the Globe[1]

PAULUS BIJL

Photographs are time, are in time, are stages for time: they have a material existence from the moment of their production until their return to dust (Edwards and Hart); a social biography during which they are used and semanticized again and again (Edwards, *Raw*); and their images are related to past, future and eternity by their observers. In this essay, I will focus on this last aspect and try to decentralize that very dominant idea that photographs show a moment that has passed. Most often, photographs are imagined to have captured a moment that was once "the present", and, when viewed at a later time, to show the this-has-been (Barthes). Yet, as we will see below, photographs can also be seen to stage the this-was-and-is-and-will-always-be (eternity, or a timeless space), the this-was (a past that was already past when the photograph was taken) and the this-will-be (the future).

I will explore these issues by looking at early antiquarian and archaeological photographs (1841-1874) in nineteenth-century Dutch cultural remembrance of a period then known as "Javanese antiquity". Java was one of the islands of the Dutch East Indies (the territory of the contemporary Republic of Indonesia), and was colonized by the Dutch from the beginning of the nineteenth century until the Japanese invasion in 1942. From at least the eighth to the sixteenth century Hindu-Buddhist cultures had been present in Java and many of the temples and statues made in that period could still be found on the island when British and Dutch interest in them started mounting, from the late eighteenth century onwards (Lunsingh-Scheurleer). I am going to look at the work of three photographers. One year after the invention of photography in 1839, the Dutch Ministry of the Colonies sent a photographer called Jurriaan Munnich (1817-1865) to Java to register its antiquities. In 1845 Adolph Schaefer (?-1873) made 66 daguerreotypes of objects in the collection of the Batavian Society for Arts and Sciences in Batavia (present-day Jakarta) and

58 of the temple of Borobudur (Moeshart). The third photographer is Isidore van Kinsbergen (1821-1905) who in 1863-7 took 332 photographs of Javanese antiquities and, in 1872-74, 65 of Borobudur (Theuns-de Boer and Asser).

All of these photographs were made in an emerging colony: during the nineteenth century, the Netherlands was on Java to establish itself as a ruler, impress its own laws, and re-arrange the mode of production for its own benefit (Spivak 6). The power balance was unequal: the Dutch colonial regime had more capital and military force than the Javanese and colonial discourse produced and legitimized the existence of these relations. When keeping in mind that power relations need to reproduce themselves constantly to remain in place (Foucault), our attention is drawn to the many ambiguities in colonial texts and images. Colonies are the products of the ideology of colonialism, and if the latter falls apart, the former will as well. The photographs were financed, made, owned, distributed and archived by people working for the Dutch colonial regime, and should be seen as producers of power relations, but as ambiguous ones. Homi Bhabha has pointed to an "underveloped passage" in *Orientalism* in which Said discusses colonial discourse as "a method of controlling what seems to be a threat to some established view of things" (104). The constructions of the Javanese past are just as much constructions of the Dutch and European pasts and the attempts to give meaning to these pasts reveal insecurities about both: Dutch observers tried to position the photographs' images in time because they did not know when they themselves were located. A number of studies on so-called colonial photography have opened up the way to seeing how photographs are "ambiguously dynamic as they function in the real world" (Edwards, *Raw* 3). These studies try to avoid an approach in which "colonialism's objects must be construed solely as essentializing texts of racial oppression and imperial governance" (Hight and Sampson 2). It is my aim in this essay to reveal these ambiguities in relation to (colonial) conceptions of time.

One way in which a photograph gains meaning is through connecting the light that marked its surface to a certain time in the past or future, or to no time at all (eternity or a timeless space). This light is then seen as already old at the moment of production, or as still to come, or as eternal. As conceptions of time are different in different periods and locations, we must ask Reinhart Koselleck's question: "how, in a given present, are the temporal dimensions of past and future related?" (3). Western modernity was inaugurated at the end of the eighteenth century alongside the rise of philosophies of historical progress, which together with the "geographical opening up of the globe" led to the conception of a world history in which "individual peoples or states, parts of the earth, sciences, *Stände*, or classes were found to be in advance of the others" (238). The Dutch and the Javanese were seen by many Dutch within the conception of the *Gleichzeitigkeit des Ungleichzeitingen* ("contemporaneity of the noncontemporaneous"; 95). Johannes Fabian addresses this (colonial) attitude among anthropologists as the "*denial of coevalness[:]* . . . *a persistent and systematic tendency to place the referent(s) of anthropology in a Time other than the present of the producer of anthropological discourse*" (31; emphasis in original). One powerful model for the relationship between the various peoples of the world was put forward by Hegel (1770-1831), who in his *Philosophy of History* mapped the emergence of Spirit from its "entombing" in the Orient (China, India, Persia, Egypt) to its Western birth and development. There were, however, several other models of temporal relationships between the peoples of the globe.

From its first public appearance in 1839, photography was connected to colonial archaeology. According to François Arago, who presented the technology on behalf of Daguerre, it could "copy the millions of hieroglyphics which cover even the exterior of the great monuments of Thebes, Memphis, Karnak" (17). Missions were undertaken in countries and colonies such as Egypt and India. Yet in Europe monuments were also photographed as part of what Elizabeth Edwards has called an "archaeological imagination": the recognition that "a salvaged dying past was essential to reading the present, which was, in its turn, based on evolutionary models of race and culture" ("Photography" 60). As we will see, the Javanese past was not always imagined as past or dead. For some there was no such thing as a Javanese past, but only an eternal present, while for others it looked just like the Dutch future.

It is possible to distinguish two major temporal positionings of the Javanese by Dutch observers: on the one hand, as being outside history and development altogether; on the other hand, as situated somewhere in the past on a developmental time line. In terms of remembrance we can say that in the second view there was actually something "in the past" to remember, while in the first there was nothing (or everything) to remember since the Javanese had always been, and would and should always be the same. H. W. van den Doel has distinguished between two main strands within the political and cultural ideologies of Dutch colonialism that help make these positions clear (*Afscheid*). Firstly, according to Van den Doel, there were the progressivists, those who believed in progress and were committed to the "ethical calling", the Dutch version of the French *mission civilisatrice*, to make the Javanese more like the Dutch while endlessly deferring their Dutchness.[2] Secondly, there were those who

adopted various conservative positions and believed in the radical difference and immutability of the Javanese. This conservatism could range
from the "frank" form of outrightly racist positions (the Javanese are seen
as different [read: of a lesser race] and should be policed and exploited) to
the ostensibly more generous forms of racism based on cultural relativism
(the Javanese are seen as different [read: exotic, mystical, sage] and should
be preserved and guided). In what follows, I will discuss how these positions could inform the reading of photography: if placed in time from a
progressivist position the photographs of antiquities were thought to
emanate *old* light, while if they were placed outside history from a conservative viewpoint they emanated *eternal* light.

   The first temporal frame of time I will discuss is the "frank" conservative one. This can be best described with the help of Benedict Anderson's
suggestion that conservatives used colonial archaeology in order for "the
native to stay native" (181; Florida 22-30). This doubling (native/native) is
important, for it points to a paradoxical situation: the native was supposed
to stay as she was, which means that she could also potentially become
who she was not. The native, in other words, was not one with him- or
herself. Initially, however, when we look at the photographs from the
conservative perspective, they function as attempts to push the Javanese
outside history, and keep them there: to fix their identity. When the two
first archaeological-photographic projects were conducted in the 1840s by
Munnich and Schaefer, the Dutch colonial regime was dominated by conservative forces. One of the central policy makers in this period was J. C.
Baud (1789-1859), who had been Governor-General, the highest position
in the Dutch colonial regime, from 1833 to 1836 and was Minister of the
Colonies from 1840 to 1848. Under Baud's authority several colonial research institutes were established and financed in order to collect the right
information to maintain the central policy aim of "profitable balance": the
Indies were seen as a "territory of profit" and the goal was to get the most
benefit at the smallest price. Both photographic projects were financed by
the Ministry of which Baud was in charge and the second also by the Batavian Society for Arts and Sciences, which was directly financed by the
Ministry. The fact that these photographs were made possible by the Ministry does not necessarily mean that they can only be semanticized in the
context of its policies, but does permit me to interpret them from its perspective. Baud never commented directly on the photographs—though
we know he discussed Schaefer's project with King William II (Hugenholtz)—but I will adopt his view on the colony to (re)construct a conservative perspective on them. In 1849 Baud said of the relationship between
the Dutch and the Javanese: "Everything is heterogeneous. We have noth-

ing in common with the Javanese. *Language, color, religion, customs, origin, historical remembrances,* everything divides Dutch people from the Javanese. *We are the suppressors, they the suppressed*" (qtd. in Kuitenbrouwer 15; emphasis in original). The assertiveness of this remark reveals its hysteria. It means that everything Javanese is by definition not Dutch and vice versa. This created a situation of dependence and a continuous deferring of both Dutch and Javanese identities, for everything that was observed about the (Javanese) other had to be countered by constructing the opposite in the (Dutch) self. The Javanese population was not only observed, however, but was also subject to processes of governance. The central idea of Dutch policy in those days was to rule the Javanese "according to their ancestral attitudes and habits" (Fasseur 45). The Javanese had to be treated as Javanese, and it is exactly this doubling that created the paradoxical situation as described above. One way to get to know the Javanese was to take photographs of what "they" had made.

Adolph Schaefer's 66 daguerreotypes of the Hindu-Buddhist statues in the Museum of Antiquities of the Batavian Society, made in 1845, now emerge as a classic registration project, aimed at framing the eternal light that would be created through the reflection of light on the antiquities. These are some examples of Schaefer's photographs.

Image 1, 2 and 3: Ganesha; a linga; and four sculptures. Photographs by Adolph Schaefer, 1845.
Special Collections, Library Leiden University.
Signatures PK-F-60.844, PK-F-60.843 and PK-F-60.844.

In the first of these, the statue of Ganesha is placed on a pedestal against a remarkably unremarkable background. Almost all of Schaefer's photographs are like this: the statues are photographed in a frontal manner, mostly alone, sometimes with two, three or four next to each other. There are no measuring rods or notes accompanying the photograph. The way Schaefer photographed these statues is in line with the drawings that illustrated the publications of nineteenth-century Dutch archaeologists. In a newspaper report from the Museum it is mentioned that Schaefer's photographs would be used as the basis for lithographs that would be collected in a catalogue, which was never published ("Mengelingen").

I have attempted to represent the conservative time frame in the following scheme (Figure 1). The motto could be: once you've photographed one thing Javanese you've photographed the whole of Java at all times. This model also shows that photographs can go far beyond functioning as indices of the "this-has-been", for here Ganesha's image functions more as a symbol of eternity. Above is the European time line, below the Javanese, separated by an impenetrable boundary. Both show no change (I have dotted them to emphasize their stability through time). The photograph of Ganesha returns endlessly on the Javanese time line as an indication of Java's eternal present.

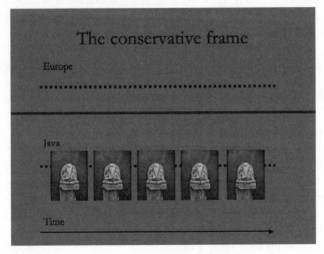

Figure 1: The conservative frame.

However, it is exactly through this photograph of Ganesha, which is itself a doubling-with-a-difference, that the Javanese become displaced, and with them the aspired fixity of Dutch identity. At the time when this photograph was taken most Javanese were no longer Hindu-Buddhists, but Muslims. Dutch observers were well aware of this, and had various theories concerning this shift: some believed that the builders of the antiquities were foreigners, while others interpreted this transition as the cultural decline of the Javanese population. What photographic projects like Schaefer's brought to light, in any case, was that Javanese attitudes and habits were subject to change. Baud also knew this, for in 1842 he said: "It is a tangible truth that a dominated people cannot, in the long run, without violence, be kept in subjection if the ruler is not bent upon governing his people with fairness and justice, and above all shows respect for the modes, habits and prejudices of the country" (qtd. in Kuitenbrouwer 25). The search for these modes, habits and prejudices, however, showed that the Javanese did not have such a stable identity, and this could have (and had) far reaching consequences for the political relations on the island.

The second type of conservatism, cultural relativism, sought to essentialize Javanese identity through connecting Java's eternal memory not to a historical, but to a metaphysical essence. In the case of the cultural relativist that I will discuss here, the critic G. P. Rouffaer (1860-1928), it was not Schaefer's photographs that facilitated this connection, but the photographs of Isidore van Kinsbergen, who made his images in the 1860s and 1870s. Van Kinsbergen, also working for the Batavian Society, was sent out to make the same kind of (scientific) photographs as Schaefer had, but returned with photographs that were theatrical. These photographs elicited very different responses from the cultural relativist Rouffaer, who was looking for eternal light, and a progressive observer, who was looking for old light and whom I will discuss later.

What Van Kinsbergen's photographs were initially supposed to look like can be glimpsed from an 1862 letter by the board of the Society. In this letter the board praised photography for being the latest scientific development, and for being efficient and cheap. It was, moreover, more reliable as a means of visual representation than any other reproductive technique: "The photographic images obtained cannot be viewed otherwise than as a very pure perspective" ("Bestuursvergadering" 523). The board was hoping for an escape from perspective and a view from nowhere. Yet, after it had seen Van Kinsbergen's first theatrical photographs, it came up with quite a different requirement for reproductions of Javanese antiquities: they had to be "alive" (*Notulen* 109). When Van Kinsbergen started his photographic project he had been active in Batavian cultural life for years. An important part of his activities took place in the theatre of Batavia. In 1851 he was hired as a peintre-décorateur for the Théâtre Français de Batavia, which allowed him to form his own theatre group in 1854. He would be active in the theatre throughout his whole life, sometimes as an actor, often as a director. The concept of theatricality can be used "to describe the 'heightened' states when everyday reality is exceeded by its representation" (Davis and Postlewait 6). In Van Kinsbergen's photographs, the statues become the actors, the images become the performance and the various respondents, the audience. These are some of Van Kinsbergen's images: one from 1863 with ancestor sculptures, one from 1865 with a rakshasa (a guard) and one from 1867 with Kala (Ganesha's protector).

Image 3, 4 and 5: Sacrificial place with ancestor sculptures and a hollow stone in Arca Domas, Bogor district, West Java; Rear of a Ganesha statue showing Kala (Ganesha's protector) in Boro, Blitar district, East Java Province; and Candi Sewu (temple complex) in Bokoharjo, Yogyakarta District, D.I. Yogyakarta district, one of the two colossal rakshasas at the east entrance. Photographs by Isidore van Kinsbergen, 1863, 1865 and 1867. KILTV/Royal Netherlands Institute of Southeast Asian and Caribbean Studies. Signatures 87643, 87756 and 87790. This caption is based on Theuns-de Boer and Asser.

The ideas of these images being "alive" and exceeding everyday reality return in Rouffaer's cultural relativist response to Van Kinsbergen's work. Rouffaer wrote about their "gripping" quality, which was facilitated by the combination of "glaring sunlight" and "mystical shadowy darkness". His connection between these images and Java's eternal essence becomes clear when he characterizes Van Kinsbergen's images of Borobudur as "the apotheosis of Buddhism, just as the Zeus of Otricoli is the apotheosis of Greek religious sense". They show something "totally and completely Indian, the most elated Indian of an amazing purity" (247). In Van Kinsbergen's photographs Rouffaer was able to find the eternal light of this Indian essence. In another article from the same year, he talks about the underestimation of Indian art in terms of "a splendid core of rich and never noticed beauty . . . that gives the best of the Indian ability, its creative power" (qtd. in Waaldijk and Legêne 23).

A cultural relativist like Rouffaer, however, was caught up in his own contradictions. In the case study of Baud and Schaefer, historical research led to the deferring of a Javanese identity, but here the shaky ground on which essential Java was imagined opens up when we consider just how Rouffaer wanted to maintain the heights of Javanese art. According to Rouffaer "our Indonesian art [...] should develop along its own path, because it has its own Indonesian beauty that is fully worthy of preservation" (qtd. in Bloembergen 254). This "own" development should be conducted with Western assistance and the purity of Indonesian art had to be established through Western means. Rouffaer's cultural relativism allows people to do what they want as long was they want what he wants them to want. His time scale is Baud's, but with a patina of benevolence (Figure 1).

A negative and progressive response to Van Kinsbergen's photographs came from the director of the Museum for Antiquities in Leiden, Conrad Leemans (1809-1893). In 1873, Leemans wrote a letter to the Batavian Society after hearing that Van Kinsbergen had been granted a second photographic assignment, namely to photograph the temple of Borobudur. Leemans was not a disinterested observer when it came to reproductions of this temple, for in that same year he published a more than 700-page account of it, accompanied by an elaborate set of drawings. In his book and letter Leemans wrote critically about photography in general, and about Van Kinsbergen's photographs in particular: "With many the contrast between light and shadow is too strong, with the result that the particularities of the original have become almost completely unknowable" (*Notulen* 103). And indeed, of the three photographs shown above, the first leaves the left part of the group of statues in the dark, the second creates a dramatic effect by picturing the statue from quite a low angle, while in the third the statue appears to be standing on a theatre stage. Leemans was not looking for statues that appeared to have lives of their own and that were placed in an eternal light: he wanted old light. This can be read in his book on Borobudur, in which he makes an elaborate comparison between the time when the temple was built and the nineteenth century. One of his basic conclusions is that there had been a fundamental change between these two periods and that it was therefore not possible to speak of one Indian mind. Leemans wanted to do historical research, and was open to the idea of change. Speculating about the future of the people of Java he wrote that the increased contact they had with "the free mind of the Western civilization" would inevitably lead to great changes (581). On the last page of his book, he celebrates the new government policies that no longer restrain the Javanese, but let them receive "the beneficial fruits of enlightenment and civilization". In contrast to Rouffaer, he was not looking for a timeless Java, but for specific knowledge of the specific period in which the Hindu-Buddhist statues and temples were made and built. His short-cut history of Java was that the island was at one time inhabited by people with a "highly developed" civilization (Hindu-Buddhism), that then Islam took over and the island plummeted into low culture, after which the Dutch entered the stage of history to give the Javanese their gifts. The type of photograph that Leemans was looking for was of the "scientific" type: straight, with equal lighting that would show all recesses of the object. The images could then be placed in a specific moment in the history of the island, namely in the Hindu-Buddhist period.

I have made a figure to visualize the way in which Leemans positioned these photographs in time (Figure 2). It shows his conception of Javanese history, progress and regression: high times during the Hindu-Buddhist period, even higher during the Dutch phase, and an all-time low in between. The type of images he appreciated (Schaefer's "scientific" ones) here stage the old light of Javanese antiquity.

The central contradiction in this model involves, on the one hand, the idea of working towards Javanese enlightenment, independence and self-governance, on the other hand, the idea that paternalist guidance is needed to achieve these goals. The ultimate objective of "self-administration under Dutch leadership", as it would later be phrased by Dutch "ethical" thinkers, says enough.

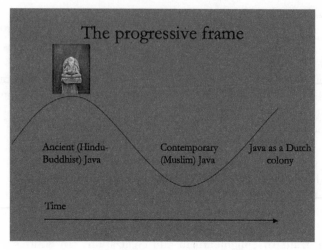

Figure 2: The progressive frame.

The last temporal frame I will discuss was endorsed by Java's first photographer Jurriaan Munnich and it represents a variation on progressivism. It differs from the frames discussed above in that the Javanese and the Dutch are not positioned as radically different or as each other's destiny, but as being different-yet-parallel. They are neither each other's Other nor noncontemporaneous contemporaries, but versions of the same *Urkultur*. Munnich was 24 when in 1840 and 1841 he made dozens of daguerreotypes of Java. Unfortunately, all of these are lost today: they were probably thrown away at some point because they were all more or less unsuccessful.

In a report from 1842, however, Munnich explicitly addressed the fact that his research into the past of Java was just as much research into the European past ("Verslag"). Walking through Java and examining its antiquities, he discovered many aspects of Western mythology. He for instance identifies statues and bas-reliefs as depicting Venus and the ship of Jason and the Argonauts, and has a clear explanation for this: just like the languages of the world, which show many etymological connections, the various mythologies of human kind are also connected. According to Munnich, the origin of mankind lies in Middle-Asia, and from that point people have spread all over the world, thereby slowly changing their images and concepts as they progress through time and space. Studying Javanese history, we could say, boils down to studying Universal History, and therefore also to Munnich's own past and that of his fellow Europeans. Yet even more important for Munnich than this idea of Universal

History seems to be the idea of Universal Decline. He was fascinated by the wear and tear of the statues and temples he came across. He connected the crumbling of the monuments to the Romantic idea that nature, in the end, will always prevail over culture, and posits this notion as a universal phenomenon: not only were the Hindu-Buddhist cultures of Java doomed to eventual decline, all cultures, including the Dutch one, would inevitably fall and wither away.

While Munnich's 1842 report on his photographic expedition is a more or less factual account of his undertakings, peppered with positive remarks on the achievements of the Dutch, Europe and the nineteenth century as a whole, an 1845 article gives us a very different Munnich. His general mood, especially near the end, cannot be called anything other than gloomy. Starting from his observations on the (often heavily damaged) monuments of the ancient Javanese he begins to wonder about the people that used to inhabit the island and after meditating on "the fate of the world" and "the brief flowering of her peoples" comes up with the question: "which faith shall await us and our greatness?" (187). This "us" can be read as "all us human beings" and indeed Munnich offers a grim picture of an old, decrepit man clinging to the past while surrounded by his grandchildren, who are not only carefree, but also careless. Yet this "us" is also, inevitably, the Dutch and their empire.

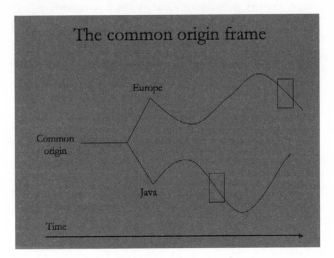

Figure 3: The common origin frame.

Munnich's world historical model can be schematized as in Figure 3. The photographs (lost and therefore represented by the squares) do not function as indices, but as symbols, namely of decline. From a common origin, both Europe and Java have emerged and go through periods of rise and decline. As both movements are universal, a declining Javanese temple can well symbolize the Dutch decline that will inevitably occur in the future. I have therefore positioned the squares on the declining slopes.

Where do we go from here? This case study opens up the questions of what happens to photographs when they are placed on different time scales and (mal)function in different political and cultural ideologies. Photographs often exceed the status of index and gain different, internally contradictory meanings. Their relationship to time is much more complex than a simple recall of the past in the present. I would like to suggest some other directions in which we can take the research on images and cultural remembrance. It would be interesting to investigate the cultural remembrances attached to photographs that were more widely disseminated, that is, over a longer period of time and among a more diverse range of groups. I am thinking of photographs that have returned throughout the twentieth and early twenty-first centuries, possibly on both sides of the (post)colonial divide. Photographs of epoch-making events such as official ceremonies, wars and other traumatic occurrences seem good starting points. These same types of images are often widely transmediated as texts and drawings, and sometimes other media such as cinema. What happens to a photograph and its possible meanings once it returns in/as another medium? The last suggestion I want to make concerns how photography may remember itself: how do, for instance, photographs of the Global South remember colonial photographs?

References

Anderson, Benedict. *Imagined Communities: Reflections on the Origin and Spread of Nationalism.* 1991. Rev. ed. London: Verso, 2006.

Arago, Dominique François. "Report." Trans. E. Epstean. *Classic Essays on Photography.* Ed. Alan Trachtenberg. New Haven: Leete's Island, 1980. 15-25.

Barthes, Roland. *Camera Lucida: Reflections on Photography.* Trans. Richard Howard. New York: Hill, 1981.

Batchen, Geoffrey. *Burning with Desire: The Conception of Photography.* Cambridge: MIT Press, 1997.

"Bestuursvergadering, gehouden den 5den April 1862." *Tijdschrift voor Indische Taal-, Land- en Volkenkunde* 4th ser. (3). 12 (1862): 503-37.

Bhabha, Homi. *The Location of Culture.* 1994. London: Routledge, 2004.

Bloembergen, Marieke. *Colonial Spectacles: The Netherlands and the Dutch East Indies at the World Exhibitions, 1880-1931.* Trans. Beverley Jackson. Singapore: Singapore UP, 2006.

Davis, Nancy C. and Thomas Postlewait. "Theatricality: An Introduction." *Theatricality.* Eds. Nancy C. Davis and Thomas Postlewait. Cambridge: Cambridge UP, 2003. 1-39.

Doel, H. W. van den. *Afscheid van Indië: de val van het Nederlandse imperium in Azië.* Amsterdam: Prometheus, 2000.

Edwards, Elizabeth. *Raw Histories: Photographs, Anthropology and Museums.* Oxford: Berg, 2001.

---. "Photography, 'Englishness' and Collective Memory: The National Photographic Record Association, 1897-1910." *Locating Memory: Photographic Acts.* Eds. Annette Kuhn and Emiko McAllister. New York: Berghahn, 2006. 53-79.

Edwards, Elizabeth, and Janice Hart. *Photographs Objects Histories: On the Materiality of Images.* London: Routledge, 2004.

Fabian, Johannes. *Time and the Other: How Anthropology Makes its Objects.* 1983. New York: Columbia UP, 2002.

Fasseur, Cees. *De Indologen. Ambtenaren voor de Oost: 1825-1950.* Amsterdam: Bakker, 1993.

Foucault, Michel. *Discipline and Punish: The Birth of the Prison.* Trans. Alan Sheridan. New York: Vintage, 1979.

Florida, Nancy. *Writing the Past, Inscribing the Future: History as Prophecy in Colonial Java.* Durham: Duke UP, 1995.

Groot, J.P.M. *Van de Grote Rivier naar het Koningsplein. Het Bataviaasch Genootschap van Kunsten en Wetenschappen 1778-1867.* Diss. Leiden University, 2006. N.p, n.d.

Hegel, G. W. F. *The Philosophy of History.* Trans. J. Sibree. Amherst: Prometheus, 1991.

Hight, Eleanor M., and Gary D. Sampson, eds. *Colonialist Photography: Imag(in)ing Race and Place.* New York: Routledge, 2002.

Hugenholtz, Wouter. *Het geheim van Paleis Kneuterdijk: De wekelijkse gesprekken van Koning Willem II met zijn minister J.C. Baud over het koloniale beleid en de herziening van de grondwet 1841-1848.* Leiden: KITLV, 2008.

Koselleck, Reinhart. *Futures Past: On the Semantics of Historical Time.* Trans. Keith Tribe. New York: Columbia UP, 2004.

Kuitenbrouwer, Maarten. *Tussen oriëntalisme en wetenschap: Het Koninklijk Instituut voor Taal-, Land- en Volkenkunde in historisch verband, 1851-2001.* Leiden: KITLV, 2001.

Leemans, C, F. C. Wilsen, and J.F.G. Brumund. *Bôrô-Boedoer op het eiland Java.* Leiden, 1873.

Locher-Scholten, Elsbeth. *Ethiek in fragmenten: Vijf studies over het koloniaal denken en doen van Nederland in de Indonesische Archipel 1877-1942.* Utrecht: HES, 1981.

Lunsing Scheurleer, Pauline. "Collecting Javanese Antiquities: The Appropriation of a Newly Discovered Hindu-Buddhist Civilization." *Colonial Collections Revisited.* Ed. Pieter ter Keurs. Leiden: CNWS. 71-114.

"Mengelingen: Daguerreotype." *Javasche Courant* 22 Feb. 1845: n.p.

Moeshart, Herman J. "Adolph Schaefer and Bordobudur." *Toward Independence: A Century of Indonesia Photographed.* Ed. Jane Levy Reed. San Francisco: Friends of Photography, 1991. 20-27.

Munnich, J. "Verslag over de Photographie gedurende het tweede gedeelte mijner reis over Java." 1942. MS. Nationaal Archief, Den Haag, Ministerie van Koloniën: Supplement, 1826-1952, nummer toegang 2.10.01.

Munnich, J. "Eenige bijdragen tot het onderzoek der oudheden op Java." *Indisch Magazijn* 2.1-2 (1845): 173-92.

Notulen van de Algemeene en Bestuurs-Vergaderingen van het Bataviaasch Genootschap van Kunsten en Wetenschappen. Batavia, 1873.

Rouffaer, G. P. "Monumentale kunst op Java." *De Gids* 4th ser. (19). 65 (1901): 225-52.

Said, Edward. *Orientalism.* 1978. New York: Vintage, 2003.

Sekula, Allan. "The Body and the Archive." *October* 39 (1986): 3-64.

Spivak, Gayatri Chakravorty. *Other Asias.* Malden: Blackwell, 2008.

Tagg, John. *The Burden of Representation: Essays on Photographies and Histories.* Basingstoke: MacMillan Education, 1988.

Theuns-de Boer, Gerda, and Saskia Asser. *Isidore van Kinsbergen (1821-1905): Fotopionier en Theatermaker in Nederlands-Indië / Isidore van Kinsbergen (1821-1905): Photo Pioneer and Theatre Maker in the Dutch East Indies.* Zaltbommel: Aprilis; Leiden: KITLV, 2005.

Waaldijk, Berteke, and Susan Legêne. "Vernieuwing van de beeldende kunsten in koloniale context 2001-1901." *Kunsten in beweging 1900-1980.* Eds. Rosemarie Buikema and Maaike Meijer. Den Haag: Sdu, 2001. 19-37.

Notes

[1] The preparation of this article was made financially possible by The Netherlands Organisation for Scientific Research (NWO).

[2] Locher-Scholten defines the ethical policy as a "policy aimed at bringing the entire Indonesian archipelago under real Dutch authority and at developing the land and people with a view to self-administration under Dutch leadership, according to a Western model" (201; translation qtd. in Bloembergen 445). Locher-Scholten situates this policy between 1894 and 1942, but "ethical" ideas had been around for a longer period of time.

The Limits of Transference:
Theories of Memory and Photography in
W. G. Sebald's *Austerlitz*

RICHARD CROWNSHAW

Austerlitz is the fictional biography of Jacques Austerlitz who arrived in England in 1939, aged four-and-a-half, as part of a *Kindertransport* from Prague. He escaped the Holocaust that claimed his parents but forgot his origins and what he had lost. His subsequent life is, for the most part, ruined, haunted by a sense of exile and loss he does not understand. Susan Suleiman would describe this novel as the fictionalisation of the plight of the "1.5 generation". The literature of the second generation—the children of survivors born after the event—is marked by the challenges of inheriting and making sense of memories of things not witnessed, or of reconstructing such experiences in the face of the silence, repression or incomprehension of the first generation. The 1.5 generation on the other hand is made up of "child survivors of the Holocaust too young to have had an adult understanding of what was happening to them, and sometimes too young to have any memory of it all, but old enough to have *been there* during the Nazi persecution of the Jews" (Suleiman 179, 181-2).

In a recent paper, Susannah Radstone argued that W. G. Sebald's novel of 2001 has been appropriated by critics as a trauma/Holocaust text in the sense that it has been read as the literal inscription or engraving of the trauma of, as Suleiman might put it, this 1.5 generation ("Trauma's Fascination"). Such readings thereby ignore the literariness of the text—its status as a novel—in favour of the literalness of trauma. Although Radstone provides no examples of such literary criticism, her critique is well founded, as it is part of her larger scrutiny of certain trends within memory studies.

Radstone argues that memory studies has been informed by postmodern approaches to historical representation that sought to deconstruct the hierarchies that governed historical thinking in which social and public experience is validated over the individual and private ("Reconceiving Binaries" 140). Put another way, the turn to memory is part of a broader, postmodern movement that saw the problematisation of the idea of the grand narrative, of "'H'istory" and its claims to universality, totality and objectivity, and its substitution by lived experience, the local, subjective and partial, which are all embodied by memory (Radstone, "Screening Trauma" 84). The turn to memory, though, has not only reinscribed a binary opposition in which memory is validated over history, it has eclipsed history altogether. The "inner world and its very processes has become predominant, and has been taken as 'the' world" (Radstone, "Reconceiving Binaries" 140). Under this academic regime, the memory in memory studies can be become over-personalised at the expense of a wider historical context and, without historical specificity, any object, discourse or practice can be taken as memory (ibid.). Given its new found authority, and indeed autonomy, memory seems to have a life, or agency, of its own, freed from historical context and specificity (Klein 136).

The fact of memory's reconstruction of the past, based on memory's partial and subjective perspective, leads to a conceptual slippage. Memory texts, be they memoirs, testimonies or monuments, are also, obviously, partial and subjective reconstructions of the past. On the basis of their common reconstructions, text and memory, which are not the same thing, are conflated. Or rather, texts are considered a direct reflection of memory's reconstructions of the past. As Radstone puts its, memory is understood as "*primarily* an inner representation of the past" ("Reconceiving Binaries" 135). By "inner" Radstone means that memory is considered the sole mediating force (ibid.). Although memory may be placed in a wider, cultural, social and historical context, the texts of memory are at the same time decontextualised by the attention paid to memory's mediation of the past rather than the mediation of representations of the past by the "institutions and discourses of the public sphere" via which memory may be "articulated" (137).

Much of Sebald's writing is characterised by an interplay of photographic (and non-photographic) images and text. In the case of *Austerlitz*, the disruptive interplay of text and image is more often than not read by critics as an analogue of Austerlitz's traumatic memory, or, as we shall see, as the performance of trauma itself. Not just a memory text in the unmediated sense—Radstone's complaint—*Austerlitz* is deemed to possess a kind of textual trauma. Prompted by Radstone's concerns, this essay explores the reception in critical discourse of the novel's remediation of photographic images and the consequent intermedial relation of text and image (Bolter and Grusin). *Pace* Radstone, and contrary to the critical consensus, this essay argues that Sebald's novel actually anticipates certain tendencies in memory (and trauma) studies—arguing not how *Austerlitz*

transmits trauma—if that were possible—but how the novel can be understood to illuminate pre-existing transferential relations that contribute
to cultural memory. It is this illumination that sheds light on how *Auster-*
litz as a memory text is itself mediated.

How might, then, intermediality be understood to present the immediacy of the past, to be unmediated reflection of traumatic memory? The
proclivities of trauma and memory studies need first to be outlined. The
conjunction of memory and trauma may seem oxymoronic, as trauma is
usually defined as that which resists remembrance. However, as the following argues, there is in trauma studies a tendency towards locating the
literal inscription of the past, which means that representations of trauma,
no matter how disrupted (symptomatic), are reified as a purer form of
memory.

The emergence of trauma studies as a discipline in the American academy in the 1990s has, in particular, been credited to the work of Cathy
Caruth, Shoshana Felman and Dori Laub. However, towards the end of
the '90s and the beginning of this decade a critical consensus had gathered
around their work sceptical of its conceptions of trauma. It is not my
intention to add to that consensus, but rather, for the purposes of this
essay, to highlight salient examples of the critique. This essay will dwell in
particular on critiques of Felman's and Caruth's conception of the performative nature of language, which is a conduit for traumatic affect
(Hungerford 73-80). To understand how trauma might inhere in language,
the temporality of trauma, according to Caruth, must be understood. For
Caruth, the American Psychiatric Association's recognition and diagnosis
of traumatic experience and its effects under the title of post-traumatic
stress disorder (PTSD) was the culmination of a long history of the relation between psychiatry and trauma, where trauma can be generally defined as "an overwhelming experience of sudden or catastrophic events in
which the response to the event occurs in the often delayed, uncontrolled
repetitive appearance of hallucinations and other intrusive phenomena"
(*Unclaimed Experience* 11). For Caruth, the pathological reaction to the
event is not defined by the nature of the event itself, because its traumatization of witnesses will vary. Nor can the pathological reaction be ac-
counted for in terms of its distortion by the personal significances attached to it by witnesses (Caruth, "Trauma and Experience" 4). "The
pathology consists, rather, solely in the *structure of its experience* or reception:
the event is not assimilated or experienced fully at the time, but only belatedly, in its repeated *possession* of the one who experiences it . . . . Thus
the traumatic symptom cannot be interpreted, simply as a distortion of
reality, nor as the lending of an unconscious meaning to a reality it wishes

to ignore, nor as the repression of what was once lived" (4-5). Instead, "the returning traumatic dream [or other intrusive response] . . . is, purely and inexplicably, the literal return of the event against the will of the one it inhabits" (5). Caruth continues, "It is this literality and its insistent return which thus constitutes trauma and points towards its enigmatic core: the delay or incompletion in knowing, or even in seeing, an overwhelming occurrence that then remains, in its insistent return, absolutely *true* to the event" (ibid.). So, the event cannot be known when witnessed and cannot be known upon its insistent return (see also Caruth, *Unclaimed Experience* 60-2). To emphasize, it is not the event itself that returns in the dream, flashback, hallucination, or other form of intrusive and repetitive behavior, but rather the failure to process the event. Repetition is the attempt to master what was missed first time round. It is the literality of the event in its missed occurrence and missed return that makes it unassimilable, resistant to symbolization, beyond representation. As Caruth puts it elsewhere, in relation to Freud's *Beyond the Pleasure Principle*, "In trauma . . . the outside has gone inside without any mediation" (*Unclaimed Experience* 59).

The pathological reaction to trauma diagnosed under the title of PTSD is, for Caruth, a symptom of a possessive history beyond possession ("Trauma and Experience" 5). This does not mean that history can simply be indirectly accessed. The event can only be experienced through what amounts to its inherent forgetting, and not through its return following forgetting. In other words, traumatic experience is inherently latent: "since the traumatic event is not experienced as it occurs, it is fully evident only in connection with another place, another time" (8, 9). Caruth deploys the idea of latency or belatedness that she finds in Freud's *Moses and Monotheism*, which guarantees the unconscious as a blank space: "If repression, in trauma, is replaced by latency, this is significant in so far as its blankness—the space of unconsciousness—is paradoxically what preserves the event in its literality" (9). Evacuated as such, the unconscious is positioned as a vehicle for trauma. Trauma has been dislocated from its historical anchor: the event and its witness. Trauma constitutes a departure from its own site (of non-origin)—a departure that is reiterated by trauma's insistent (non)return. What then becomes of the witness? A crisis of witnessing engendered by trauma, which calls the origins of historical (empirical) knowledge into question, demands of history a new kind of listening to the witness of trauma: "the witnessing, *precisely*, of impossibility" (8-10). It is in this witnessing of witnessing that trauma, having departed from its site of (non)origin, threatens "'contagion'": "the traumatisation of the ones who listen" (ibid.). As Caruth might put it, that which has departed from the site of individual trauma threatens an arrival in collective memory of events not witnessed directly (*Unclaimed Experience* 67). If trauma cannot be witnessed, the traumatic event can only take place through its belatedness, through the witnessing of the witness (Caruth, "Trauma and Experience" 11). The momentum of belatedness means that if the traumatic event cannot be known in its own right, it is more likely to be known or rather felt in other histories, as it is enacted as part of other events and incorporated into the history of those events. "The traumatic nature of history means that events are only historical to the extent that they implicate others" (Caruth, *Unclaimed Experience* 18). Indeed, the "endless *inherent necessity* of repetition" brought about by the survival of trauma might well lead to the "formation of history as the endless repetition of previous violence" (63).

Contagion finds, according to Caruth, its model in Freud's version of Jewish tradition in *Moses and Monotheism*, but the very idea of contagion ultimately collapses the differences between history and memory (in the sense that witnessing is constituted by a relationship to text rather than history), and it is around that text that collective memories form of events not historically, that is, directly, witnessed (see also Leys 285). The vehicle for contagion is language. Caruth finds in the aporias that she discerns in Freud's explanatory and prefatory notes to *Moses and Monotheism*, not only the traumatic ramifications or repetitions of Jewish historical experience, the inception of which is Mosaic, but also a repetition, beyond representation, of Freud's departure from Vienna in 1938 under threat of Nazi persecution. So, it is the threat of Nazism and an unfolding Holocaust, and its resonance in a longer Jewish history of trauma, that is (un)registered in the aporias of literary language. In which case, as Leys puts it, any space is capable of registering trauma (290). Amy Hungerford develops the logic of Caruth's argument further: language and traumatic experience become the same thing. Language's failure of reference—its falling impact—turns it into a site of trauma (Hungerford 81-3). Historical trauma is reduced to a textual trace, and textual trauma supersedes history. So, *Moses and Monotheism* is marked by Freud's departure from Austria for England in 1938, but the site of trauma is the text itself. Literary language as such is able to transmit trauma from one person to another because it has been severed from any prior relationship between (direct) witness to historical trauma and his or her testimony. "By cutting experience free from the subject of experience, Caruth allows trauma not only to be abstract in the extreme but also, by virtue of that abstraction, to be transmissible" (Leys 297). If the text is traumatic, the contagion of trauma extends to the act of reading. Trauma's contagion, which spreads via the language community, has the potential to victimize all who are affected by the language of trauma, thereby confusing distinctions between victim and perpetrator, and those who would relate to each category of historical actor (Felman 297).

Felman's conception of testimony—the "literary—or discursive—mode *par excellence* of our times" (5)—develops the idea that trauma can be conveyed by language: Caruth's "fantasy about memorisation . . . made possible by the deconstructive emphasis on the materiality of the signifier" (Hungerford 84). Felman defines testimony thus: "As a relation to events, testimony seems to be composed of bits and pieces of a memory that has been overwhelmed by occurrences that have not settled into understanding or remembrance, acts that cannot be constructed as knowledge nor assimilated into full cognition, events in excess of our frames of reference" (5). Testimony cannot offer a "totalizable" account of those events. Testimonial language does "not possess itself as a conclusion, as constation of a verdict or the self-transparency of knowledge." It is instead a "performative speech act" addressing historical "action" that "exceeds any "substantialized significance"; its "impact . . . dynamically explodes any conceptual reifications and any constative delimitations" (ibid.).

For example, according to Felman, the poetry of Paul Celan "strives to defetishize his language and to dislocate his own aesthetic mastery, by breaking down any self-possessed control of sense and by trying to disrupt any sense of unity, integrity or continuity of conscious meaning" (37). Through the deformation of words, phrases and syntax, through the insertion of space and thereby silence between and within words, through the breakdown of poetic sound, Celan attempts to convey the experience—his— of witnessing that which resisted witnessing and the attribution of conscious meaning. "Through their very breakdown, the sounds testify, henceforth, precisely to a knowledge they do not possess, by unleashing, and by drifting into, their own buried depths of silence" (ibid.). Celan's experience as witness is not in doubt, nor is the testimonial nature of his poetry. What might be problematic here is the embodiment of trauma in language. It is the conflation of traumatic memory—no matter how inaccessible that memory is, as in "sounds testify . . . to a knowledge they do not possess . . . drifting into . . . their buried depths of silence"—and language, positing language as witness, which is problematic here. As in Caruth's concept, trauma, then, is endlessly transmissible.

As Hungerford argues, that language can embody rather than represent trauma reveals a certain irony about the deconstructionist origins of much trauma theory. The very rejection of language as representational by deconstructionism gives way to a kind of sacralisation of language as just that, not a representation of trauma but the trauma itself in terms of language's embodiment or performance of trauma's disruptions (see also Ball

1-44). This positioning of trauma shifts the focus of Holocaust studies away from the survivors' acts of survival in the camps to their acts of witnessing, in which anyone, potentially, can participate. "The implications of that deconstructive shift from language as representation to language as performance—apparent in the idea that survivors can be produced on the basis of trauma that is experienced by being read—suggests that Felman's evident concern with the actual violence experienced in the Holocaust may be unnecessary to trauma theory at its most abstract level" (Hungerford 80). The logic of Felman's argument about the participatory nature of trauma is that the direct experience of the camps is exemplary (in the extreme but exemplary nonetheless) rather than unique in that it illuminates a crisis of language and identity at the "very core of our common life" (ibid.). As the contagion of trauma spreads throughout the language community, it is language that institutes or perhaps constitutes a series of traumatized identities—and the experience of traumatic events in history merely exemplifies a trauma that has already been felt at the core of identity.

Despite the critical backlash, trauma studies in a canonical form—recognisable by the contagion of trauma and over-identification with the witness whose experience can be shared via language and culture—has had a pervasive effect on literary analysis. This theoretical climate might explain readings of *Austerlitz* that find in it a textual trauma. The texture of trauma could be found in the interplay of photographs and text that is a feature common to Sebald's texts. The photographs included in the narrative of *Austerlitz* seem to belong mostly to its eponymous protagonist, and have been arranged by the narrator to illustrate the narrative of Austerlitz's recollection of his own life, the origins of which he had forgotten. The relationship between text and image casts doubt on the referential ability of each sign system, as if each were inadequate and in need of shoring up, or perhaps as if they ought to interrupt each other's referential claims. The relationship between text and image is, then, more dissonant than consonant. (Not only is the code of realism habitually brought to photographic images cast into doubt, the actual provenance of the image becomes dubious. The image's illustrative status seems arbitrary and the reader is often left unsure of whether the image actually refers to what the text implies.) It is this dissonance that might resonate with a traumatic failure of reference.

With these uncertainties in mind, this essay takes up a recent reading of *Austerlitz* that finds in the narrative its "optical unconscious". The phrase is Benjamin's and not one that Carolin Duttlinger uses, but it describes the way that Austerlitz uses photographs both to reveal and conceal his past—at least according to Duttlinger. Duttlinger modifies Ulrich Baer's conception of photography's ability to represent a moment of trauma. For Baer, photography, in its relation to the Holocaust and to case studies of nineteenth-century hysteria, generates a "mechanically recorded instant that was not necessarily registered by the subject's own consciousness," thereby enabling access to "experiences that have remained unremembered yet cannot be forgotten" (7-8). The catalyst for Duttlinger's modification can be found in Austerlitz's recollection of a fainting fit during a trip to Paris in the 1950s, after a visit to the veterinary museum at Maisons-Alfort. During the trip, Austerlitz had taken hundreds of pictures of the Parisian *banlieues*. I use Duttlinger's quotation of the text because of her reference to the original German. For Austerlitz, this was

> the first of several fainting fits I was to suffer, causing temporary but complete loss of memory [*Auslöschung sämtlicher Gedächtnisspuren*], a condition described in psychiatric textbooks . . . as hysterical epilepsy. Only when I developed the photographs I had taken that Sunday in September at Maisons-Alfort was I able . . . to reconstruct my buried experiences. (qtd. in Duttlinger 159)

The photographs stand in for memories of what has been forgotten. Duttlinger points out that "Sebald in the original uses the term '*Gedächtnisspuren*', 'memory-traces', to describe the protagonist's memory loss. The term alludes to Freud's famous formulation in *Beyond the Pleasure Principle*, 'consciousness arises instead [literally: in the place] of a memory-trace [*Erinnerunsspur*]' . . . , a statement which marks the core of Freud's theory about the breach between consciousness and memory in trauma" (Duttlinger 159). Duttlinger argues that Sebald positions photographic images as a "protective shield from the stimuli it simultaneously stores, inaccessible to memory. In a variation of Freud's phrase, then, consciousness here 'arises in the place of the photographic image'" (160). This may explain Austerlitz' obsession with taking photographs: they regulate his psychic life for him.

Before returning to Duttlinger's reading, it is important to note that the status of the image evolves in the novel, following Austerlitz's attempted remembrance of his origins. Austerlitz journeys to Prague in search of traces of his parents, where he finds an old family friend and former nanny, Věra. Věra gives Austerlitz two photographs, which had slipped, years ago, from a copy of Balzac's story of Colonel Chabert, possibly lent to Agáta who placed them there in "the last weeks before the Germans marched in" (256). Věra at first thought one of them might be of Agáta and Maximilian (Austerlitz's parents) on the set of a provincial theatre before the war (perhaps in Reichenau or Olmutz) on which Agáta performed (265-6). The other is of Austerlitz, dressed for a ball, taken in February 1939, six months before he left Prague (259). Austerlitz is struck by Věra's observation that these photographs had "the impression of something stirring in them, as if one caught the small sighs of despair . . . as if the pictures had a memory of their own and remembered us, remembered the role that we the survivors, and those no longer among us had played in our former lives" (258). Věra's suggestion is that the photographs are haunted by the referents (subjects) they bring back to life—and haunting for those who view them.

In the haunted and haunting nature of these images is an unmistakable reference to Roland Barthes' *Camera Lucida*. As Barthes would have it, the photographic image constitutes a form of witnessing: "I call 'photographic referent' not the optionally real thing to which an image or a sign refers but the necessarily real thing which was placed before the lens, without which there would be no photograph" (76). The referent is not in doubt, but its representation can appear chimerical, because the "intractable" "that-has-been" of the referent is "absolutely, irrefutably present, and yet already deferred" (76-7). Put another way, photographs anticipate the death of their referents. "*This will be* and *this has been;* I observe with horror the anterior future of which death is at stake. By giving me the absolute past of the pose (aorist), the photograph tells me death in the future. What pricks me is the discovery of this equivalence . . . . Whether or not the subject is already dead, every photograph is this catastrophe" (96). In this sense the photograph reanimates its referents, turns them into living corpses, as Barthes might have it (78). It is the reality-effect of the photograph, the viewer's confusion of sign and referent, that enhances the perception of reanimation:

> the photograph surreptitiously induces belief that it is alive, because of that delusion which makes us attribute to Reality an absolutely superior, somehow eternal value; but by shifting this reality to the past ("that-has-been") the photograph suggests that it is already dead. Hence it would be better to say that Photography's inimitable feature (its *noeme*) is that someone has seen the referent (even if it is a matter of objects) in *flesh and blood*, or again *in person*. (Barthes 78)

However, if we look more carefully at Austerlitz's reaction to and Sebald's contextualization of these photographs, something different emerges. They are interleaved in Balzac's novel about the return of Colonel Chabert, who, knocked unconscious at the battle of Eylau and interred in a mass grave, rose from the dead and returned years later to reclaim his wife, estate and name (394). Risen from the dead, he is unrecognisable and his claim to life seems arbitrary and in need of authorisation by the lawyer

Derville. The other photograph, that of Austerlitz, is verified by his grand-father's inscription on its reverse and later by Věra's confirmation (259). As in Chabert's story, witnesses are needed to corroborate history; the past and past objects cannot speak for themselves (that is, they are not autonomous). Although photographs are inscribed with the agency of witnessing (the act of photographing the past event), they cannot witness themselves. In response to the photograph of the couple who might be Agáta and Maximilian, Austerlitz projects a befitting drama onto the mountain scenery of the set: *"Wilhelm Tell*, or *La Sonnambula*, or Ibsen's last play"* (257). Ironically, the photograph turns out not to be of his par-ents. Of the photograph of himself, Austerlitz could not "recollect myself in that part" (259). Although unrecognisable to himself, "I always felt the piercing, inquiring gaze of the page boy who had come to demand his dues, who was waiting . . . for me to accept the challenge and avert the misfortune lying ahead of him" (260). It is therefore Austerlitz who ani-mates these photographs with a life they do not possess on their own.

In the case of the photograph taken on a theatre set, as Duttlinger points out, photography acts as an "auxiliary representational framework", enabling both an "imaginary, emotional engagement with the experience of trauma"—a possible confrontation with his parents and therefore his lost traumatic origins—but also a displacement of that experience into a "fictitious and anonymous photographic context" (163). Photography, then, does not so much record what is unavailable to conscious percep-tion, but it acts as a shield by "providing a substitute for those experiences and facilitates the viewer's retrospective, imaginary engagement with inci-dents which were never experienced, witnessed or photographed in the first place" (Duttlinger 163).

Although Duttlinger has not collapsed fiction and traumatic memory, the gap between them closes in her reading. On the one hand, she argues that *Austerlitz* is a fictional illustration or modelling of the relationship between the photographic image and traumatic memory in which photog-raphy constitutes "a mode of visual testimony that accompanies the pro-tagonist's quest for his repressed past" (170). On the other, "the discourse on photography in *Austerlitz* cannot be reduced to a theoretical, cultural or aesthetic exploration, since it derives its complexity as well as its literary potential from the fact that it also figures as a symptom of the protago-nist's traumatised psychological disposition" (156). Figuring as a symptom of trauma, those photographic images and the ideas that surround them somehow exceed or disrupt their own theorisation. That the novel's pho-totextuality figures as a traumatic symptom that exceeds theorization lends a certain autonomy or agency to the text. Arguably, Duttlinger's reading implies that the text not only reflects but performs a trauma that threatens to break the bounds of its own literary and figurative nature. This essay argues that Sebald does not align text and trauma but rather encourages a series of theoretical readings. The ideas ascribed to photography by Austerlitz and his narrator imply the author's deployment of various theoretical models, and theoretical exploration of photography and memory. The provocation of certain theoretical responses means that readers find themselves following theoretical *formulae* by which the text's traumatic nature can be, supposedly, elicited. However, it is this very formulaic route that ultimately separates trauma and text.

Although it might appear that *Austerlitz* frustrates a Barthesian reading—the images considered by Austerlitz do not have a life of their own; it is his gaze that (re)animates their subjects—the temporality of these images actually follows Barthes to the letter. Austerlitz's search for the true image of his mother echoes Barthes' highly subjective search for an image of his mother. This subjectivism is focused by the puncta of the photographic image. "A photograph's punctum is that accident which pricks me" (Barthes 27). This "wound" will disturb the "studium", the cultural field occupied by photographer and viewer that allows the recognition of the photographer's intentions and which makes the image generally meaningful (ibid.). The detail, the partial object, in the image that constitutes the punctum and which may overwhelm the photograph as a whole, disturbing its cultural meaning—"the studium is ultimately always coded, the punctum is not" (51)—is wholly in the eye of the beholder:

> Whether or not it is triggered, it is an addition: it is what I add to the photograph and *what is nonetheless already there* . . . . Hence to give examples of the punctum is, in a certain fashion, to *give myself up*. A detail overwhelms the entirety of my reading; it is an intense mutation of my interest, a fulguration. (Barthes 55, 43)

When it comes to a historical understanding of the image, "there exists another punctum (another 'stigmatum') than the 'detail'. This new punctum, which is no longer of form but of intensity, is Time, the lacerating emphasis of the noeme ('that-has-been'), its pure representation" (Barthes 96). In other words, "*that* is dead and *that* is going to die" (ibid.). Disturbing the cultural field (the studium), this temporal punctum does not make the image available for memory work, or rather mourning, in that the image marks loss, not the redemption of loss through cultural meaning.

> I cannot transform my grief [writes Barthes], I cannot let my gaze drift; no culture will help me utter this suffering which I experience entirely on the level of the image's finitude (this is why, despite its codes, I cannot *read* a photograph):

the Photograph—my Photograph—is without culture: when it is painful, nothing
in it can transform grief into mourning. And if dialectic is that thought which
masters the corruptible and converts the negation of death into the power of
work, then the photograph is undialectical: it is a denatured theatre where death
cannot 'be contemplated', reflected and interiorised. (Barthes 90)

So, it is the very subjective process that animated the photographic image
in the first place in the name of the remembrance of the lost that disrupts
that remembrance. It is for this reason that "Not only is the Photograph
never, in essence, a memory (whose grammatical expression would be the
perfect tense, whereas the tense of photograph is the aorist), but it actually
blocks memory, quickly becomes a counter-memory" (ibid.). Barthes cannot exhibit "The Winter Garden Photograph", the true image of his
mother—the idea of photography's essence is an impossible science given
the way that photographs are animated—because its punctum exists only
for him. Therefore, the failure of the image as a memory prop exists only
for him. Like Barthes, Austerlitz pursues the mother-image, and it count-
ers memory work for both melancholics. Sebald's staging of a Barthesian
melancholia, though, does not conflate literature and memory as if they
were the same thing. It rather establishes a pretext for Austerlitz's memory
work and therefore *Camera Lucida* as the novel's intertext.

The novel also suggests a Benjaminian reading, with similar effect.
Austerlitz obtains a copy of the Nazi propaganda film made of the Theresienstadt ghetto in preparation for a Red Cross visit, which was successfully designed to create the illusion of better conditions for the ghetto's
prisoners. In the film *Der Führer schenkt den Juden eine Stadt*, or rather a
patchwork of surviving scenes, Austerlitz hopes to find an image of his
mother, who was sent to Theresienstadt before her fatal deportation far-
ther east. Typically, and as with other images related to his parents, Austerlitz frames his viewing of these images with his dramatic imagination,
underscoring the unreliable nature of the images, their propensity for
dissimulation. So, before seeing the film, he imagines his mother as "a
saleswoman in the haberdashery shop, just taking a fine pair of gloves
carefully out of one of the drawers, or singing a part of Olympia in the
Tales of Hoffmann which . . . was staged in Theresienstadt in the course of
the improvements campaign" (343). As Duttlinger points out, without
realizing the import of this thought, Austerlitz's imagination is complicit
with the Nazi's strategy of illusion in which the brutal realities of the
ghetto were veiled by Nazi propaganda (167). Initially, the film reveals
nothing of his mother, just a series of images that "seemed to dissolve
even as they appeared" (345). However, by making a slow-motion version

in which the original 14 minutes are extended to an hour, "previously hidden objects and people" emerge (345). The slow-motion version reveals damage to the film stock that was "hardly noticed before, [but which] now melted the image from its centre or from the edges, blotting it out and instead making patterns of bright white sprinkled with black which reminded me of aerial photographs taken in the far north, or a drop of water seen under a microscope" (348). The deceleration of the moving image effectively returns it to a series of composite frames. Austerlitz's reading of the film recalls—and rather deliberately, I argue—Walter Benjamin's sense of the optical unconscious.

Benjamin describes how "photography reveals the physiognomic aspects of visual worlds which dwell in the smallest things meaningful yet covert enough to find a hiding place in waking dreams" ("A Small History" 243). Elsewhere, Benjamin elaborates:

> The enlargement of a snapshot does not simply render more precise what in any case was visible, though unclear: it reveals entirely new structural formations of the subject . . . . Evidently a different nature opens itself to the camera than opens to the naked eye—if only because an unconsciously penetrated space is substituted for a space consciously explored by man. The camera introduces us to unconscious optics as does psychoanalysis to unconscious impulses. (Benjamin, "The Work of Art" 229-30)

Austerlitz's microscopic view allows him to see flaws in the film that "disrupt and undermine the coherence of its staged, deceptive reality" (Duttlinger 160). What is more, the deceleration allows the emergence of a figure, in the audience of a musical performance, whom Austerlitz believes to be his mother: "at the left-hand side, set a little way back and close to the upper edge of the frame, the face of a young woman appears, barely emerging from the black shadows around it, which is why I did not notice it at all at first" (350). Austerlitz believes her to be his mother. Duttlinger also seems to confirm this identification: "Austerlitz thus finally discovers his mother" (169). Despite the theatrical setting, which is a reminder of the photographic image's inherent ability to stage reality, as well as a reminder of its particular use here within the fictions of Nazi propaganda, both protagonist and critic invest in the image's purported reference. The only danger to this referentiality is, for both protagonist and critic, the fleetingness of the arrested image.

Duttlinger's corroboration seems a little spurious and against Sebald's intentions, and it even overrides the contrary evidence that she identifies. Austerlitz's description of his mother-image, specifically her jewellery, does not match the image itself. Duttlinger reads this as Sebald's statement on the precariousness of photographic reference in general (or of this illustration in particular) rather than the wilfulness of Austerlitz's interpretation (169). Duttlinger also overrides her own very useful exploration of the reference to Louis Darget. The slow-motion film transforms its subjects into ghostly versions of themselves:

> They seemed to be hovering rather than walking, as if their feet no longer quite touched the ground. The contours of their bodies were blurred and, particularly the scenes shot out of doors in the broad daylight, had dissolved at the edges, resembling . . . the frayed outlines of the human hand shown in the fluidal pictures and electrographs taken by Louis Draget [sic]. (348)

Darget (not Draget) "assumed that every living being emanates invisible rays which could be made visible on the photographic plate. His technique involved the physical contact between the referent's hand and the photographic plate and was later extended to so-called 'mental photography', which aimed at the photographic depiction of invisible fluids emitted by the sitter's thoughts and emotional states" (Duttlinger 168). Duttlinger reads the allusion as a figure of the inextricability of the visible and the invisible in the photographic image (ibid.), which as I argue, in Benjaminian terms, is the immanence of the optical unconscious in conscious perception. Duttlinger had earlier argued that the photographic image functioned in Sebald's text as a displacement of or substitution for the traumatic event that cannot be known by its protagonist and which remains unconscious. Now her argument suggests, via the allusion to Darget, the immanence of the unconscious and what resides in it. Indeed, the emergence of the mother-image is not just the restitution of a forgotten part of Austerlitz's life, but also the return of a history of his traumatic origins: a history that entailed her death, his survival, and the subsequent repression of those events.

Surely, the Darget-like characteristics of the decelerated film hint not at the emergence of what had until recently resided in the unconscious, that is, Agáta, but at Austerlitz's metaphysical desire to conjure up that referent. So, rather like Barthes' punctum, which can only exist in the eye of the beholder, the ghostly emanations of the image are, likewise, not the intrusion of the unconscious but of another form of latency. As Benjamin explains: "the beholder feels an irresistible urge to search such a picture for the tiny spark of contingency, of the Here and Now, with which reality has so to speak seared the subject, to find the inconspicuous spot where in the immediacy of the long-forgotten moment the future subsists so eloquently that we, looking back, may rediscover it" ("A Small History" 243). Benjamin relates the optical unconscious to memory work to come, provoked by the apprehension of a provocative aspect of the image. This of course is a subjective projection of a provocation onto the image and onto the past moment of its making. Given Sebald's Benjaminian scheme, the Theresienstadt image of Agáta remains unverifiable; the only verifiable image that Austerlitz does find of her is in the Celetná theatrical archives in Prague, in the records for 1938 and 1939 (353). Even this image has to be treated with suspicion, given the readiness with which Věra identifies it. If all images have so far proved unreliable, the immediate verification of this one seems conspicuous. More important, though, than identifying the limits and excesses of Austerlitz's historical imagination is the theoretical terrain on which this takes place—on which Sebald orchestrates Auster- litz's responses to the past. The fact of the allusion to another theory is as important as what the theory does. In other words, a series of intertexts keep the memory work done in this novel within theoretical bounds, thereby generating an isomorphic rather than contagious relationship between memory and text. In fact, Duttlinger's elaborations on the ema- nations that flow from subject to image recall once again Barthes' *Camera Lucida* as an intertext: the "umbilical cord [that] links the body of the pho- tographed thing to my gaze: light though impalpable, is here a carnal me- dium, a skin I share with anyone who has been photographed" (81).

If Duttlinger's reading implies the text comes close to performing memory work, Samuel Pane locates trauma within the text itself: "The trauma that emerges upon their viewing of photographic images does not reside exclusively in the subject of the photographs they [Austerlitz and his narrator] consult throughout the novel, but rather it seems to reside in the photographic medium itself" (39). Furthermore, "Since photographic media in *Austerlitz* is inherently traumatic, there can never be any complete recovery and documentation of the narratives of that past. Hence, narra- tive itself in *Austerlitz* must also be traumatic; it constantly returns to pho- tographic images and constantly fails in its search for commensurability with human experience" (Pane 41).

Pane draws on Caruth's conception of trauma in which repetition— compulsion - in this case focused on the photographic images obsessed over in the text—is the belated and literal return of an event missed first time round. Repetition is the attempt at mastery that fails second time round. In addition, Pane draws on Barthes to think through Caruth's con- ception of belatedness. The punctum is realised belatedly, after its viewing (48). In other words, it is the initial failure to see an image's punctum and then the affect of that failure afterwards (with the image out of sight), and the punctum's resistance to naming or to the symbolic code, which sug- gests a failure of witnessing on the viewer's part. The compulsion to mas-

ter what cannot be seen spreads from protagonist to narrator and ultimately to author and novel: "Narrative desire merges with trauma theory
at the nexus of the narrator's implication in the thrust of Austerlitz's initial
act of narration. In effect, Sebald's novel is the product of the narrator's
collusion with Austerlitz's need to tell . . . though he cannot name the
desire in which he participates. He cannot resist the narrative desire that
drives him repeatedly back to photographic images" (42). For Pane, then,
trauma resides in the text.

As Radstone has argued, the merging of text and trauma precludes the
consideration of articulation and mediation. Put another way, Pane's theoretical route to historical trauma actually dislocates the text from the specific historical circumstances of remembrance. So, where Pane suggests
the reader's (necessarily failed) witnessing of the text's trauma, Bernhard
Malkmus argues that the instability of the text's images locates the reader
historically. As Malkmus argues: "It is often impossible to determine
whether the images function as a trigger of memory or whether they serve
as a subsequent condensation of the rhizome of linguistic associations
governing the stream of consciousness in the text" (214). The status of the
photographic images seem to oscillate between the "concrete" and "abstract", never functioning as "mere illustrations", "but they also entangle
the reader in a subtext of interpretation and anticipation. Images are both
trigger and residua of memory, they transcend and undermine temporal
(narrative) categories and simultaneously establish an idiosyncratic
mnemoscape from where the reader's act of remembering can depart"
(ibid.). The instability of the images and their disruption of the text create
a space within the text for the reader's own memory work, or rather for
the intersection, staged by the novel, of personal and collective memory
(ibid.).

Malkmus places the novel firmly in the context of post-1989 German
conceptions of history. The self-consciousness of German historical
memory work after 1989 testifies to the untenability of *posthistoire*, and the
inhabitation of Sebald's in-between spaces between text and image, created by the interrelations of text and image, is, for Malkmus, a means of
contributing to and sustaining a form of memory work that relates individual memory to collective memory and *vice versa* (214). The necessary
rethinking after 1989 of Germany's previous commemorative cultures
(Eastern and Western), the identities they had produced in relation to the
past, and of the normalising effect those cultures had on the past—a re-
consideration of the legacy of Nazism and of questions of historical responsibility—was a matter for individual and collective memory. For
Malkmus, Sebald offers a kind of template for an individual intervention

in collective memory: "He evokes stories of recontextualisation as a constant realm of translation between idiosyncratic condensations of historical memory and its return into collective topicality" (216). This does not mean to say that the novel frames unmediated access to the past (either for the individual or the collective): "the perception of reality and the past is always already shot through with contexts that have to be reconstructed" (215). Sebald's approach to historical memory is Benjaminian in that memory is the medium of the exploration of the past, rather than the instrument by which the past is retrieved. So, in other words, fragments and objects of the past have to be considered in terms of the changing contexts by which they are remembered, and those contexts also need historicising (215, 216). So, Sebald's text constitutes a realm of "translatability and convertibility between non-sensory and sensory correspondences, text and image, context and object" (215). In other words, the text demonstrates the layers of mediation involved in the work that constitutes cultural memory in that fragments and objects of the past found in the text are converted or translated by the memory work they focus. In turn, that memory work is contingent on its operational contexts. Given its internal dynamics, the novel issues protocols for its own use as an object of memory—a usage pre-empted and provoked by the "author . . . [-]voyeur, who detects idiosyncratic correspondences he can textually process as allegories of cultural memory" (ibid.).

The diegetic and extra-diegetic dialogue between the individual and the collective orchestrated by the novel does not suggest that memory work has or should reach its conclusions. Malkmus, following Lyotard, argues that "'traumatisation'" is the only adequate response to the Holocaust because it opens up a non-space of representation, whereas the symbolization of experience means an "infinite chain of potential interpretations. A sign can be paradigmatically exchanged or syntagmatically reshuffled, it inevitably draws attention away from what it signifies to how it signifies, from experience to medium" (225). The space of non-representation is once again found in the punctal nature of the photographic image that marks a return of the event in non-symbolic form (229), but which is also the means of individual and idiosyncratic participation in a cultural memory for the protagonist, narrator and reader. "It is from the angle of this punctum that the spectator revitalises the whole photograph. It triggers a memoire involuntaire, an empathy with history that allows a re-entry into history through a revealing moment captured in a second" (228).

Malkmus goes some way to stemming the universalization of trauma otherwise found in *Austerlitz*. Although the affectiveness of the image provokes the reader as well as narrator and protagonist, positioning the reader as witness to a kind of textual trauma, this positionality is historically located. Indeed, the reader's memory work is not unbounded but has to negotiate the relationship between German author, narrator (implicitly German) and Jewish émigré protagonist: "The painstaking diligence with which the narrator/Sebald reassembles Austerlitz's story and redesigns his historical mnemoscape of wartime Europe can be read as a voice of a German deeply affected by the omnipresence of history, a person who knows that oblivion is stronger and has largely covered up all the historical evidence" (223).

Nevertheless, trauma still resides in the text. Such is the logic of Malkmus' argument, and that is confirmed by his reading of the visual motif of images of eyes found near the beginning of the novel. They represent "the uncanny-familiar gaze of history out of the dark" (234). They suggest that the reader, narrator and author are witnessed by Austerlitz and the history of which he is conscious and unconscious. In other words, the text seems to anticipate us, or so we imagine, because its photographic images return to us familiar histories and those that are unfamiliar and beyond our grasp. Such is the traumatic nature of photography with its "primordial quality of something real, outside systems of representation" (ibid.). Again, the text is agentic. Not only that, while Malkmus ascribes to these images an affectiveness that is associated with and which essentialises the photographic image, these are not in fact photographs.

The images of human eyes are those of the faces of Wittgenstein and the artist Jan Peter Tripp. They are both reproductions of the artwork of Jan Peter Tripp. It is unclear whether they belong to the narrator's photographic collection, or Austerlitz's. More likely, the images could be drawn from the author's own collection, after all Sebald and Tripp had been collaborators, life-long friends, and Sebald had written essays on Tripp's work (see Sebald and Tripp, *Unrecounted*; Sebald, "As Day and Night"; Sebald, "*Scomber scombrus*"). What is to be made of what seems like an authorial intervention, or such an explicit declaration of intertextuality? Sebald writes of Tripp in relation to Barthes:

> Roland Barthes saw in the by now omnipresent man with a camera an agent of death, and in photography something like the residue of life perpetually perishing. What distinguishes art from such undertaker's business is that life's closeness to death is its theme, not its addiction. It confronts the extinction of the visible world in an interminable series of reproductions by the deconstruction of phenomenal forms. Accordingly, Jan Peter Tripp's pictures, too, have always an analytical, not synthesising tendency. The photographic material that is their starting point is carefully modified. The mechanical sharpness/vagueness relationship is

suspended, additions are made and reductions. Something is shifted to another place, emphasised, foreshortened or minimally dislocated. Shades of colour are changed and at times those happy errors occur from which unexpectedly the system of a representation opposed to reality can result (Sebald, "As Day and Night" 84).

Sebald positions Tripp's aesthetics as an antidote to Barthes' melancholy phenomenology of the photographic image. Under the auspices of this phenomenology, as we have seen, the realism of the image serves to dislocate the referent, to present absence, which means, as Sebald might have it, that loss is universalized—subsuming particular historical losses. Tripp's "deconstruction of phenomenal forms" through the modification of photographic pretexts generates a critical distance from the affectiveness of the photographic image. Implicit in this is Sebald's wariness that traumatic loss, which, as we have seen, has been found traumatic in so many renditions of Barthes, resides in the text, from where it can contaminate the reader. Where others have found the text traumatic, agentic, a reflection of trauma, or its analogue, Malkmus has at least positioned its affectiveness within a specific cultural history of memory. He has shown how the text is mediated by the discourses of a wider public sphere that allow the articulation of the past. Nevertheless, the logic of his argument ultimately locates trauma in the text. What is needed is a rethinking of the idea of the transference of trauma, which can be found in the work of Dominick LaCapra.

LaCapra's concern with the universalization of trauma—contagion—via its representation is that it engenders endless mourning or melancholia. The object of memory is transvaluated from a negative sublime—something that defies representation—into a positive sublime, which becomes the basis (cathection) of individual and group identity (LaCapra, *Writing History* 23). To put it another way, endless mourning is overly-focused on the aporia that structure the representation of trauma, detaching them from their specific historical referents to the extent that structural absences or traumas subsume historically specific losses or traumas (ibid.). (The critique of trauma studies with which this essay began reached parallel conclusions.)

The universalization of loss "makes of existence a fundamentally traumatic scene" affecting all relations (LaCapra, *Writing History* 23-4). The basis of identity is then foundation-less (without historical specificity), which means the collapse of any measure of the relation between identities and their traumas: the "relation between differentiated experiences of agents and subjects in the past and the differentiated experiences of observers or secondary witnesses" (37). Given the groundlessness of identity, an over-identification with the victim and victim's trauma, the very thing that has facilitated this groundless condition, becomes, ironically, the only means by which identity can be regrounded—by which history can be pursued. While this may appear as a sacrifice of the self to the historically othered victim, it is in fact the sacrifice of that other in the service of self-identification—an oblation that repeats the very logic of the sacrificial scapegoating of Nazism's victims (24, 30-1). Under Nazism, this was a form of role-reversal, in which the victim represented that part of the (Nazi) self that had to be expunged. In memorialization, the continuation of a sacrificial logic also continues this universalization of the victim. In fact, the excess of generosity in which the self is offered "elides the problem of the victim" (24). What is needed is a "middle voice" by which the writer can articulate historical experience in a mode that remains, through incomplete and disrupted representation, faithful to the witness's perspective, without confusing structural and historical trauma. Modulated as such, the middle voice is able to differentiate (or articulate the differences between) subject positions—primarily between perpetrator and victim, but also between direct and secondary witness—that would otherwise remain confused in a generalized scene of trauma: an "undifferentiated scene of horror and negative sublimity, a scene beneath or beyond ethical considerations" (26-7).

The middle voice recognises the transference of trauma, understood as the way in which "problems and processes active in the texts or artefacts we study are repeated in displaced and often disguised or distorted form in our very accounts of them" (LaCapra, *Representing the Holocaust* 111). Furthermore:

> The Holocaust presents the historian with transference in the most traumatic form conceivable—but in a form that will vary with the difference in subject-position of the analyst. Whether the historian or analyst is a survivor, a relative of survivors, a former Nazi, a former collaborator, a relative of former Nazis or collaborators, a younger Jew or German displaced or distanced from more immediate contact with survival, participation, collaboration, or a relative "outsider" to these problems will make a difference even in the meaning of statements that may be formerly identical. (LaCapra, *Representing the Holocaust* 46)

Recognizing the transference of trauma, then, LaCapra insists on the specification of its origins and affect. Empathy is called for rather than identification, where identification is the "unmediated fusion of self and other in which the otherness or alterity of the other is not recognised and respected" (LaCapra, *Writing History* 27, n31). This fusion is akin to

Kleinian "projective identification" in "which aspects not acknowledged in the self are attributed to the other. It may also involve incorporation, in which aspects of the other are taken into or encrypted in the self" (27). With empathy, "one does not feel compelled or authorized to speak in the other's voice or take the other's place, for example, as surrogate victim or perpetrator," and this is fundamental to an ethical stance toward the other (27-8). An empathic middle voice seeks to articulate "modulations of proximity and distance, empathy and irony with respect to different 'objects' of investigation", and given the importance of retaining the historical referent and historically grounded identity, "it need not be understood as ruling out all forms of objectivity and objectification" (30, 35).

What then does the middle voice sound like or, when transcribed, look like, and just how is it articulated? LaCapra does not suggest that there is a stylistic formula (14), but that an adequate voice (or form of historical representation) illuminates one's pre-existing implication in transferential relations. It is the aporetic nature of the middle voice that opens up a space in which the pre-existent relationship of the addresser and addressee (writer and reader) to trauma can be elicited and explored. This is fundamentally different from the idea of the text actually transmitting trauma. It is in this space that a differential relationship to the traumatic event can be established, perpetrators can be distinguished from victims, witnesses from secondary witnesses, the universalization of trauma and its victims stemmed, and relationships to the traumatic event illuminated rather than just claimed. LaCapra, then, admits the reverberations of the traumatic, but calls for a more modulated representation of affect. If the middle voice entails "an often disconcerting exploration of disorientation, its symptomatic dimensions, and possible ways of responding to them", then the "crucial issue is how one responds to or comes to terms with that initial positionality—and here one confronts the issue of how to deploy various modalities of acting out, working over, and working through" (189, 36). Indeed, if the middle voice foregrounds one's subject position, it allows a thinking through of the ethical ramifications of the perspectives that emanate from that position. Although the middle voice is not inherently traumatic—trauma does not inhere in language and discourse—it provides an index to traumatization, and in doing so it allows engagement with, critical distance from and self-reflexivity towards transferential relations rather than their disavowal. In short, the middle voice generates a sense of "empathetic unsettlement."

By anticipating theories of trauma and loss that might otherwise elicit trauma in the text, Sebald's phototextuality acts more as a prophylactic to trauma's contagion rather than as a conduit. A traumatic text would suggest an ability to share the victim's experience. In LaCapra's terms, this "identification" by German author and narrator with Jewish Holocaust victim would have entailed a dangerous sacrificial logic. The text's provocation of trauma and then its revocation sound like the kind of irony advocated by LaCapra that checks proximity to trauma with distance, acting out with working through. This is not to say that trauma inheres in the text or that the text traumatizes the reader, but that its provocations and revocations—its hollowing out—affords the reader not an opportunity to indulge in a contagious trauma, (over)identification, but the space to locate his pre-existing positionality in relation to trauma.

Austerlitz's intermediality has evoked the disruptive dynamics of trauma and thereby anticipated theories that would find trauma in the text, but it has also opened up a textual space in which pre-existent transferential relations and identities can be located. What other light might *Austerlitz's* intermediality—its remediation of photographic images—shed on memory and trauma studies? The evocative, indeed provocative phototextuality of the novel recalls the critiques of trauma studies with which this essay began. The tendency to see such novels as the unmediated reflection of traumatic memory overlooks the particularity of the text itself: for example, its generic, formal, and rhetorical properties, as well as the literary discourses, histories and traditions that attend and inform textual practice (Radstone, "Memory Studies" 30-39). It is the textual—in this case phototextual or intermedial—properties that inform reception. As Kansteiner argues, reception is all too often neglected in the study of memory. Memory texts may be authorized by the institutions and discourses of the public sphere, but there is often a discrepancy between the intentionality of the authorizing agents, the intentions of that text's author or authors, the text itself, and the text's reception or consumption. As Kansteiner reminds us, texts can be read against their authors' intentions, or not consumed at all as significant memory texts despite their intentions, and the medium of the text can refract or dislocate those intentions. Therefore, memory studies needs to pay increasing attention to the hermeneutical triangle of object, maker and consumer (Kansteiner, "Finding Meaning" 197). That the affectiveness of intermediality is depen-dent on reception (with all its contexts and contingencies) is a less than obvious statement given the way that theories of traumatic memory have essentialized the photographic image—as discussed above, the image is rendered essentially melancholic—and/or found the interplay of word and image inherently affective. (This essay's discussion of transference has gone some way in locating potential scenarios of reception.) A consideration of intermediality, then, has demonstrated that the dynamics of memory are better understood by, as Kansteiner might put it, a triangular hermeneutics. Otherwise, memory is hypostatized - located in one medium of representation or another, or in the discourses, agencies and institutions that mediate and authorize memory texts, or in their receptive or not so receptive subjects rather than found in the relations between the constituent parts of cultural memory.

References

Baer, Ulrich. *Spectral Evidence: The Photography of Trauma*. Cambridge: MIT Press, 2002.

Ball, Karyn. "Trauma and its Institutional Destinies." *Cultural Critique* 46 (2000): 1-44.

Barthes, Roland. *Camera Lucida: Reflections on Photography*. Trans. Richard Howard. London: Cape, 1982.

Benjamin, Walter. "The Work of Art in the Age of Mechanical Reproduction." *Illuminations*. By Benjamin. Trans. Harry Zohn. London: Fontana, 1992. 211-44.

---. "A Small History of Photography." *One Way Street, and Other Writings*. By Benjamin. Trans. E. Jephcott and K. Shorter. London: Verso, 1997. 240-57.

Bolter, Jay David and Richard Grusin. *Remediation: Understanding New Media*. Cambridge: MIT Press, 2000.

Caruth, Cathy. "Trauma and Experience: Introduction." *Trauma: Explorations in Memory*. Ed. Cathy Caruth. Baltimore: Johns Hopkins UP, 1995. 3-12.

---. *Unclaimed Experience: Trauma, Narrative, and History*. Baltimore: Johns Hopkins UP, 1996.

Duttlinger, Carolin. "Traumatic Photographs: Remembrance and the Mechanical Media." *W. G. Sebald: A Critical Companion*. Ed. J.J. Long and Anne Whitehead. Seattle: U of Washington P, 2004. 155-74.

Felman, Shoshana. "Education and Crisis, or the Vicissitudes of Teaching." *Testimony: Crises of Witnessing in Literature, Psychoanalysis, and History*. Ed. Shoshana Felman and Dori Laub. New York: Routledge, 1992. 1-56.

Hungerford, Amy. "Memorizing Memory." *The Yale Journal of Criticism* 14.1 (2001): 67-92.

Kansteiner, Wulf. "Finding Meaning in Memory: A Methodological Critique of Memory Studies." *History and Theory* 41.2 (2002): 179-97.

Klein, Kerwin Lee. "On the Emergence of *Memory* in Historical Discourse." *Representations* 69 (2000): 127-50.

LaCapra, Dominick. *Representing the Holocaust: History, Theory, Trauma*. London: Cornell UP, 1996.

---. *History and Memory After Auschwitz*. London: Cornell UP, 1998.

---. *Writing History, Writing Trauma*. Baltimore: Johns Hopkins UP, 2001.

Leys, Ruth. *Trauma: A Genealogy*. Chicago: U of Chicago P, 2000.

Malkmus, Berhnhard. "'All of them Signs and Characters from the Type-Case of Forgotten Things'—Intermedia Configurations of History in W. G. Sebald." *Memory Traces: 1989 and the Questions of German Cultural Identity*. Ed. Silke Arnold-de Simine. Oxford: Lang, 2005. 211-44.

Pane, Samuel. "*Trauma Obscura*: Photographic Media in W. G. Sebald's *Austerlitz*." *Mosaic* 38.1 (2005): 37-54.

Radstone, Susannah. "Screening Trauma: *Forrest Gump*, Film and Memory." *Memory and Methodology*. Ed. Susannah Radstone. Oxford: Berg, 2000. 79-110.

---. "Reconceiving Binaries: The Limits of Memory." *History Workshop Journal* 59 (2005): 134-50.

---. "Trauma's Fascination." Psychoanalysis and History Seminar. Institute of Historical Research, University of London. 22 Nov. 2006. Lecture.

---. "Memory Studies: For and Against." *Memory Studies* 1.1 (2008): 30-39.

Sebald, W. G. *Austerlitz*. Trans. Anthea Bell. London: Penguin, 2002.

---. "As Day and Night, Chalk and Cheese: On the Pictures of Jan Peter Tripp." Sebald and Tripp 78-94.

---. "*Scomber scombrus* or the Common Mackerel: On Pictures by Jan Peter Tripp." *Campo Santo*. By Sebald. Ed. Sven Meyer. Trans. Anthea Bell. London: Hamish Hamilton, 2005. 169-72.

Sebald, W. G., and Jan Peter Tripp. *Unrecounted*. Trans. Michael Hamburger. London: Hamish Hamilton, 2004.

Suleiman, Susan Rubin. *Crises of Memory and the Second World War*. Cambridge: Harvard UP, 2006.

Digital Network Memory

Andrew Hoskins

1. Memory "On-the-Fly"

The media metaphors of memory are as seductive in their apparent longevity as they are plentiful. They have a history of their own, from Plato's "wax tablet" (although he later rejected this same model) and other versions of memory as writing, through photography and the physicality and fixity of film and magnetic tape, to the mobility and instantaneity of "flash memory". The metaphorical tension at least appears through the frequent treatment of memory as either indelible and immovable or as something that is not available to the human or machinic processes of capture, storage and retrieval. Douwe Draaisma for example, states: "One metaphor turns our recollections into fluttering birds which we can only catch at the risk of grabbing the wrong one, the next one reduces memories to static and latent traces". Is it then that this disjuncture has become more pronounced and our understanding of memory has become more obscured with the rapid advance of digital media and technologies and their associated memory discourses and practices? For, as Draaisma continues: "With each new metaphor we place a different filter in front of our perception of memory" (230). In taking "network" as a metaphor for the highly mediated and mediatized memory of today, however, I do not seek merely another "filter" to our perception of memory, but rather to make visible the crucial paradigmatic shift that is needed (and underway in places) in the study of media and communications. For instance, Mizuko Ito takes the notion of "networked publics" to refer to a "linked set of social, cultural, and technological developments", thus replacing the passive and the consumptive connotations of "audience" and "consumer" (2-3). In other words, if the individual as consumer of media is complemented if not challenged by the individual as producer and user (thus, "pro-sumer", see

Merrin) then the relationship between media and memory is similarly transformed.

Contemporary memory is principally constituted neither through retrieval nor through the representation of some content of the past in the present. Rather, it is embedded in and distributed through our sociotechnical practices (see Bowker; Van House and Churchill; and Grusin, *Premediation*). Thus the use of Web sites and services such as *MySpace*, *Facebook* and *Twitter* allow users to continually display and to shape biographical information, post commentaries on their unfolding lives and to interact publicly or semi-publicly with one another through messaging services in real-time or near real-time. Other "dynamic" so-called "Web 2.0" platforms include file sharing systems, for example *Flickr* and *YouTube*, which mesh the private and the public into an immediate and intensely visual and auditory present past. The very use of these systems contributes to a new memory—an emergent digital network memory—in that communications in themselves dynamically add to, alter, and erase, a kind of living archival memory.

So, in this essay, I argue for a more temporally and spatially adequate perspective on memory that deliberately highlights the dynamics of mediated memory as something created when needed, driven by the connectivities of digital technologies and media, and inextricably forged through and constitutive of digital social networks: in other words, a new "network memory".

The actual and potential transformative power of media and their associated technologies to render memory (in all its apparently isolated or collective and cultural configurations) static and enduring has been both acclaimed and bemoaned. The neurobiologist, Steven Rose, for example, contrasts the memory-keeping of early human societies with the memorial processes of today. In the oral cultures of the former, memories needed to be constantly trained and renewed, with select individuals afforded the considerable responsibility of "retelling" the stories which preserved the common culture. Rose argues that "[p]eople's memories, internal records of their own experiences, must have been their most treasured—but also fragile—possessions" (60). Moreover, the moment of each storytelling was unrepeatable: "Then, each time a tale was told it was unique, the product of a particular interaction of the teller, his or her memories of past stories told, and the present audience". In contrast, Rose argues, new technologies challenge both the uniqueness and dynamics of human memory: "A videotape or audiotape, a written record, do more than just reinforce memory; they freeze it, and in imposing a fixed, linear sequence upon it, they simultaneously preserve it and prevent it from evolving and transforming itself with time" (61).

By extension, the same technologies and media shape (and shape our understanding of) the nature, function and potential of the "archive". Here, the idea of the archive as a "repository" or "store" is influential in contemporary media-memory discourses. Diana Taylor, for example, outlines the presumed fixity of the archive: "'Archival' memory exists as documents, maps, literary texts, letters, archaeological remains, bones, videos, films, CDs, all those items supposedly resistant to change" (19). So, the very forms of many traditional media evoke a permanency in their storage potential as "available" to future times.

One response to the acclaimed "fixing" potential of media is that this idea is too easily embroiled in the association of the apparent permanence of a given medium with the durability of the memory. Uric Neisser for instance cautions over the metaphorical comparing of memory with a "permanent medium of storage". He argues: "Such a comparison seems harmless enough, but once the metaphor is in play we tend to endow memory itself with properties that only the medium really has: permanence, detail, incorruptibility" (81).

More specifically, as archival, media also work to totalizing effect by providing a common blanket for present and future perspectives on the past. Jan Assmann hints at (or even reinforces) this problem in defining two modes of "cultural memory" so that memory operates: "first in the mode of potentiality of the archive whose accumulated texts, images, and rules of conduct act as a total horizon, and second in the mode of actuality, whereby each contemporary context puts the objectivized meaning into its own perspective, giving it its own relevance" (130). A similar binary is more concretely evident in Rose's distinction between the fallible and dynamic "organic" or "human" memory and the "artificial" memory of media.

In this essay I argue that the distinctions between the totalizing and the contextual, the permanent and the ephemeral, the archive and narrative, are less effectual when memory is embedded in networks that blur these characteristics. The digital media of most interest here are principally the internet and the array of technological advances that have transformed the temporality, spatiality, and indeed the mobility of memories. Even the dynamics of the emergent field of memory studies seem unable to keep pace with what I propose here is part of a new digital temporality of memory. Although the term "new" is readily applied to a range of late modern phenomena it is appropriate in this context. "New memory" (Hoskins, "New Memory"; *Televising War*; and "Television") is "new" in its continually emergent state propelled through the metaphors and media and technologies of the day, but simultaneously these same media reflexively shape a reassessment of the nature and the very value of remembering (and forgetting) under these conditions. Perhaps this contributes to a contemporary ecology of "metamemory" where discourses and debates attempt to reconcile or to challenge the function or purpose of particular cultural memory markers—objects, exhibitions, museums etc.—which serve to "stand in" for and potentially become more durable than the memory they purport to engender and to encourage.

This essay seeks to extend the application of new memory in our digital media ecology through proposing that the very condition of remembering is increasingly networked but also actively and re-actively constructed on-the-fly and that, notably, memory is characterized by its mediated or mediatized *emergence*[1] through a range of everyday digital media.

The metaphor "on-the-fly" is also found in the field of computing. To provide one example from the area of programming computer audio and electro-acoustic music, being developed at Princeton:

> On-the-fly programming (or live coding) is a style of programming in which the programmer/performer/composer augments and modifies the program while it is running, without stopping or restarting, in order to assert expressive, programmable control for performance, composition, and experimentation at runtime. (Wang and Cook)

On-the-fly memory is a constructive version of memory that builds on and indeed requires previous moments out of which it emerges, accumulates and also acquires new characteristics with and in each passing moment. For instance, one of the pioneers of the psychology of memory, Fredric Bartlett, writing over three-quarters of a century ago, used the metaphor of the playing of a skilled game to illustrate the "constructive character of remembering":

> We may fancy that we are repeating a series of movements learned a long time before from a text-book or from a teacher. But motion study shows that in fact we build up the stroke afresh on a basis of the immediately preceding balance of postures and the momentary needs of the game. Every time we make it, it has its own characteristics. (204)

The treating of memory (and forgetting) as forged through a momentum of changing times, as the relationship between the now and the most recently connected moment, is an important starting point in the search for a more temporally-adequate account of human memory. However, memory on-the-fly is more than a cumulative trajectory of past moments which feeds into and shapes each present anew. For instance, personal biography intersects with history in an implicit way, locating the unfolding details of everyday life in terms of the events of the larger society—history in the making. The unfolding details of daily life have a "once through" quality, in which the mundane and momentous actions and events of people's lives carry them forward even as the continuous present seems to slide relentlessly into the past. Each moment is lived and experienced as what Harold Garfinkel (186) calls "another next first time", namely as a recognizable and sequentially located new moment, a patterned new moment that can be understood because of its similarity to previous moments and because of its place in the joint unfolding of biography and history (Boden and Hoskins).

One can begin to realize just how instructive Garfinkel's ethnomethodology is in accounting for the relationship between media and memory in terms of the shift in focus from media content to that of sociotechnical practices. This is part of a wider shift underway between what I will set out as "two phases of mediatization".[2] Indeed, Garfinkel's "another next first time" is similar to the title of Lisa Gitelman's excellent book on how media function simultaneously as subjects and instruments of inquiry: *Always Already New*. How then to best characterize and interrogate memory that is continually affected by (and expressed through) digital media in that there is an ongoing negotiation of the self and culture through and interplay with the emergent technologies of the day to shape a past that is "always already new"?

The tension between the traces of the past versus the contingencies of the present in the production of memory is even more profound with the onset of the digital media. This is because of the ways in which digital networks simultaneously enable a massively increased availability of all-things-past (which Chris Anderson calls "the long tail") and the heightened connectivity of, and in, the present. Furthermore, the construction of memory in everyday life is "imbricated" not only in digital recording technologies and media but also in the standards and classifications resulting from their growth that inevitably and often invisibly regulate our sociotechnical practices (see Bowker and Star 2). To go further, technological advances have provoked a reevaluation of the relationship between media and consciousness.

There is a history to these developments. Grusin (*Premediation*), for example, observes that "even media and cultural theorists have begun to argue that humans have historically co-evolved with technology, distributing their cognitive and other functions across an increasingly complex network of technical artifacts". And, one of the driving features of the transformation of these relationships is a "technological unconscious" (Clough; M. Taylor; Thrift; Hayles; and Grusin, "Publicity"). Hayles (drawing on Thrift) defines this as "the everyday habits initiated, regulated, and disciplined by multiple strata of technological devices and inventions" (138). For a long time, the relationship between the broadcast media and "mass audiences" of the first phase of mediatization was theorized in terms of linear models of communication—"influence" and the legacy of "effects" research unfortunately still clings to the teaching of and scholarship in the discipline of Media and Communication Studies in places. (A corollary in memory studies is a long legacy of the term "collective", although this issue is beyond the parameters of this essay.) Today, however, digital technologies and media penetrate and "mesh" with our everyday. As Roger Silverstone observes, "media . . . define a space that is increasingly mutually referential and reinforcive, and increasingly integrated into the fabric of everyday life" (5).

In other words, contemporary memory is thoroughly interpenetrated by a technological unconscious in that there occurs a "co-evolution" of memory and technology. Memory is readily and dynamically configured through our digital practices and the connectivity of digital networks. There is a kind of ambient quality to this shaping of memory in the present through the "very basic sendings and receivings of sociotechnical life—and the modest but constant hum of connection and interconnection that they make possible" (Thrift 175). The increasingly digital networking of memory not only functions in a continuous present but is also a distinctive shaper of a new mediatized age of memory. Hayles, for instance, argues that "the unconscious has a historical dimension, changing in relation to the artefactual environment with which it interacts" (138) and Bowker suggests that "[e]ach new medium imprints its own special flavor to the memories of that epoch" (26).

With these arguments in mind, it is useful to distinguish between the "two phases of mediatization" mentioned above. I will first develop this idea before moving on to address some of the key phenomena that are transforming cultural memory and that are defining of the current and "second" phase.

2. Media, Memory, and Miscellany

Shifts in the form and the potential of the archive contribute to the infrastructural changes of the so-called new media and are indicative of a move across two distinct (but overlapping) phases of mediatization. The first phase is characterized by the traditional organization of "Big Media" (Gillmor) and elite institutions which were seen by some commentators on cultural memory as proliferating, overbearing and hierarchically-organised archives. For instance, Nora argues that such archival accumulations produced a "terrorism of historicized memory" (14). The second phase of mediatization, however, delivers a "long tail" (Anderson) of the past (images, video etc.) whose "emergence" into future presents is contingent in terms of the when, but also in terms of its access by whom. David Weinberger calls this the "third order" of information, involving the removal of the limitations previously assumed inevitable in the ways information is organized. (The "first order" is the actual physical placing or storage of an item and the "second order" is that which separates information about the first order objects from the objects themselves such as the card catalogue.) Weinberger argues that "the 'miscellanizing' of information not only breaks it out of its traditional organizational categories but also removes the implicit authority granted by being published in the paper world" (22). Thus, under these conditions, the archive appears to have new potential, liberated from its former inherently spatial and to some extent institutional constraints. Indeed, the traditional materiality associated with the artefactual archive has been challenged by the fluidity, reproducibility, and transferability of digital data. In this way archives as they have become increasingly networked have become a key strata of our technological unconscious, transcending the social and the technological. For instance, as Van House and Churchill observe: "Archives sit at the boundary between public and private. Current archives extend well beyond a person, a space, an institution, a nation state. They are socio-technical systems, neither entirely social nor technical" (306).

A key trend in this regard is the ways in which the archives have become networked—part of a new accessible and highly connected network memory. Thus, the archive can even be seen as a medium in its own right as it has been liberated "from archival space into archival time". That is to say, the idea of the static archive as a permanent place of storage is being replaced by the much more fluid temporalities and dynamics of "permanent data transfer" (Ernst 52). Whereas in the broadcast era mass media were stored in the archival space of the vault or library subject to the material conditions of order, classification and retrieval (i.e. access), it is connectivity that becomes of primary significance to the digital archive as an unequivocally "mass" medium.

Elsewhere, I have written on the "collapse of memory" (Hoskins, "Television"), which was a condition brought on by the "emerging new structures of temporality generated by the quickening pace of material life on the one hand and by the acceleration of media images and information on the other" (Huyssen 253). The mass media effaced the past through the imposition of (visual and aural) immediacy in their mediation of events and particularly through the real-time lens of television news. This describes one consequence of the first phase of mediatization, in which the broadcast media ushered in a perpetual and pervasive present, but one that included the recycling of past images, sounds, and events, through a prism of the instantaneity of real-time or at least the televisual stylistics and discourse of pseudo real-time reporting. Although television has been characterized as possessing an embedded "liveness" as a property of the medium itself (i.e. television is always "on") the Internet is itself a temporally dynamic networked archival infrastructure which makes it a qualitatively different mechanism of memory. Ernst for example, argues: "Within the digital regime, all data become subject to realtime processing. Under data processing conditions in realtime, the past itself becomes a delusion; the residual time delay of archival information shrinks to null". Although Ernst sees the memory cultures of the material archive-centred European cultural memory co-existing with the emergence of "transfer-based" trans-Atlantic media (52) the inevitable advance of the latter both over and into the former produces a fissuring of cultural-media memory. I will now briefly outline one example.

The materiality of European cultural memory (which seems to be the basis for Aleida Assmann's model of the canon and the archive, see below) is exemplified by the Imperial War Museum London's (IWM) "permanent" Holocaust exhibition that was opened in 2000. Its advisory group pursued a purist narrative, perhaps contrasting with Holocaust and other museums elsewhere in the world that have embraced more centrally the technologies that today heavily mediate representations of the past. They sought out authentic objects of and from this event to provide "real signs" (Hoskins, "Signs") of the Holocaust (rather than employing post-Holocaust discourses, representations and other interpretations of this event). This is not to say that the exhibition is without electronic media—there are plenty of screens, film, video, sounds, images, etc.—but the ethos of the exhibition advisors seems best reflected in the objects and the artefacts. In this example, as Huyssen argues: "Even when the museum uses video and television programming in supplementary and didactic ways . . . it offers an alternative to channel flicking that is grounded in the materiality of the exhibited objects and in their temporal aura" (32).

In December 2002, two-and-a-half years after the opening of the Holocaust Exhibition, its very antithesis opened on the floor above, also at the IWM. The Crimes Against Humanity Exhibition contains no arte-facts or objects, but rather presents a narrative of (other) contemporary genocides entirely through the use of screen media. It occupies a space of only a very small proportion of the Holocaust Exhibition and is housed in the bright and modern atrium of the IWM.

In terms of the dominant modalities of representations in and through these two exhibition spaces, the former (artefactual) relates to the visualiz-ing of the Holocaust as an event unique and incomparable and appropri-ate to representations that deliver a relatively fixed narrative. However, the latter (entirely screen and database) mediates events (genocides) witnessed in an era in which television—and journalism—are increasingly pervasive first drafters of history, and so more easily negotiable as subject to the flux and revisions of "data transfer". These developments form only part of a trajectory of the co-evolution of technology and memory (and forgetting). As the networks and infrastructures of media connect and transform, new possibilities and dangers emerge that modulate the dynamics of cultural memory, which in turn require newly adequate conceptualisations, and it is to these questions that I now turn.

3. Time of the Archive?

One of the key emergent binaries in the theorization of cultural memory which, as I shall argue, is only partially useful as an explanatory model of the new dynamics of the distribution of memory, is that of active versus passive remembering (and forgetting). Aleida Assmann proposes two modes of cultural memory in that "[t]he institutions of active memory preserve the *past as present* while the institutions of passive memory pre-serve the *past as past*" (98, emphasis in original). Assmann uses the differ-ent spaces of the museum to illustrate this distinction; actively circulated memory is represented by that which is on show and visible to public visitors, what she terms the "canon", whereas "passively stored memory" is comprised of those objects stored and currently not on display, which she calls the "archive" (98). This model, however, is most applicable to a highly material form of cultural memory, and does not adequately account for the dynamics of digital data (including database technologies and the Web) in challenging public spatial display (and material existence) as a signifier of canonicity. I will now explore the significance of current socio-technical practices for the potential of present and for future archives.

The fissuring of cultural-media memory then is intensifying as the modus operandi of history of the second phase of mediatization is increasingly digital. The productions of memory and the data used to forge history are made in an ongoing present. As was mentioned earlier, they also work to totalizing effect by providing a common blanket for present and future perspectives on the past. World Wide Web has ushered in a temporality in its production of events that mediatizes memory in new ways.

Despite its archival promise, the Web does not merely produce an interweaving of past and present, but a new networked "coevalness", of connectivity and data transfer. For example, Gitelman envisages the Web involving "a public variously engaged in reading, selecting, excerpting, linking, citing, pasting, writing, designing, revising, updating, and deleting, all within a context where the datedness of these heterogeneous *interpretive* acts remains inconsistently perceived or certain" (147, emphasis in original). The temporality of the web is emergent and continuous as opposed to the temporality of other media, which render our experiences of events as "punctual" (see Warner). Compare that, for example, with the circulations of publications and broadcast media—and even "24-hour" news which, paradoxically, is highly punctuated around the cycle of clock-time, often incorporated into its semiotic display.

This is not just an issue of web pages, for example, being vulnerable to continual updating and permanent disconnection from the network and/or deletion, and thus not available for discovery and restoration to their original state, or any one of their former states. Digital and digitized data as with the content of any emergent media is ultimately vulnerable to obsolescence, beyond recovery without the availability of the technological tools compatible with its creation.

The changes in temporality associated with the Internet are illuminated through attempts to capture and preserve it. The Wayback Machine (www.archive.org) attempts to perform such an operation in attempting to provide an archive of the Internet on the Internet. On its home (search) page it announces "Welcome to the Archive" and it is labelled as a "non-profit" venture that is "building a digital library of Internet sites and other cultural artefacts in digital form". However, the Wayback Machine fails to deliver the punctual logic of the archives of other media even though it presents pages according to the date of their capture. So, whereas the media of television, film and print are rendered relatively punctual in their datedness of production, publication, and circulation, and which is embodied in the cultures of their reproduction and archiving (including remediated on the Internet) there is not a universal and reliable temporally-located "shared sense of Web publication as an event". Indeed, this is made apparent with the seeming presentness of the past that the Wayback

Machine seeks to capture and to recover, in that "there is something oddly and unidentifiably present about the past to which the Wayback Machine promises to transport its users" (Gitelman 137).

However, in addition to the difficulties inherent in capturing, storing and reproducing the instantaneity of the real-time effects of Web pages, Gitelman points to the "cultural logic of timelessness" associated with online publication projects such as the William Blake Archive which is "helping to make a new medium authoritative in a sense by co-opting cultural authority, by entwining the new means and existing subjects of public memory" (141). Indeed the Blake Archive is promoted as "a hybrid all-in-one edition, catalogue, database, and set of scholarly tools capable of taking full advantage of the opportunities offered by new information technology" (www.blakearchive.org/blake/archive.html). So, when such projects aim to incorporate, for example, "as much of Blake's pictorial and literary canon as possible" (ibid.), what are the prospects for a greater transference between or even a blurring of Aleida Assmann's modes of "active" (canon) and "passive" (archive) memory? It is the case that the Internet represents a huge accumulation of archival memory, in Assmann's terms, in that its storage capacity "has by far exceeded that which can be translated back into active human memory" (104). Yet, at the very least the temporality of the Web and other communications technologies and the fluidity of digital content, are transforming the archival properties and cultures in which individual, social and cultural memories are invested. Thus, the idea of active memory equating to the preservation of the "past as present" and passive memory as the preservation of the "past as past", fails to address the function of the continuous networked present of the Web and other digital media through which memory and technology co-evolve, including the co-existing of previously more distinct modes of cultural memory, for instance: the "private" and the "public".

More broadly, the significance of the archive in shaping the potential for "memory work" is evident in the field of contemporary journalism that for Barbie Zelizer, "tends to produce mnemonic work through those news organizations with the most extensive archives" (84). The digital is at the very least an accelerant of this process and one can extend this argument to archives in general and point to the blurring of amateur and professional journalism and the rise of the so-called "citizen journalist" (see Gillmor).

4. The Future of Cultural Memory

The future of both active and passive memory, to the extent that one finds these categories usable, is also being determined by the massive shift to personal expression ushered in by the internet and via other means of digital recording and communication. The nature and potential for the representation and historicisation of people's lives has been transformed. For example, much of the information that biographers have conventionally accessed, and displayed and/or stored in archives and museums was in the form of hard copy, whereas today the traces of people's lives are increasingly found in their digital communications. There are a number of potential consequences of our emergent and everyday sociotechnical practices for the voracity, preservation, and circulation of such data and thus on cultural remembering and forgetting. Not only does the unprecedented accessibility of this digital data make it more vulnerable to manipulation, but its potential to be rediscovered in future times is very much reduced in comparison with the materiality of its hard-copy predecessors. So, emails, text-messages, and social networking sites, for example, holding the content of a great mass of private and semi-public communications, may seem readily-accessible today, but what are the prospects for the survival of such data in a form and to an extent that is usable in cultural memory? Paul Arthur, for example, argues:

> the correspondence between people is increasingly distributed, impermanent and complexly interlinked. One person's social networking web page on a networking service is likely to be characterised by short, code-laden communications from "friends", and the idea of "correspondence"—with the to and fro of information between people—has been lost and replaced by an unpredictable kind of multiple commentary… The future historian may be confronted with an apparent void of information on lives that were in fact richly documented, but only through fleeting digital entries on security encrypted online services.

The instantaneity and simultaneity of some forms of digital communication and the systemic deletion of many (i.e. email programmes set to permanently delete mail messages after a fixed period) contribute to the diminishment in the number of unintentional textual traces we leave behind, notably those which were once much more material, storable (although open to different types of degradation) recoverable and open to future interpretations and reinterpretations. The temporality, fluidity and availability of digital data more generally—from text messages to emails, photographs and video, through to web pages—has facilitated a much more revocable (and some would argue chaotic) basis for the building of future cultural memory.

For instance, the temporality of images themselves is changing and as research by Van House and Churchill has shown, photos are actually becoming less archival: "while people do still make archival images, many are treated as ephemeral and transitory, including being used for image-based communication, in effect visual or multimodal messaging" (298). Thus the images made of and in everyday life that will shape tomorrow's personal and public memory, are vulnerable to the shifts in today's sociotechnical practices enabled through the highly fluid, transferable and erasable memory-matter of digital data.

It may be that the very prospects for the deletion and disconnection of what I have called digital network memory will actually afford the material objects (and metaphors) of cultural memory, of photographs, magnetic tape, letters, monuments, etc. greater significance. Can then the immateriality of network memory and an investment in and preservation of a materially-authentic past co-exist? Will the "tagging" of images in *Flickr* ultimately shape what will become the equivalent of "canon" and "archive" for those we share our photographs with?

To develop conceptual frameworks or models that are adequate to the genuinely dynamic and ongoing shifts in the formation of cultural and other memories is highly challenging, and no more so than in relation to material memory where it persists. But a fundamental reorientation in theory and in method is needed to address the rapid co-evolution of memory and technology, and the shifting (and non-punctual) times of the Internet need to be fully implicated in any temporally-responsive interrogation of the rise and impact of digital network memory.

References

Anderson, Chris. *The Long Tail: How Endless Choice is Creating Unlimited Demand*. London: Random House Business, 2006.

Arthur, Paul. "Saving Lives: Digital Biography and Life Writing." Garde-Hansen, Hoskins and Reading (forthcoming).

Assmann, Aleida. "Canon and Archive." *Cultural Memory Studies: An International and Interdisciplinary Handbook*. Eds. Astrid Erll and Ansgar Nünning, in collaboration with Sara B. Young. Berlin: de Gruyter, 2008. 97-107.

Assmann, Jan. "Collective Memory and Cultural Identity." Trans. John Czaplicka. *New German Critique* 65 (1995): 125-133.

Bartlett F.C. *Remembering: A Study in Experimental and Social Psychology*. Cambridge: Cambridge UP, 1932.

Boden, Deirdre, and Andrew Hoskins. "Time, Space and Television." Culture and Identity: City, Nation, World. Second Theory, Culture & Society Conference. Berlin. 11 Aug. 1995. Presentation.

Bowker, Geoffrey C. *Memory Practices in the Sciences*. Cambridge: MIT Press, 2005.

Bowker, Geoffrey C. and Susan Leigh Star. *Sorting Things Out: Classification and its Consequences*. Cambridge: MIT Press, 2000.

Clough, Patricia Ticineto. *Autoaffection: Unconscious Thought in the Age of Teletechnology*. Minneapolis: U of Minnesota P, 2000.

Draaisma, Douwe. *Metaphors of Memory: A History of Ideas About the Mind*. Trans. Paul Vincent. Cambridge: Cambridge UP, 2000.

Ernst, Wolfgang. "The Archive As Metaphor: From Archival Space to Archival Time" *Open* 7 (2004): 46-53.

Garde-Hansen, Joanne, Andrew Hoskins, and Anna Reading, eds. *Save As . . . Digital Memories*. Basingstoke: Palgrave Macmillan (forthcoming).

Garfinkel, Harold. "Two Incommensurable, Asymmetrically Alternate Technologies of Social Analysis." *Text in Context: Contributions to Ethnomethodology*. Eds. Graham Watson and Robert Seller. London: Sage, 1992. 175-206.

Gillmor, Dan. *We The Media: Grassroots Journalism, By the People, For the People*. Sebastapol: O'Reilly, 2006.

Gitelman, Lisa. *Always Already New: Media, History and the Data of Culture*. Cambridge: MIT Press, 2006.

Grusin, Richard. "Premediation." *Criticism* 46.1 (2004): 17-39.

---. "Publicity, Pornography, or Everyday Media Practice? On the Abu Ghraib Photographs." *Open* 13 (2007): 46-60.

---. *Premediation*. Forthcoming.

Hayles, N. Katherine. "Traumas of Code." *Critical Inquiry* 33.1 (2006): 136-157.

Hoskins, Andrew. "New Memory: Mediating History." *The Historical Journal of Film, Radio and Television* 21.4 (2001): 191-211.

---. "Signs of the Holocaust: Exhibiting Memory in a Mediated Age." *Media, Culture & Society* 25.1 (2003): 7-22.

---. *Televising War: From Vietnam to Iraq*. London: Continuum, 2004.

---. "Television and the Collapse of Memory." *Time & Society* 13.1 (2004): 109-127.

---. "The Mediatization of Memory." Garde-Hansen, Hoskins and Reading.

Hoskins, Andrew and Ben O'Loughlin. *War and Media: The Emergence of Diffused War*. Cambridge: Polity, 2009.

Huyssen, Andreas. *Twilight Memories: Marking Time in a Culture of Amnesia*. London: Routledge, 1995.

Ito, Mizuko. "Introduction." *Networked Publics*. Ed. Kazys Varnelis. Cambridge: MIT Press, 2008. 1-14.

Johnson, Steven. *Emergence: The Connected Lives of Ants, Brains, Cities and Software*. London: Penguin, 2002.

Merrin, William. *Media Studies 2.0*. Swansea, n.d. Web. 11 Jan. 2008. <http://mediastudies2point0.blogspot.com>.

Neisser, Ulric. "Memory with a Grain of Salt." *Memory: An Anthology*. Eds. Harriet Wood, Harriet Harvey and A.S. Byatt. London: Chatto & Windus, 2008. 80-88.

Nora, Pierre. "Between Memory and History: 'Les Lieux de Mémoire'." *Memory and Counter-Memory*. Ed. Natalie Zemon Davis and Randolph Starn. Spec. issue of *Representations* 26 (1989): 7-24.

Rose, Steven. *The Making of Memory: From Molecules to Mind*. London: Bantam, 1993.

Sawyer, R. Keith. *Social Emergence: Societies as Complex Systems*. Cambridge: Cambridge UP, 2005.

Silverstone, Roger. *Media and Morality: On the Rise of the Mediapolis*. Cambridge: Polity, 2007.

Taylor, Diana. *The Archive and the Repertoire: Performing Cultural Memory in the Americas*. Durham: Duke UP, 2003.

Taylor, Mark C. *The Moment of Complexity: Emerging Network Culture*. Chicago: U of Chicago P, 2002.

Thrift, Nigel. "Remembering the Technological Unconscious by Foregrounding Knowledges of Position." *Environment and Planning: D: Society and Space* 22 (2004): 175-90

Van House, Nancy and Elizabeth F. Churchill. "Technologies of Memory: Key Issues and Critical Perspectives." *Memory Studies* 1.3 (2008): 295-310.

Wang, Ge and Perry R. Cook. "On-the-fly Programming: Using Code as an Expressive Musical Instrument." *Sound Lab*. Princeton University, June 2004. Web. 16 June 2008. <http://soundlab.cs.princeton.edu/-publications/on-the-fly_nime2004.pdf>.

Warner, Michael. *Publics and Counterpublics*. New York: Zone, 2002.

"The Wayback Machine." *The Internet Archive*. N.p., n.d. Web. 12 Sept. 2008. <http://www.archive.org/index.php>.

Weinberger, David. *Everything is Miscellaneous: The Power of the New Digital Disorder*. New York: Times, 2007.

The William Blake Archive. Lib. of Cong., 8 May 2008. Web. 13 July 2008. <http://www.blakearchive.org/blake>.

Zelizer, Barbie. "Why Memory's Work on Journalism Does Not Reflect Journalism's Work on Memory." *Memory Studies* 1.1 (2008): 79-87.

Notes

[1] See also the uses of "emergence" in the marking of more dynamic models of a range of contemporary phenomena: Johnson, 2001; Sawyer, 2005, and Hoskins and O'Loughlin.

[2] The first phase of mediatization involves the forms, practices and experiences associated with the dominant media and institutions of the broadcast era, and particularly television. The second phase interconnects and overlaps with elements of the first, but is distinctive in that it requires a shift in how we approach and formulate the very relationship we have with media. Notably, this is owing to its much more immediate and extensive interpenetration with the everyday on an individual, social and continual basis (see Hoskins, "Mediatization"; and for a detailed development of this model as applied to warfare, see Hoskins and O'Loughlin).

II. Remediation

Remembering across Time, Space, and Cultures: Premediation, Remediation and the "Indian Mutiny"[1]

ASTRID ERLL

1. Sites of Memory, Premediation, and Remediation

The "Indian Mutiny" is a *lieu de mémoire*, a site of memory which has emerged from the history of British colonialism. It is the result and a sign of the cultural contact and the various conflicts between Englishmen and Indian people in nineteenth-century India. The "Mutiny" was a rebellion against British rule which broke out in northern and central India in Spring 1857. It started indeed as a mutiny of discontented sepoy regiments, i.e. Indian soldiers in the service of the East India Company (which had, by that time, annexed the greater part of the sub-continent). But the soldiers' uprising speedily turned into a "popular revolt"[2], which also involved the tax-drained Indian peasants and disinherited Indian princes. One year later, in 1858, the British had re-established power, with an hitherto unknown cruelty—for example, burning whole villages, and executing every single man in them, in order to avenge British victims and to deter any other rebels. In the history of British imperialism in India, the revolt turned out to be a watershed. It led to the transformation of an informal Empire, which had been controlled for more than a hundred years by the East India Company, into the formal empire under the British crown: the British Raj in India, which would not end until almost a hundred years later, with Indian Independence in 1947.

As a shared site of memory, the "Indian Mutiny" carries great significance in British as well as Indian memory cultures. In both countries, the uprising had (and in many cases still has) assumed the dimensions of a national myth. From an Indian nationalist perspective, the revolt of 1857/58 is a foundational event in that it is understood as the first heroic revolt against foreign rule, which would lead to the freedom struggle and then to independence.[3] From a British imperialist perspective, the revolt marks the beginning of and provides the legitimation for the British Raj. In the colonizers' view, with their uprising, the sepoys had shown up the need for a strong British government on the Indian subcontinent (see Metcalf).

As these two different narratives already indicate, the events of the years 1857/58 are not only a shared site of memory, but also very much a contested one. This contestation begins with the question of how to describe the Indian rebellion—a question that tends to be resolved rather differently in Great Britain and in India. While most British historians (even today) adhere to the somewhat derogatory term "Indian Mutiny" (thus implying insubordination and treachery on the Indian side), people in India usually prefer other terms, such as "Indian rebellion", "Indian uprising", or even "the first war of Indian independence".

Lieux de mémoire provide, as Pierre Nora maintains, "a maximum amount of meaning in a minimum number of signs"[4]. In order to explain how such a condensation of meaning works, Ann Rigney has introduced the term "convergence" into the discourse of cultural memory studies.[5] Cultural memories tend to "converge and coalesce" into a *lieu de mémoire* (Rigney, "Plenitude" 18). Stories, iconic images and topoi about the past flow together and are conflated into a site of memory. One hundred and fifty years of remembering the "Indian Mutiny" show that the sources from which meaning "flows" into this site of memory are of three different kinds. They include 1) different media representing the event (newspaper articles, official and unofficial histories, novels, photography, movies etc.), 2) different periods of recent history (e.g. the ages of imperialism and post-colonialism) and 3) different cultural contexts (British, Indian and many hybrid formations, such as nineteenth-century "Anglo-India" or the Indian diaspora in today's multicultural Britain).[6]

Thus, rather than as a static, fixed repository or a storehouse of memory, the *lieu de mémoire* should be conceived of, in the words of Ann Rigney, as "a self-perpetuating vortex of symbolic investment" ("Plenitude" 18). But the convergence and condensation of meaning into a site of memory is only one direction of the process by which *lieux de mémoire* come into being. In fact, those individual rememberers who are confronted with a site of memory (standing in front of a memorial, participating in a commemoration, or just hearing the word "Indian Mutiny") will usually want to *unfold* meaning, to associate certain images and narratives with the specific site. For example, the Victorians, and indeed up to the mid-twentieth century, mainstream British culture associated the term "Indian Mutiny" with images of ferocious sepoys raping English women, with British cantonments on fire, with heroic Highland soldiers charging into battle, and with narrative plots such as "last-minute rescue" and "last stand", "faith and delivery" and "virtue rewarded". However, the name of the event alone, or just one "Mutiny" painting or memorial obviously cannot suffice to evoke all these associations. They can only serve as "cues" which trigger different memories in each observer, different images and narratives of the past that are already part of his or her semantic memory.[7] And such memories can only come to the fore if the rememberer has read some Mutiny novels, seen a documentary on TV, watched a movie, listened to grandparents' stories of the event or was taught its history in school: in short, if he or she is part of a "media culture"[8] in which representations of the "Indian Mutiny" are constantly being circulated.

This article will focus on the importance of media in creating and disseminating notions about the "Indian Mutiny" and thus in constructing, maintaining and transforming a site of memory which has been shared by British and Indian people over a time span of one and a half centuries. Proceeding from the idea that it is the "convergence" of medial representations which turns an event into a *lieu de mémoire*, I will delineate some of the intermedial networks which produced the "Indian Mutiny" as a site of memory. I wish to draw particular attention to the diachronic dimension of these networks, or more precisely: to two basic processes of convergence which can be called "premediation" and "remediation".[9]

By using the term "premediation" I draw attention to the fact that existent media which circulate in a given society provide schemata for new experience and its representation. In this way, the representations of colonial wars premediated the experience of the First World War; and medial representations of the First World War, in turn, were at first used as a model for understanding the Second World War. But it is not only representations of earlier events that shape our understanding and remembrance of later events. Media which belong to more remote cultural spheres, such as art, mythology, religion or law, can exert great power as premediators, too. In the Western world, the Bible and Homer's epics have premediated historical experience for many centuries. Today, our expectations and meaning-making are often shaped by popular movies.[10]

By the term "remediation" I refer to the fact that especially those events which are transformed into *lieux de mémoire* are usually represented again and again, over decades and centuries, in different media. What is known about an event which has turned into a site of memory, therefore, seems to refer not so much to what one might cautiously call the "actual event", but instead to a canon of existent medial constructions, to the narratives, images and myths circulating in a memory culture. The rebellion of 1857/58 is a perfect example of this memory-making interplay of pre- and remediation.

In what follows I will take a—necessarily highly selective—look at the pre- and remediation of some of the topoi and narratives which are closely connected to the "Indian Mutiny". Probably the most tenacious notions about the rebellion centre on mini-narratives, such as "rape and revenge" and "treachery and massacre", as well as around some names and places fraught with meaning, such as "Nana Sahib", "Satichaura Ghat" and "Bibighar". Newspaper articles, eyewitness accounts, historiographical works, novels and movies (among many other media) have contributed to infuse these elements of the "Mutiny" myth with meaning, and they continue to do so. The following is a reconstruction of some of the horizontal and vertical lines of representation, which connect British imperial myth-making with colonial Indian counter-memory, and popular Hollywood stories with images of the revolt created in India's post-colonial Bolly-wood. It is the attempt to show how—via premediation and remediation—cultural memory operates across time, space and cultures.

2. Atrocity Stories and Premediation: the British Press of 1857

That the colonial British memory culture of the nineteenth century turned the events of 1857/58 into a foundational myth, which contributed to grand-scale imperial self-fashioning and helped legitimize British rule in India, is well known (see Brantlinger; Chakravarty). With the help of exaggerated newspaper articles, biased historiography, and more than one hundred hugely popular "Mutiny" romances, a colonial narrative was created which had little to do with the actual events. The imperial myth prominently features the themes of Indian treachery, of terrible Indian atrocities and—as far as the British side is concerned—of extreme heroism ("every man a hero, every woman a man", as one source phrases it).[11] From the colonizers' perspective, Indians had betrayed British benevolence by turning against their just, liberal and progressive rulers. Back at home, in England, the rumours of massacres and the rape of British women struck at the heart of Victorian sensibilities. "Rape" became a symbol of what was understood as the Indians' transgressive assault against the British nation.[12]

None of the elements of memory just mentioned can stand up to historical enquiry, even if one relies solely on British sources. The elements of the British myth are at best debatable, more often utterly wrong. For example, most of the rape stories belong to the "fictions connected with the Indian Mutiny" as Edward Leckey pointed out as early as 1859. More-over, what was often forgotten was that some British atrocities preceded as well as surpassed those of the Indians, as Edward Thompson showed in detail in 1925. The British site of memory called "Indian Mutiny"—up to 1947, and in a residual way also after Indian independence—is a case in point for the selectivity, unreliability and political functions of cultural memory. And it is the product of a powerful British media culture.

The earliest and most important medium which turned the Indian up-rising into a site of memory was the British press in the years 1857/58. In many newspaper articles one can sense an awareness that the current events already belonged to "world history". Back in London's Fleet Street, where information about what happened in the faraway colony was scarce and unreliable, a rhetoric of prospective memory fashioned the events in India as a foundational, almost mythical event, and as an important lesson for "many generations to come". The British press was also an important generator of those bloodcurdling atrocity stories which shape the image of the "Mutiny" in Britain to this day. Some examples may give a taste of the atrocity stories which were disseminated by British newspapers. The fol-lowing text was originally published in the *Bombay Telegraph* and reissued in the *Times*:

> Children have been compelled to eat the quivering flesh of their murdered par-ents, after which they were literally *torn asunder* by the laughing fiends who sur-rounded them. Men in many instances have been mutilated, and, before being absolutely killed, have had to gaze upon the last dishonour of their wives and daughters previous to being put to death. But really we cannot describe the bru-talities that have been committed; they pass the boundaries of human belief, and to dwell upon them shakes reason upon its throne. If ever a nation was made the instrument of an insulted Deity, that nation is England; and we trust that she will strike and spare not. (*The Times*, 17 Sept. 1857: 9)

Apart from the curious rhetorical device of introducing a topos of un-speakability (after *everything* seems to have been said), it is striking that this article ends with a fervent call for revenge. It is thus an early example of the rape-revenge plot connected with the "Indian Mutiny", which can be found in most late-nineteenth-century "Mutiny" romances, and which popular British memory would become obsessed with, until even late in the twentieth century.

Along these soon conventionalized lines (treachery, massacre, mutila-tion, rape) went also the following atrocity story, again taken from the *Times*, which presents a veritable chamber of horrors:

They took 48 females, most of them girls of [sic] from 10 to 14, many delicately nurtured ladies, – violated them and kept them for the base purposes of the heads of the insurrection for a whole week. At the end of that time they made them strip themselves, and gave them up to the lowest of the people to abuse in broad daylight in the streets of Delhi. They then commenced the work of torturing them to death, cutting off their breasts, fingers, and noses, and leaving them to die. One lady was three days dying. (*The Times*, 25 Aug. 1857: 6) [13]

But where did these wild fantasies of rape and mutilation originate? The fact that a host of similar atrocity stories emerged simultaneously in many different places supports the idea that they are a result of premediation. Some of the atrocity stories seem to go back to the then current literary fashion of "Gothic horror". Most of them seem related to a Christian imagination, with its medieval and early Renaissance visions of hell, such as can be found in the works of Dante and Shakespeare or—especially when it comes to children roasting over fire—in Hieronymus Bosch's paintings. All of these are texts, genres and images which an uninformed public resorts to in order to imagine and make sense of an exotic and dangerous reality which is barely understood. Such processes of premediation usually do not take place intentionally, though. Widely available media often provide their schemata inconspicuously. Premediation is a cultural practice of experiencing and remembering: the use of existent patterns and paradigms to transform contingent events into meaningful images and narratives.

3. Mediating and Remediating "Satichaura Ghat": From Eyewitness Account to Historiography

As I have stated earlier, atrocities, massacre and rape are a staple element of "Mutiny" memory to this day. A striking example of how a host of different medial representations—from eyewitness-accounts, newspaper articles and historiography to novels, paintings and movies—converged and coalesced over a large time span into a powerful (yet in India and Britain rather differently interpreted) *lieu de mémoire* is the massacre of the "Satichaura Ghat", which took place in Cawnpore (Kanpur) on June 27, 1857.

Cawnpore was one of the British stations besieged by Indian rebels during the revolt (the other famous one is the Lucknow Residency). Under the leadership of the rebel prince Nana Sahib the Indian sepoys offered General Wheeler and the British residents of Cawnpore safe passage from their besieged entrenchment (the so-called "Wheeler's entrench-ment"). They led them to the Ganges river, where boats were waiting for the defeated colonizers to take them to Allahabad, but fire was opened from an ambush as soon as the British boarded the boats. Several hundred British people were killed: the men instantly; the women several weeks later, after having been taken hostage in a nearby house called "Bibighar". The women's dead bodies were thrown into a well, which, under the name of the "Well of Cawnpore", has been turned into one of the best-known memorials of the British in India.

These seem to be the facts that can be established about "Cawn-pore".[14] To this day, our knowledge of the Satichaura Ghat massacre rests on merely two primary sources. Of the four male British survivors only two, Mowbray Thomson and W. J. Shepherd, wrote down their memories; the Indian rebels did not leave behind any written documents. What is a difficult situation for historians[15], though, may prove to be a good oppor-tunity for media and cultural memory studies, because the meagre body of first-hand source material makes "Satichaura Ghat" an excellent labora-tory to observe how the mediation and remediation of an event occurs.

Mowbray Thomson's Mutiny memoir, *Story of Cawnpore*, appeared in 1859. It has become, as Gautam Chakravarty (111) correctly observes, a "founding template", a text that almost all later remediations of the mas-sacre refer back to. Thomson was in one of the boats at the *ghat* (shore) when they were under fire and he survived by swimming down the Ganges river, by literally "beating the water for life" (Thomson 168).[16]

The other account of the Cawnpore massacre, W. J. Shepherd's, ap-peared in Lucknow as early as 1857, under the title *A Personal Narrative of the Outbreak and Massacre at Cawnpore during the Sepoy Revolt of 1857.* This is the first account to be published about the Satichaura Ghat massacre. However, Shepherd did not actually witness the massacre, but managed to escape the Wheeler's entrenchment as a spy dressed in Indian costume. (His masquerade was quickly discovered by the Indians and he was subse-quently taken hostage by the Maratha chief Nana Sahib.) What he writes about "Satichaura Ghat" and "Bibighar" is therefore based on hearsay, and much seems to be wrong.[17] Nevertheless, Shepherd's account had a great impact on memory culture—because it appeared very early and be-cause long passages from it were published in *The Times* (in November 1857). Shepherd's story was thus represented in *the* Victorian mass me-dium; as such it was widely circulated and readily available to British audi-ences.

Because of its early appearance Shepherd's account (but not Thom-son's, which was not published until 1859[18]) could enter the best-known historiography of the revolt, Charles Ball's popular, and often jingoistic, *History of the Indian Mutiny*. Ball's book is an example of what may be called "instant history-writing". It tells the story of the revolt even before the fighting was officially ended. Through their lack of hindsight and their determination to record every available representation of the revolt for future memory, such works of history fulfil, as Gautam Chakravarty (20) points out, "a mediatory function", "distilling a mass of heterogeneous primary material comprising letters, diaries, memoirs, newspaper reports, telegrams, civil and military despatches, parliamentary debates and, sometimes, rumour, and so preparing the ground for history writing in subsequent decades."[19]

Figure 1: "Massacre in the Boats off Cawnpore", in Ball, *History of the Indian Mutiny* (1858), 336.

Charles Ball's *History of the Indian Mutiny* is one of the most widely distributed, most richly illustrated, and certainly most popular histories of the revolt. Because of its extensive circulation, it has become an important source for narratives and images of the "Indian Mutiny". Ball's famous "Satichaura Ghat" illustration, for example (see figure 1), is actually one of the most frequently reproduced images of the rebellion, even today (and often enough without any comment as to its source or its ideological implications); the "Ulrica Wheeler" myth, a story about the youngest daughter of General Wheeler, who is said to have killed several sepoys after being abducted by them and in order to "save her honour", also finds popular expression in one of Ball's illustrations (see figure 2).

Figure 2: "Miss Wheeler defending herself against the sepoys at Cawnpore", in Ball, *History of the Indian Mutiny* (1858), 380.

Ball drew largely on Shepherd's writing with whole pages of his *History* consisting of quotations taken from Shepherd's account in *The Times* (with Ball sometimes correcting obvious errors). Ball's history is therefore an extensive and literal remediation of Shepherd's eyewitness account. With its wide distribution and huge popularity, the *History of the Indian Mutiny* transported Shepherd's story of "Cawnpore" into late nineteenth- and early twentieth-century memory cultures.

What is striking about Ball's *History* is its high degree of repetitiveness. For example, the episode of how British soldiers found the massacred bodies of English women and children in a well near the "Bibighar"—in what was to become the "Well of Cawnpore"—is told several times, each time by quoting a different eyewitness.[20] Such repetitions certainly have an authenticating function. Moreover, they effect an amplification of certain episodes of the revolt, thus preparing the ground for the emergence of a site of memory. In Ball, we find the process of convergence and coalescence condensed into one single medium.

In the following two sections I will examine how those early representations of the Cawnpore massacres, which were themselves interlinked in many complex ways, became an object for remediation in the late nineteenth century. How were the images and narratives created by Shepherd, Ball and Thomson turned into the fundament of a *shared* site of memory, i.e. how did British *and* Indian writers refer to "Satichaura Ghat" and "Bibighar"? The next section will move on to a different symbolic system: to literature and to the most prominent literary genre of the nineteenth century, the novel.[21]

4. High Imperialism, Remediation, and Variation: Henty's Popular Novel *In Times of Peril* (1881)

The most important and also, as far as cultural memory is concerned, most resonant period of British "Mutiny" writing is the latter part of the nineteenth century, an age of self-confident and aggressive imperialistic self-fashioning—not least in the medium of literature. In the 1880s, and even more so in the 1890s, the number of published "Mutiny" novels reached a peak. The literary market was flooded by popular romances and juvenile fiction addressing the events of 1857; examples include G. A. Henty's *Rujub the Juggler* (1893), H. C. Irwin's *A Man of Honour* (1896), J. E. Muddock's *The Great White Hand* (1896) and Flora Annie Steel's *On the Face of the Waters* (1897). The turn from eyewitness account and history-writing to fiction and the greater freedom of representation associated with the latter result in a further amplification of the "Indian Mutiny" as a site of imperial memory. The "vicious" Nana Sahib's troops become more and more numerous; British soldiers appear more and more heroic; English women by the hundreds are abducted, raped and/or killed by lecherous sepoys. This "larger than life" version of the "Indian Mutiny" (prepared and supported by other contemporary media of cultural remembering, such as paintings, sermons, odes, monuments and popular historiography) would thus enter popular memory and prove very persistent. Even a hundred years later, in contemporary British narrative history, traces of the high-Victorian myth-making can still be discerned.[22]

In 1881, G. A. Henty, one of the empire's most productive bards and successful "recruiting officer for a generation of schoolboys" (Turnbaugh 735) published *In Times of Peril*, a juvenile adventure novel with a highly propagandistic, didactic and, not least, memorial dimension. The fictive teenage protagonists, the brothers Dick and Ned, take part in every major campaign of the "Indian Mutiny". They experience the siege and the storming of Delhi; they spend time in the Lucknow residency among the besieged and later take part in General Campbell's so called "second relief"; they even witness the Satichaura Ghat massacre of Cawnpore:

> Dick and Ned Warrener were in one of the boats which were still ashore when the treacherous sepoys burst from their hiding-place. "The scoundrels!" burst from Ned indignantly; while Dick, seeing at a glance the hopelessness of their position, grasped his brother's arm.
> "We must swim for it, Ned, Take a long dive, and go under again the moment you have got breath."
> Without an instant's delay the brothers leaped into the water, as dozens of others were doing; and although each time their heads came up for an instant the bullets splashed around them, they kept on untouched until they reached the centre of the stream. (149-50)

Interesting with regard to this scene is not only the fact that the narrator's account of the boys' adventure echoes *Story of Cawnpore* quite precisely, thus making the novel one of the numerous remediations of Thomson's textual "founding template". What Dick and Ned can see with their own eyes, while they (just as Thomson described it) are "beating water for life" (Dick tells his brother that they must "swim for it") and have reached the middle of the Ganges, is also a strikingly precise ekphrasis of Ball's Satichaura Ghat-illustration (see figure 1):

> They looked back, and saw the sepoys had many of them entered the river up to their shoulders, to shoot the swimmers; others on horseback had ridden far out, and were cutting down those who, unable to swim far, made again toward shallow water; while cannon and muskets still poured in their fire against the helpless crowds in the boats. (ibid.)

What is rather strange, however, is that whereas the literary narrative thus evokes the well-known illustration in Charles Ball's *History*, the novel's own illustration of this scene (see figure 3) seems to refer to a different point in the timeline of the massacre. The image, which can be found in the first edition of *In Times of Peril*, can be interpreted as a remediation of Ball's famous Satichaura Ghat image.[23] But more interesting are the differences between Ball's and Henty's illustrations. The moment in time which is depicted in Henty is the beginning of the massacre: the British are looking, surprised and shocked, in the direction from which the gunfire seems to come. The illustration in Ball's *History*, on the other hand, shows a later point in time, when the sepoys have followed the British into the water and many British are being killed.

This particular choice that is made in the novel's visual representation of the massacre fits well within its overall structure. Although the narrative does feature scenes in which British people are killed, the illustrations of *In Times of Peril* tell a different story: apart from the "Satichaura Ghat" illustration, with its one single figure in the boat that was apparently shot by the sepoys (see figure 3), none of the novel's nineteen images represent the British being violated in any way. On the contrary, the illustrations of *In Times of Peril* usually show colonizers successfully taking action. It is therefore the active and heroic part of the imperial "Mutiny" myth which is amplified by a specific blend of textual and visual remediation and variation. And this is of course a very appropriate kind of remembering in a novel which was clearly meant to instil imperialist values and norms in its young readers.

OPENING FIRE ON THE BOATS.

Figure 3: "Opening Fire on the Boats", in Henty, *In Times of Peril* (1881), 148.

5. Affirmative Remediation and Subversive Premediation in Indian English Literature: Dutt's *Shunkur* (1877/8)

The corpus of Indian representations and remediations of the "Mutiny" in the nineteenth century is less clearly defined and accessible than its British counterpart. Presenting an Indian perspective on the revolt was a dangerous thing to do for Indian novelists and historians under the Raj. It was only in 1909, that is, more than fifty years after the revolt, that the nationalist classic by Vinayak Damodar Savarkar, *The Indian War of Independence*, was published—and immediately banned by the British. Savarkar's pamphlet points to the enormous potential of "1857/58" as a foundational event of an Indian nationalist memory culture, a potential to which Karl Marx had already drawn attention in 1858 when he called the rebellion the "first Indian war of independence" and emphasized the fact that for the first time in history Hindus and Muslims fought side by side against foreign rule.

Not only because of British censorship, but probably also because of the low literacy rate in the nineteenth century, some of the most powerful media of Indian memory of "1857/58" are to be found not in historical and literary writings, but mainly in oral media, such as ballads and songs. The collections of Scholberg and Joshi show that there were many ballads about Indian heroes of the revolt, such as the Rani of Jhansi, Tantya Tope, and Kunwar Singh. With regard to literary representations of "1857/58" R. Veena maintains that the British had "complete control not only over Indian territory but also over the literary 'space' within which to write about it. It was only after Independence that the literary space was opened up to accommodate the Indian perspective(s) on the events of 1857" (1). Nevertheless, leafing through Scholberg's extensive bibliography one realizes that there *are* Indian texts about the revolt which were published before 1947, in fact throughout the nineteenth and the early twentieth centuries. These have not, as far as I can see, been systematically analyzed. Nor have they even entered a canon of cultural memory on which Indians would draw (Indian novelists and historians, also those of the Subaltern Studies group, usually refer back to the imperial media representations, even if they set out to deconstruct them). Considering the fact that the Indian texts recorded in Scholberg's bibliography are written in Indian regional languages such as Assamese, Bengali, Gujarati, Hindi, Kannada, Marathi, Oriya, Persian, Punjabi, Sindhi, Tamil, Telugu and Urdu, it becomes clear that an understanding of Indian memory cultures and their medial representations of "1857/58" must be an interdisciplinary project, one which would have to bring together scholars of various languages and literatures as well as cultural historians, who have engaged with regional-language literature on 1857. The works of Scholberg and Joshi moreover show that it is important to broaden the medial basis of such a "memorial historiography", integrating Indian newspaper articles, letters, ballads, songs, images, and literary texts as representations of "1857/58" in their own right.

One of the best-known Indian works of fiction in English to have represented the events of 1857/58 is Shoshee Chunder Dutt's short novel *Shunkur*, published in 1877/8.[24] Shoshee Chunder Dutt (1824-1886) belongs to the famous Dutt family, a Bengali middle-class, Anglicized family of poets, journalists and historians.[25] His writing can be placed at the beginning of the Bengal Renaissance. However, unlike more overtly nationalist Bengali writers, such as Bankim Chandra Chatterjee, Dutt did not turn to Bangla at some stage in his career but chose to write exclusively in English throughout his life. In fact, "Shoshee's seemingly ambiguous poetic investment in the culture of the colonizer has meant that his prose, while representing some of the earliest fiction in English by a South Asian, has received scant attention in nationalist, Marxist and postcolonial literary histories" (Tickell 8). It is the aim of the following interpretation to uncover, with the help of concepts such as remediation and premediation, some of the anti-colonial criticism that even such an "elite Indian-English literary response" (ibid.) may express.[26]

Two main story lines can be distinguished in *Shunkur*. One is about Nana Sahib; the other is about the fictive character Shunkur. The Nana Sahib story features the Cawnpore massacres—as we have seen, a key element of the British memory of the "Indian Mutiny". Here, Dutt closely follows the topoi and narratives of the imperial media culture: Nana Sahib is depicted as an evil, decadent and lecherous villain. The fictive story about Shunkur, however, is quite another matter. It begins in the Indian village Soorájpore. A young Indian woman shows compassion for two British soldiers on the run after the massacres at the Satichaura Ghat and offers them shelter in her house. The soldiers, Mackenzie and Bernard, however, reciprocate the good deed by raping the woman, who is so ashamed that she commits suicide. Her brother and her husband, Probhoo and Shunkur, find her dead body when they return from the market and vow revenge. They get involved in the revolt, fight on Nana Sahib's side, and find the rapists in the end. They kill the British villains and then, as their revenge is fulfilled, return to their village.

Shunkur is a good example of remediation on various levels. The way Nana Sahib is characterized as a villain and the introduction of the rape-revenge plot are striking examples of how British representations of the "Indian Mutiny" were remediated in Indian writing. Moreover, Dutt closely follows the British conventions of selection and heightening: there are lengthy descriptions of the massacres at the Satichaura Ghat and in the Bibighar; and even the myth of "Ulrica Wheeler" is repeated in *Shunkur* (for Ball's illustration see figure 2). The sheer extent of Dutt's remediation becomes evident when his description of the Cawnpore massacres is compared with W. J. Shepherd's account in *The Times*:

The women and children, most of whom were wounded, some with three or four bullet shots in them, were spared and brought to the Nana's camp, and placed in a pukka building called "Subada Ke-Kothee".	Of the women and children several were wounded, and some of these were released from their sufferings by death, while the rest were confined in a puccá-house called "Subádá Kothee".
(Shepherd, *The Times*, 7. Nov. 1857: 7)	(Dutt 107)
One young lady, however, was seized upon (reported to be General Wheeler's daughter) and taken away by a trooper of the 2nd Light Cavalry to his home, where she at night, finding a favourable opportunity, secured the trooper's sword, and with it, after killing him and three others, threw herself into a well and was killed.	One young lady only had been seized upon previously by a trooper of the 2nd Light Cavalry, and carried off to his own quarters, where she was violently treated; but, finding a favourable opportunity, she rose up at night, and securing her ravisher's sword, avenged herself by killing him and three others, after which she flung herself into a well, and was killed.
(Shepherd, *The Times*, 7. Nov. 1857: 7)	(Dutt 107)

Quite obviously, Dutt has copied Shepherd's account and integrated it into his literary text.[27] Such forms of plagiarism are no anomaly in the history of remediating "1857/58" though. As we have seen, Ball copied long passages from Shepherd's account into his *History of the Indian Mutiny* and Henty drew on and amalgamated the representations of Thomson and Ball in only one page of his *In Times of Peril*. In *Shunkur*, however, the unmarked integration of British eyewitness accounts (along with all the imperialist stereotypes about Nana Sahib and "Cawnpore") is especially striking, because it seems that this nominally "Indian" version of the revolt is to a large extent nothing more than a remediation of British representations. The plagiarism can be understood as an example of "audience-tuning"[28] in the production of cultural memory: the adjustment of communication to (parts of) an intended audience. It serves as a medial *captatio*

benevolentiae, indicating to a British readership, to which the novel was obviously also addressed,[29] that *Shunkur* is a "proper and authentic" account
of the Mutiny, even though it was written by a colonial subject. What
Homi Bhabha would call an instance of "colonial mimicry" is an effect of
cross-cultural memory, and it operates by remediation. The novel thus
may appear as yet another expression of a British dominated memory
culture, one that stabilizes the imperial *lieu de mémoire* through constant
transcription, even across the boundaries of colonizer and colonized.

The story line which features Shunkur's revenge, however, unfolds
quite a different dynamics. It is a subversive version of Indian counter-
memory. First of all, the adventures of Shunkur and Probhoo are an early
representation of the "peasant armed", whom revisionist historiography
of the revolt "discovered" only after 1947 and then turned into a central
subject matter.[30] Dutt's fictional narrative imaginatively represents the
lived experience of the host of peasants and small landowners, who took
part in the revolt, but whose testimony did not circulate within nineteenth-century British and Indian elite memory cultures, because their
memories were never written down in letters or autobiographies (as almost all of the English witnesses' were) and thus not coded in one of the
leading media of those cultures. Secondly, *Shunkur* inverts the British rape-
revenge plot. Now it is the Indian woman, and not the English woman,
who is assaulted and must be revenged.

With regard to the simultaneous presence of British and Indian perspectives on the revolt in *Shunkur*, Meenakshi Mukherjee concludes that
"Dutt takes special care to distribute sympathy evenly between the British
and the Indians. If officers like Bernard and Mackenzie are despicable
enough to rape the woman who has given them shelter, Nanasaheb's
treachery and promiscuity are foregrounded as if to provide a balance in
villainy" ("The Beginnings" 95). Such an interpretation can certainly be
backed up by looking at the authorial narrator's comments, who is at pains
to politely but firmly revise some British misconceptions about the revolt.
However, I would argue that the Shunkur story line goes beyond such a
conciliatory endeavour, and that it does so yet again by a medial dynamics.
Except in this case, it is a canonical text of *Indian* memory cultures that the
novel draws on. *Shunkur* can be read as a story of the Indian Mutiny which
is premediated by the Indian epic *Mahabharata*'s mythical narrative about
the beautiful Draupadi, who was married to the five brothers of the Pan-
dava family: one of Draupadi's five husbands gambled away his land, his
brothers and his wife to the family of their cousins, the Kauravas. As a
slave in the service of the Kauravas Draupadi is almost raped by her husbands' cousins Duryodhana and Dushasana (but the Lord Krishna shows

compassion and restores her garments as fast as they are torn). Draupadi's husband Bhima vows revenge and kills the cousins in the end. As Pamela Lothspeich has shown, the glorification of Draupadi as an allegory of "Mother India" can be traced back to late colonial Hindi literature, when many Draupadi parables were produced. Early twentieth-century drama, for example, drew on the myth of Draupadi's violation and used it as an allegory for the conquest of "Mother India" by the British. If we assume that *Shunkur* is an early version of such parables, then its rape-revenge plot is not only an inversion of a powerful British "Mutiny" topos; it has in addition a mythological dimension, which carries a proto-nationalist subtext—a subtext which the British reader would not necessarily expect or understand, if one goes by the medial mimicry on the text's surface.

Mukherjee points out that "Shunkur's vendetta against those who raped his wife is made out to be a purely personal matter with no political overtones" ("The Beginnings" 95). This is what especially the ending of the novel seems to point to. Shunkur's last words are: "there is no further motive for the life we were obliged to adopt; let us go back to our cheerless home" (Dutt 158). When read according to the conventions of western-realist narratives of the nineteenth century, this is indeed a return to the apolitical sphere, just as one would find it, for example, in some works of European poetic realism of the time. Understood in this way, *Shunkur* neither comments on politics nor on the process of British-Indian history. But if we regard the novel as being premediated by the *Mahabharata*, then it is possible to decode from the literal story an allegorical dimension: After the "rape of Mother India" has been avenged and the perpetrators MacKenzie and Bernard (obviously standing for British imperialism) are taken to account, there is indeed nothing else to do than to "return home", that is, to try to resume the old ways of living. The novel's allegorical premediation thus defies the British "Mutiny" myth and represents an alternative memory. It provides a glimpse of a "future past" of the revolt of 1857/58—the vision of an avenged "Mother India"—and inscribes it into an Indian site of memory.

6. "Mutiny" in Hollywood:
Michael Curtiz' *The Charge of the Light Brigade* (1936)

In the twentieth century, the "Indian Mutiny" continued to be constructed and reconstructed as a *lieu de mémoire*. New media (such as film, radio, television and the internet) as well as an altered geopolitical landscape (decolonization, Indian independence in 1947) were responsible for new and altered forms of "symbolic investment" into the site of memory.[31] Critical essays, such as Edward Thompson's *The Other Side of the Medal* (1925) and F. W. Buckler's *The Political Theory of the Indian Mutiny* (1922), revisionist historiography, such as Eric Stokes's *The Peasant Armed* (1981) and Ranajit Guha's *Elementary Aspects of Peasant Insurgency* (1983), have challenged the imperial and Indian nationalist canons of events, heroes and narrative structures, cherished myths and topoi. In the realm of literature, there has been a considerable increase of revisionist historical novels dealing with the Indian Mutiny (e.g. Farrell's *The Siege of Krishnapur*, 1972), of representations of the revolt in Indian English writing (Khushwant Singh's *Delhi*, 1989), in novels emerging from the Indian diaspora (Vikram Chandra's *Red Earth and Pouring Rain*, 1995) and from multicultural Britain (Zadie Smith's *White Teeth*, 2000). What they all have in common is that they move away from the imperial adventure and romance model of narrating the "Indian Mutiny" (which Henty's novels are a good example of) and open up new ways of remembering the revolt by using new narrative forms of representation (such as unreliability, multiperspectivity, tales within tales etc.).[32] In the remaining sections of this article, however, I will have a look at what has arguably become one of the most powerful media of symbolic investment into "sites of memory": popular cinema.[33]

Many of the most popular movies about imperial history emerged from the so-called "Cinema of Empire" (Richards) during the 1930s and 1940s. But interestingly, it was not the British but rather the American film industry which set out to remember the "Indian Mutiny": Michael Curtiz' *The Charge of the Light Brigade* (1936) is a classic of the Empire Cinema made in Hollywood, and it is a striking cinematic version of the "Mutiny". Although the name "Cawnpore" never appears in this movie, with its plot of Indian treachery and rebellion *The Charge of the Light Brigade* certainly belongs in the long line of "Mutiny" remediations. More than five minutes of the film show a massacre of British civilians by Indian soldiers, a massacre which takes place after a long siege of an English station has ended and safe passage has been offered to the British by a rebellious Indian prince. There is, once again, a British spy dressed in native garment who tries to leave the besieged station undetected, but is found out and killed by the rebels; even the rape motif so dear to the British newspapers is integrated into the movie, when a Sikh tries to abduct the heroine.

As the title of the movie, with its open reference to Alfred Lord Tennyson's famous poem about the Crimean War, already indicates, Curtiz' movie actually conflates two British sites of imperial memory, the "Indian Mutiny" and the "Crimean war". It is therefore a good example of further processes of convergence. To the Hollywood producers and American audiences, memories of British imperialism were foreign and not relevant to their identity. Thus, separate historical events could easily be amalgamated into one single topos of "violence and the British Empire". And apparently, their temporal sequence could also be altered: in Curtiz' movie, the Mutiny of 1857/58 precedes the Crimean War of 1854-56.

The fact that "Mutiny" narratives migrated to the Hollywood cinema of the 1930s points to yet another basic process of memory in media cultures: the "Mutiny" had by then turned into a powerful premediator. It had become a narrative schema which could be used to create successful stories. In this sense the "Indian Mutiny" is not only a *lieu de mémoire* shared by the British and the Indian people, but can be seen as a transnationally available pattern of representation.[34] As a trans-cultural schema, the "Indian Mutiny" has become decontextualized. In 1930s Hollywood, "Mutiny" does not refer to a specific historical event, perceived in a clearly demarcated spatio-temporal context and related to cultural identity. It has instead been turned into a narrative template used to tell stories of good and evil, valour and treachery—carrying with it, however, the ideology of a form that was created in the context of British imperialism.[35]

But while in the United States the "Indian Mutiny" was used as an effective narrative schema for entertainment and box-office successes, the British government in India was rather sensitive about the revolt as a theme of popular cinema. As Prem Chowdhry (29) points out in his study on the historical reception of the Empire Cinema, *The Charge of the Light Brigade* was "considered by British officials in India a 'painful reminder of Indian history which was better left unrecalled'".

It is for such political reasons that no "Mutiny" film emerged from the *British* Cinema of Empire during the 1930s and 1940s. Producers were very interested in the "Mutiny" as a theme, but British censorship intervened, for example in 1936 when plans for a movie called *The Relief of Lucknow* were made. The president of the British Board of Film Censors (BBFC), Lord Tyrrell, warned: "The B.B.F.C. has been advised by all the authorities responsible for the government of India, both civil and military, that in their considered opinion, such a film would revive memories of the days of conflict in India which it had been the earnest endeavour of both countries to obliterate with a view to promoting harmonious cooperation between the two peoples" (qtd. in Richards 42). And two years later, an official of the Government of India wrote about the same issue:

> May I say how extraordinarily dangerous I think any such film would be in India today. In the first place young nationalist India is extraordinarily sensitive about

the whole Mutiny episode. To them it was the first wave of national movement for independence. . . . It would most certainly provoke a crop of films from Indian companies setting forth the Indian version of the Mutiny, and it would be extraordinarily difficult for the Government of India to censor or suppress them if it had allowed a British film of the Mutiny to appear. Further, Hollywood has long been itching to use the Mutiny as a theme . . . There will be no means of stopping Hollywood from pouring out versions of its own which would probably infuriate both Britain and India (qtd. in Chowdhry 30-31).

In these remarks, we can sense the power exerted by popular media memory and the fear that British officials had in the face of the Indian independence movement during the 1930s, firstly, of cinematic counter-memory made in India, and secondly, of an uncontrollable Hollywood machine, which might appropriate and commodify the memory of 1857/8 without considering its political implications for Britain and India.

7. Bollywood "Films Back": Ketan Mehta's *The Rising* (2005)

My final example of "Mutiny" remediation is one of the most recent and most widely distributed representations of the revolt: Ketan Mehta's Bollywood movie *The Rising* (2005). There is a current renaissance of historical themes, and more specifically, of nineteenth-century settings in Bollywood[36] which has also witnessed the production of a film about the Indian rebellion. With the release of *The Rising*, a film about Mangal Pandey, the first mutineer of 1857, there is once more a powerful mass medium involved in the representation of the Indian rebellion. Just like the newspapers of the nineteenth century, movies—and especially Indian Bollywood movies—reach large parts of the populace. Bollywood is not only the most powerful film industry in Asia; it also exports its products to Europe and the US, where especially members of the Asian diaspora make for large audiences.

The Rising is a clear instance of what may be called "filming back". It revises some of the most tenacious of the British myths: instead of a drugged and ragged rioting sepoy (as borne out by colonial historical records) we see a proud and utterly sober Mangal Pandey (and when he consumes cannabis—"bhang"—, he does so in the company of his British friend Gordon). While British accounts centre on the rape of English women, *The Rising* depicts an organized setting up of brothels by the East India Company, where abducted Indian women have to be at the service of British soldiers. And whereas British historiography tends to describe the rebellion of 1857 as unorganized and chaotic, *The Rising* gives an account of a carefully planned, concerted action.

This alternative version of the "Mutiny" presented by the movie drew some criticism, especially in Britain. In interviews given to several British newspapers in the summer of 2005, the historian Saul David criticized the film, which was partly funded by the UK Film Council, for what he saw as its "historical inaccuracy".[37] But of course, *The Rising* is a *fictional* medium of remembrance. It is moreover part of the Mumbai film industry, which is famous for its highly melodramatic plots and black-and-white characterization, an aesthetic that starkly contrasts with classical Hollywood realism. Had it created a story in line with British military historiography, it would have failed dramatically *as a movie* (a movie, at that, directed primarily at Indian audiences). Cultural memory is produced not only by different media (oral speech, written documents, film) but also within different symbolic systems (art, history, religion). Each of these has specific characteristics and limitations. A fictional film, even if it is a "history film", cannot be judged by using criteria which are derived from "history" as an academic discipline, because movies function according to a different symbolic system. This does not mean, however, that the production of cultural memory through literature, movies and the arts cannot be criticized. What is needed is a different methodology, one which allows us to address (adapting Fredric Jameson's expression) the "ideology of memorial form", through, for example, an analysis of narrative voice, perspective structures, character constellations, the use of imagery or (as in the following) intermedial structures and references.

The central message of *The Rising* is its linking of revolt and independence—in 1857 and 1947 respectively—as two national sites of memory. This linkage, which is prevalent in popular post-colonial Indian memory cultures[38], is made in *The Rising* verbally and visually. At the beginning of the movie, the following words appear on the screen:

> The man who changed history
> his courage inspired a nation
> his sacrifice gave birth to a dream
> his name will forever stand for FREEDOM

A key scene of the film is a British massacre of Indian peasants (see figure 4). Historically, this episode is not recorded, or at least not as having taken place during the time immediately preceding the outbreak of the mutinies in spring 1857. It does evoke, however, the time *after* the "Mutiny", the cruel British campaigns of counter-insurgency in 1858. Moreover, the episode recalls and inverts the British Satichaura Ghat myth, a technique similar to Dutt's inverted rape narrative. Finally, this scene is related to the palimpsest of new memories and medial representations which have emerged since Indian independence. It draws on the iconographic memory connected with the Indian freedom struggle, because it quite clearly is a visual echo of the Amritsar massacre in the Jallianwala Bagh (1919), which was similarly represented in countless movies about British India—the version most popular worldwide can be found in Richard Attenborough's *Gandhi* of 1982 (see figure 5). The episode, in short, condenses the complex of "colonial violence" into one image.

Figure 4: The Rising (2005): massacre of Indian peasants

Figure 5: *Gandhi* (1982): representation of the Jallianwala Bagh massacre of 1919

It is in line with so many historical cross-references that we find in the final credits of *The Rising* the image of Mangal Pandey cross-faded with well-known images of Gandhi's freedom movement: Indians on a protest march, probably footage from the Quit India campaign of 1942 (see figure 6). This is an apt visualization of the intermedial processes which are at the basis of all *lieux de mémoire*: images, topoi and narratives about the past are brought together and "cross-faded", condensed into a single site of memory. Such a creation of a "maximum amount of meaning in a minimum number of signs" is made possible through the repeated representation of historical events, usually across the whole spectrum of culturally available media.

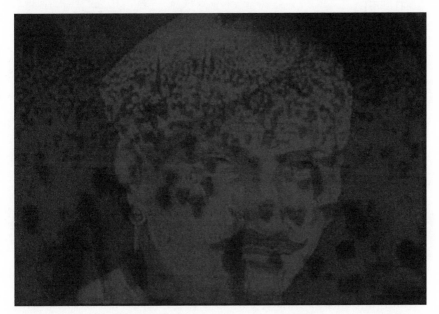

Figure 6: *The Rising* (2005): Cross-fading of the image of Mangal Pandey with footage of Indian protest marches of the 1940s

Lieux de mémoire derive their meaning only within the context of (increasingly globalized) media cultures. Medial representations surround, constitute and modify sites of memory. They function according to different media specificities, symbolic systems and within ever changing sociopolitical constellations. Medial representations of the past, moreover, refer to one another, pre-form and re-shape cultural memories. And they do so across the boundaries of time, space, and culture. In this sense, all *lieux de mémoire* (and not only those "belonging" to two different nations) are "shared sites of memory": they are shared by different social classes, political camps, generations, religious groups and regional cultures (above as well as below the level of the national), and not least by different media cultures—with their specific practices of representation and reception.

References

Ball, Charles. *The History of the Indian Mutiny: Giving a Detailed Account of the Sepoy Insurrection; and a Concise History of the Great Military Events which Have Tended to Consolidate British Empire in Hindostan.* 2 vols. London, [1858?].

Bolter, Jay David, and Richard Grusin. *Remediation: Understanding New Media.* Cambridge: MIT Press, 1999.

Brantlinger, Patrick. *Rule of Darkness: British Literature and Imperialism, 1870-1914.* Ithaca: Cornell UP, 1988.

Chakravarty, Gautam. *The Indian Mutiny and the British Imagination.* Cambridge: Cambridge UP, 2005.

Chowdhry, Prem. *Colonial India and the Making of Empire Cinema: Image, Ideology and Identity.* Manchester: Manchester UP, 2000.

Dutt, Shoshee Chunder. "Shunkur: A Tale of the Indian Mutiny." *Bengaliana: A Dish of Rice and Curry and Other Indigestible Ingredients.* By Dutt. Calcutta, 1885. 84-158.

Echterhoff, G., E.T. Higgins, and S. Groll. "Audience-Tuning Effects on Memory: The Role of Shared Reality." *Journal of Personality and Social Psychology* 89.3 (2005): 257-76.

Erll, Astrid. *Kollektives Gedächtnis und Erinnerungskulturen.* Stuttgart: Metzler, 2005.

---. "'Re-writing' as Re-visioning: Modes of Representing the 'Indian Mutiny' in British Literature, 1857 to 2000." *Literature and the Production of Cultural Memory.* Eds. Astrid Erll and Ann Rigney. Spec. issue of *European Journal of English Studies* 10.2 (2006): 163-85.

---. *Prämediation-Remediation: Repräsentationen des indischen Aufstands in imperialen und post-kolonialen Medienkulturen (von 1857 bis zur Gegenwart).* Trier: WVT, 2007.

Erll, Astrid, and Ansgar Nünning, in collaboration with Sara B. Young, eds. *Cultural Memory Studies: An International and Interdisciplinary Handbook.* Berlin: de Gruyter, 2008.

Erll, Astrid, and Stephanie Wodianka, eds. *Film und kulturelle Erinnerung: Plurimediale Konstellationen.* Berlin: de Gruyter, 2008.

Gandhi. Dir. Richard Attenborough. 1982. Columbia TriStar, 2003. DVD.

Grusin, Richard. "Premediation." *Criticism* 46.1 (2004): 17-39.

Guha, Ranajit. *Elementary Aspects of Peasant Insurgency in Colonial India.* 1983. Durham: Duke UP, 1999.

Hastings, Chris, and Beth Jones. "Lottery-Funded Film Under Fire for Anti-British Bias." *Sunday Telegraph* 14. Aug. 2005: 8.

Henty, George Alfred. *In Times of Peril: A Story of India. With Nineteen Illustrations.* London, 1881.

Herbert, Christopher. *War of No Pity: The Indian Mutiny and Victorian Trauma.* Princeton: Princeton UP, 2008.

Hibbert, Christopher. *The Great Mutiny, India 1857.* 1978. London: Penguin, 1980.

Joshi, Puran Chandra, ed. *1857 in Folk Songs.* New Delhi: People's Publishing House, 1994.

Kaye, Sir John William, and George Bruce Malleson. *History of the Indian Mutiny of 1857-8.* 6 vols. London, 1897.

Leckey, Edward. *Fictions Connected with the Indian Outbreak of 1857 Exposed.* Bombay, 1859.

Lothspeich, Pamela. "Unspeakable Outrages and Unbearable Defilements: Rape Narratives in the Literature of Colonial India." *Postcolonial Text* 3.1 (2007): n. pag. Web. 14 Aug. 2008. <http://postcolonial.org/>.

Marx, Karl. *The First Indian War of Independence.* 1858. Smaller Collections. Moscow: Foreign Languages Pub., 1960.

Metcalf, Thomas R. *Ideologies of the Raj.* Cambridge: Cambridge UP, 1995.

Mukherjee, Meenakshi. *The Perishable Empire: Essays on Indian Writing in English.* New Delhi: Oxford UP, 2000.

---. "The Beginnings of the Indian Novel." *A History of Indian Literature in English.* Ed. Krishna Arvind Mehrotra. London: Hurst & Company, 2003. 92-102.

Mukherjee, Rudrangshu. *Awadh in Revolt, 1857-58: A Study of Popular Resistance.* Delhi: Oxford UP, 1984.

---. *Spectre of Violence: The 1857 Kanpur Massacres.* London: Viking, 1998.

Nora, Pierre, ed. *Les lieux de mémoire.* 3 vols. Paris: Gallimard, 1984-1992.

Ray, Rajat Kanta. *The Felt Community: Commonality and Mentality before the Emergence of Indian Nationalism.* Delhi: Oxford UP, 2003.

Richards, Jeffrey. *Visions of Yesterday.* London: Routledge and Kegan Paul, 1973.

Rigney, Ann. *The Rhetoric of Historical Representation: Three Narrative Histories of the French Revolution.* Cambridge: Cambridge UP, 1990.

---. "Plenitude, Scarcity and the Circulation of Cultural Memory." *Journal of European Studies* 35.1 (2005): 11-28.

Sabin, Margery. *Dissenters and Mavericks: Writings about India in English, 1765-2000*. Oxford: Oxford UP, 2002.

Savarkar, Vinayak Damodar. *The Indian War of Independence, 1857*. 1909. New Delhi: Rajdhani Granthagar, 1970.

Scholberg, Henry. *The Indian Literature of the Great Rebellion*. New Delhi: South Asia, 1993.

Sharpe, Jenny. *Allegories of Empire: The Figure of Woman in the Colonial Text*. Minneapolis: U of Minnesota P, 1993.

Shepherd, W. J. *A Personal Narrative of the Outbreak and Massacre at Cawnpore During the Sepoy Revolt of 1857*. Lucknow, 1857.

Stokes, Eric T. *The Peasant Armed: The Indian Revolt of 1857*. Ed. C.A. Bayly. Oxford: Clarendon, 1986.

Taylor, P. J. O., ed. *A Companion to the 'Indian Mutiny' of 1857*. Delhi: Oxford UP, 1996.

The Charge of the Light Brigade. Dir. Michael Curtiz. 1936. Warner Home Video, 1989. Videocassette.

The Rising: Ballad of Mangal Pandey. Dir. Ketan Mehta. 2005. Yash Raj Films, 2005. DVD.

Thompson, Edward. *The Other Side of the Medal*. London: Hogarth, 1925.

Thomson, Mowbray. *The Story of Cawnpore*. London, 1859.

Tickell, Alex. "Introduction." *Shoshee Chunder Dutt: Selections from Bengaliana*. Ed. Alex Tickell. Nottingham: Trent, 2005. 7-22.

Tulving, Endel, and Fergus I. M. Craik, eds. *The Oxford Handbook of Memory*. New York: Oxford UP, 2000.

Turnbaugh, Roy. "Images of Empire. G. A. Henty and John Buchan." *Journal of Popular Culture* 9.3 (1975): 734-40.

Veena, R. "The Literature of the Events of 1857: A Postcolonial Reading." *Writing in a Post-colonial Space*. Ed. Surya Nath Pandey. New Delhi: Atlanti, 1999. 1-9.

Ward, Andrew. *Our Bones Are Scattered: The Cawnpore Massacres and the Indian Mutiny of 1857*. London: Murray, 1996.

Notes

[1] An earlier version of this paper appeared in Indra Sengupta Frey, ed. *Memory, History and Colonialism: Engaging with Pierre Nora in Colonial and Post-colonial Contexts. Bulletin of the German Historical Institute London.* London, 2009. I would like to thank Indra Sengupta Frey for many helpful and

instructive comments on that earlier manuscript, from which the present article has also very much profited.

[2] For this argument see R. Mukherjee, *Awadh in Revolt*.

[3] For a thorough historical analysis of this idea see Ray.

[4] Qtd. in Rigney, "Plenitude" 18. For a detailed account of the *lieux de mémoire*-project see Nora.

[5] For an overview of terms, concepts and approaches to cultural memory see Erll and Nünning.

[6] For a history of British and Indian memories of the "Indian Mutiny" from 1857 to the present see Erll, *Prämediation*.

[7] "Semantic memory" is our knowledge system ("the world is round", "the First World War started in 1914"); it can be distinguished from "episodic memory", which refers to our lived experience ("my first day at school"; "how I witnessed the fall of the Berlin Wall". For such terms of cognitive psychology see Tulving and Craik.

[8] I use the term "media culture" to accentuate the medial production of culture: the fact that every intersubjective notion of reality is based on communication and medial representation. Thus, the focus is directed towards the specific possibilities and restrictions of representation connected with those media that are available in a given society. In this sense, cultural memory, too, is the product of medial processes (see Erll, *Kollektives Gedächtnis*).

[9] The term "remediation" (and later also "premediation") was introduced in the context of new media theory; see Bolter and Grusin; and Grusin. It was Ann Rigney who proposed combining the concept of "remediation" with cultural memory studies. In what follows I will use Bolter and Grusin's concepts "premediation" and "remediation" as an inspiration, but also depart significantly from their use of these terms in order to accommodate them to the specific concerns of my cultural studies approach to memory.

[10] On "9/11", many of those who saw the planes crashing into the World Trade Centre were reminded of the movie *Independence Day*; while George W. Bush revealed the premediating force of the Christian tradition when he distinguished between "good and evil states", "light and darkness" and called for a "crusade" against the terrorists.

[11] *Calcutta Review* (LXI 1858: v). This is of course the dominant myth, created by a powerful imperial memory culture, which (and this is important for the approach delineated here) made an impact on British as well as Indian cultures. At the same time, there were certainly dissident voices in

England which were highly critical of the British role in India (see Sabin; and Herbert).

[12] For a detailed and intriguing analysis of the figure of woman and the topos of rape in connection with the "Mutiny" see Sharpe.

[13] Jenny Sharpe has pointed out that the "eye-witness" who was responsible for this story was soon afterwards exposed by Karl Marx in the *New York Daily Tribune* as "a cowardly parson residing at Bangalore, Mysore, more than a thousand miles, as the bird flies, distant from the scene of the action" (Sharpe 66; and Marx).

[14] See R. Mukherjee, *Spectre of Violence*; and Ward.

[15] One way of dealing with this situation is reading the available, often biased sources "against the grain". For this method see Guha; and R. Mukherjee, *Awadh in Revolt*.

[16] Later, Thomson exclaims: "how excellent an investment that guinea had proved which I spent a year or two before at the baths in Holborn, learning to swim!" (190). "Learning to swim" has, as P.J.O. Taylor records, become one of the well-remembered anecdotes connected with the "Indian Mutiny" (191-2).

[17] See Taylor (304-5). For Shepherd's reverberative error concerning the place to which the British women and children were brought after the massacre at the Satichaura Ghat see this article, below.

[18] Ball does include, however, an earlier eyewitness account written by Thomson, misspelling his name as "Thompson" (see Ball 384).

[19] This also shows clearly that historiography is inherently a "genre of remediation", a text type grounded on the integration of oral and written documents and other media of representation; or, as Ann Rigney puts it: "the historian's claim to speak with the authority of reality is paradoxically linked to his use of *other* discourses" (*Rhetoric* 13).

[20] See Erll, *Prämediation* 71-2.

[21] This move is made in order to show how remediation occurred not only across a spectrum of different media, but also across the spectrum of different symbolic systems. History, politics, literature, religion and law were most important in the creation of the "Indian Mutiny" as a site of memory. It would also be interesting, for example, to ask what types of premediation and remediation we find at the basis of Kaye and Malleson's multivolume historiographical standard work on the Indian Mutiny.

[22] For example, in Christopher Hibbert's historiography with the telling title *The Great Indian Mutiny*, which was published in 1978.

[23] This assumption is supported by the fact that here, too, the form of the boats is *not* historically correct: the boats offered by Nana Sahib to the British had roofs which were to protect the white-skinned colonizers from the fierce Indian sun on their long ride to Allahabad (see Ward 301). But the roofs appear neither in Ball's image nor in most of its remediations.

[24] Being Calcutta-based Bengalis, Shoshee Chunder Dutt and his family were not eyewitnesses of the "Mutiny", which took place in Awadh. *Shunkur* is therefore an imaginative version of the revolt, just like most of the British 'Mutiny' novels.

[25] The historian Romesh Chunder Dutt is Shoshee Chunder Dutt's nephew.

[26] On Shoshee Chunder Dutt's writing see also M. Mukherjee, *The Perishable Empire*.

[27] He also copied Shepherd's mistake: Shepherd (and by extension Ball and Henty, but not Thomson) falsely assumes that the women were brought into the "Subádá Kothee" (instead of the nearby "Bibighar").

[28] This is a concept developed in social psychology; see Echterhoff, Higgins and Groll.

[29] Dutt is one of the first Indian writers to be published both in India and in Britain, thus reaching educated Indian elites and "Anglo-India" (the British then living in India) as well as an interested public back in the "colonial centre", Great Britain.

[30] Notably in Eric T. Stokes's historiography *The Peasant Armed*; see also Guha; R. Mukherjee, *Awadh in Revolt*. In this respect, *Shunkur* can also be placed in the tradition of Bengali literature on "peasant suffering", which was developed into a powerful trope of Bengali fiction from the mid-nineteenth century onwards, especially by Dinabandhu Mitra's influential drama *Nil Darpan* [The Mirror of Indigo] (1858-1859). I am grateful to Indra Sengupta-Frey, who drew my attention to this fact.

[31] These new forms emerged alongside traditional and conventionalized ways of representation. There were (and still are) many representations of the "Indian Mutiny" which rely on the received patterns of British imperial memory. We find them in popular novels, film, and historical works.

[32] For a history of literary representations of the "Indian Mutiny" see Erll, *Prämediation* and Erll, "Re-writing".

[33] For the theory and methodology of the "memory film", see Erll and Wodianka.

[34] In fact, the "Mutiny", and especially the figure of Nana Sahib, had soon become a favoured subject of popular entertainment all over the world. In

nineteenth-century Germany, for example, Theodor Fontane wrote about the Indian revolt, and in France, Jules Verne.

[35] In 1930s Hollywood, the "Cinema of Empire" is structurally and ideologically not very different from the major American genre of that time, the Western. According to the film historian Jeffrey Richards, "Americans do seem to have responded to Britain's folk myths in the same way that Britain responds to America's, the Westerns. There is in fact an area of cross-reference between the two genres. ... Ideologically, American films of Empire were little different from British films of Empire" (3-4).

[36] Another hugely popular Bollywood movie set in nineteenth-century colonial India is *Lagaan* (2001).

[37] For example in an interview given to the *Sunday Telegraph* (14 Aug. 2005), which appeared under the sensational title "Lottery-funded film under fire for anti-British bias" (Hastings and Jones).

[38] For a critical assessment of this version of Indian history see Ray.

Towards a Memory Dispositif:
Truth, Myth, and the Ned Kelly *lieu de mémoire,* 1890-1930[1]

LAURA BASU

1. From Site to Dispositif: *Lieux de mémoire* Reconsidered

The concept of "memory site", though deployed regularly, has been generally under-theorized since initially addressed in Pierre Nora's *Lieux de mémoire.* The term has been especially overlooked by the field of media studies, and has been taken up predominantly by those interested in literal locations of memory (e.g. Winter). Taking Australia's best known bushranger Ned Kelly as a case study, this article will begin to examine the processes by which a memory site may develop and function over a period of time through the processes of mediation and remediation. The article will thus contribute to a more thorough understanding of the workings of cultural memory in relation to media representation. It will conclude by suggesting the concept of a *memory dispositif* as a potentially fruitful avenue of research for the field, after exploring one important aspect of that dispositif, namely the *media dispositif.*

Nora describes *lieux de mémoire,* or sites of memory, as places (literal or symbolic) where "memory crystallizes and secretes itself". *Lieux de mémoire* develop in the wake of the erosion of *milieux de mémoire.* The latter are "real environments of memory" associated with tradition, custom and "the repetition of the ancestral". The former, on the other hand, are constructed sites of externalized or "false" memory, which arise due to "a movement toward democratization and mass culture on a global scale" ("Between" 7). According to Nora, we are, with the help of mass media, distanced from "the realm of true memory", and it is precisely because of this distance or externalization that we feel compelled to construct sites of memory; "if we were able to live within memory, we would not have needed to consecrate *lieux de mémoire* in its name" (8).

What exactly are *lieux de mémoire*? Nora's category is very broad. He tells us that there are concrete memory sites such as cemeteries, museums and anniversaries, and more "intellectually elaborate ones" such as the notions of generation and lineage. Memory sites can be portable, topographical, monumental; there are public sites of memory and private ones, "pure sites" and "composite sites", sites that are dominant and sites that are dominated. The list goes on. What is clear is that "the most fundamental purpose of the *lieu de mémoire* is to stop time, to block the work of forgetting, to establish a state of things, to immortalize death, to materialize the immaterial—just as if gold were the only memory of money—all of this in order to capture a *maximum amount of meaning in the fewest of signs*" (19, emphasis added). Memory sites can be "anything administering the presence of the past within the present", and they only exist to the extent of their capacity for metamorphosis, "an endless recycling of their meaning and an unpredictable proliferation of their ramifications" (19-20).

Using Foucault's scarcity principle, Ann Rigney argues that memory sites "are defined by the fact that they elicit intense attention on the part of those doing the remembering and thereby become a self-perpetuating vortex of symbolic investment (this process recalls Foucault's reference to an 'internal proliferation of meaning')". Sites of memory help to reduce "the proliferation of disparate memories" and provide "common frameworks for appropriating the past" (18). They can serve to concentrate or conflate memories, whereby "memorial layers" are formed; Rigney gives as an example of this the celebration of 11 November in Britain, which has now become an occasion "not just for commemorating the end of World War 1 in its specificity, but more generally an occasion for commemorating British casualties in various wars" (19). Rigney, like many other cultural memory scholars now, moves on from Nora's notion that sites of memory, with all the mediatization and externalization they entail, are somehow "false" or "unnatural", asking instead "what if uses of 'external' sources of information are no longer seen as regrettable manifestations of memory loss, but as the order of the day?" (14). Likewise, it is not my interest here to oppose sites of memory to some form of "natural", "organic", "good" memory, but to examine in more detail how exactly a memory site may form and evolve over time, and in particular how it may produce, organize and transmit meaning, in terms of the mediatizations that are so essential to its existence.

Instead of focussing on one medium in isolation, the concept of the memory site allows us to examine how various medial processes and the *interactions between* media technologies, genres and products combine to form "a self-perpetuating vortex of symbolic investment" that may absorb and proliferate certain meanings pertaining to aspects of both the past and the present, without ignoring the importance of medium specificity. In this sense, it would be useful to consider a memory site as comprising a *media dispositif,* which can be seen as integral part of a larger *memory dispositif.* My concluding suggestion regarding the memory dispositif concept does not constitute a dismissal of the value of the memory site, but should be seen rather as a reconceptualistion, emphasizing an additional, crucial aspect of the dynamics of cultural memory.

The term "dispositif", often translated as "apparatus", usually refers to a constellation of heterogeneous elements within a system; Foucault's use of the concept moreover emphasizes *"the nature of the connection…between these…elements"* (Foucault 194, emphasis added), the interplay between which results in a specific historical formation producing power structures, knowledge and subjectivity. Foucault was never exhaustive about the exact nature of the dispositif, but the model is now being taken up by such fields as international development (Brigg) and media studies (Kessler). Deleuze, in an essay on Foucault, describes the dispositif as "a tangle, a multilinear ensemble" and again stresses the importance of the lines and traces between any given configuration of elements, "like vectors and tensors" (159). Although not the emphasis of this article, an important feature of the dispositif is that it has a "dominant strategic function", responding to an "urgent need" (Foucault 195). Thinking about a memory site as dispositif allows us to move beyond looking at individual texts or media as they relate to cultural memory and to see a site of memory as being made up of a conglomeration of heterogeneous media texts, the specific relationships between which determining the nature and functions of the memory site at a given time.

The historical personage and story of Ned Kelly is a memory site which has, through relentless (inter)medial representation since the late nineteenth century, managed to survive more successfully than any other figure from Australian history. After a brief introduction to the Kelly case, and a description of the initial construction of the site by the press, the article will detail some of the ways in which the media dispositif component of this site developed during an important period of its evolution, 1890-1930, and its effects. It will focus on two texts, specifically the police memoir *The Last of the Bushrangers* from 1892 (Hare) and an early film, *The Story of the Kelly Gang* from 1906, and the relationships of each with other texts. It will identify a few of the specific medial processes and interactions that took place in this phase, and will describe how, as a result, ideas of truth and myth were produced, and coincided and merged to form one of a nation's most important and contested sites of memory.

2. Ned Kelly: the Formation of a Memory Site

Ned Kelly was born in Beveridge in 1855 to Irish, working-class parents. His father, "Red", was transported for cattle stealing, while his mother, Ellen, immigrated with her family. Kelly was part of a large family or clan, which settled in the Australian colony of Victoria as rural selectors, where its members were in constant conflict with the police. The real trouble started in 1878 when a police constable named Fitzpatrick accused Ned and members of his family of assault. Ellen Kelly was imprisoned for the offence, on very unreliable evidence. To escape arrest, Ned and his younger brother Dan fled to the bush, where they were later joined by two others, Joe Byrne and Steve Hart. The situation worsened in October 1878, when the men ambushed and killed three policemen at Stringybark Creek near Mansfield. Now legally declared outlaws, the four men became known as the Kelly gang. During the following eighteen months, the gang staged two elaborate bank robberies, at Euroa and Jerilderie. Events came to a climax in June 1880 when Joe Byrne killed close friend and double agent Aaron Sherritt, after which the Kellys faced a dramatic showdown with the police at Glenrowen, where the gang wore its now iconic home-made armour. Ned was injured and captured at this time, and the other three were killed. Ned Kelly was put on trial and hanged on 11 November 1880, at the age of twenty-five.

In Australia, Ned Kelly remains a potent site of memory, over 125 years after his execution in 1880, and the story has been represented time and again in almost every existing medium. The case is thought of as a highly controversial, factually ambiguous and emotionally fraught one. Even recently, Ned Kelly writers and scholars have continued to remind us that "125 years after Ned's death, opinions are usually either black or white. In general terms, the masses see Ned as either a merciless killer who unforgivably chose to take up arms against society, or as a national hero who was the embodiment of the Australian spirit" ("About Ned Kelly").

It was the press from the Australian colonies that initially established the Ned Kelly memory site while it was reporting on the events as they were taking place. The relative immediacy associated with the press even at this time, its comparatively uninterrupted and repetitious informational streams, not to mention its status as the "fourth estate", enabled it to effectively assemble a media event marked for future remembrance, and lay strong foundations on which to erect a site of memory. There were heterogeneous voices concerning the Kellys, delivered in heterogeneous media such as ballads and letters composed by the gang members themselves and their sympathizers, and plays. However, the ability of the press to incorporate all of them amounted to a totalizing force; it allowed for Ned to be taken up in a number of different ways, but almost all within the boundaries set by the mainstream press. Although the press was generally very anti-Kelly, it set up a binary opposition between forces—those of "law and order" on the one hand and of the Kellys on the other, who were perceived as having many sympathizers who were linked to a certain section of Australian society, the "lower orders". A powerful binary opposition was therefore produced *internally* to the press, and it was this internal dialectic that contributed considerably to the production of an enduring site of memory, fuelled by tension and controversy. The press can therefore almost be seen as its own quasi-autonomous media dispositif, but only due to its ability to cannibalize and incorporate other, disparate, media and voices.

It is not the initial press construction of the memory site that I would like to discuss here, however, but two media representations from a slightly later stage in its development. The years 1890-1930 saw a decline in press interest, at least of course in terms of current events. But this did not signify a decrease in media attention; on the contrary the Kelly story was taken up fervently by other media technologies and genres, and the memory site showed no signs of dying out. The site was continued and developed predominantly by books: memoirs, popular histories and novels. There were also a number of Kelly plays and a couple of serials in newspapers. In addition at least three films about the Kelly gang were made and exhibited during this time. Again, although there were some pro-Kelly voices during this time, the most powerful media were anti-Kelly, particularly the histories and memoirs (of which not one came from a Kelly sympathizer). There remained a great deal of government censorship around the site, so although it paid to keep representing the Kelly gang and contributing to its legend it was wise to come down firmly on the side of law and order whilst doing so. The films and plays were often designated by the authorities as pro-Kelly, though they contained ambiguities in this respect, and usually moralized during their glorification of the criminals. These films and plays were associated with the "lower orders", which were (apparently) more likely to identify with the Kellys, and many of them were banned. (As with the initial press construction of the site, when media used by working-class "sympathizers" were censored, there appears to be an intimate connection between particular media usage and class divisions.)

The period 1890-1930 is an important and unique one in the progression of the site. It is a phase in which the Kelly events had ceased to be current or ongoing: by around 1890 any fears that had been entertained concerning outbreaks and rebellions from surviving sympathizers had dissipated. Kelly had thus moved decidedly into the realm of memory proper, but only just; the events very much remained within living memory, and most of the matter published on the subject constitutes first-person accounts. By about 1930 most of the participants or eyewitnesses had died, and the memory site entered a new stage. 1890-1930 were also eventful years for Australia. The 1890s saw increased urbanization in the colonies, and a severe depression. Perhaps partly due to these occurrences, it was also a decade of intense informal nation-building, carried out by cultural producers within the urban centres, such as Henry Lawson and Banjo Patterson, but revolving around the figure of the bushman, a figure who remains an important part of the Australian national identity today. Federation in 1901 signified the formalization of the nation-state, which became embroiled in the Boer War and then the First World War. The battle at Gallipoli remains, after the genocides accompanying invasion, perhaps the deepest trauma for the nation, and possibly its most powerful site of memory. Post-war reconstruction precipitated the Crash of 1929, which hit both the industrial and agricultural sectors in Australia, and which is where our era comes to an end. In what follows I will examine one book and one film from this period, two nodes within the media dispositif, in terms of their relational lines with other primary Ned Kelly products.

3. Media Interplay: Veracity, Incorporation, Contestation

Probably the most striking feature of all the Kelly texts that together develop the memory site between 1890 and 1930 is their determined insistence upon their own authenticity or authority, and therefore on their proximity to the realities of the Kelly gang events. Nora tells us that one of the necessary conditions for the formation of a memory site is a "will to remember" ("Between" 19). After the initial press frenzy of 1878-1880, the will to remember was certainly maintained, and remains to this day. Perhaps the strongest impetus for remembrance in all the Kelly representations in the phase 1890-1930 was the desire to sell the truths at the heart of the Kelly affair and to assert utmost authority in revealing those truths.

One only has to look at the names of some of these texts to understand how important the qualities of authenticity and authority are to them: "The Kelly Gang from Within" (Cookson), *The True Story of the Kelly Gang of Bushrangers* (Chomley), *The Complete Inner History of the Kelly Gang and Their Pursuers* (Kenneally), and "The Kelly Raid on Jerliderie by one who was there" (Elliott), to name but a few. Together the texts clamour to be recognised in this way, in often-hostile competition with each other. However, as will be seen in what follows, each bid for veracity also always entails the incorporation of other texts, either in an appropriation of these qualities in the other, or to undermine the other in support of its own.

The Last of the Bushrangers was first published in 1892 and written by Francis Augustus Hare. It is a popular history of the Kelly gang saga, but is moreover a memoir. Superintendent Hare was one of the major players in the Kelly affair, as a policeman who was twice persuaded to lead the hunt for the outlaws. The book is probably the most important of all the printed Kelly matter for this phase of the memory site; it was popular, republished several times, and was used and referred to by many of the other texts. As a memoir, the book has strong claims to veracity. However, the text also incorporates a number of other texts, and enters into relationships of authority with them.

The first point is that Hare's book is to a great extent a reaction to the findings of a Police Commission, which was set up to investigate the circumstances of the Kelly outrage, and in particular the conduct of the police forces involved in the pursuit of the gang, and which published a lengthy report in 1882. The Commission was in no way independent; of the eight persons involved in the enquiry, six were Members of Parliament. The report fell far short of criticizing the police force as an institution, however some members were severely criticized for their inefficiency, incompetence, cowardice and in-fighting. Although *The Last of the Bushrangers* does not often make explicit reference to the Commission report, it can be understood as a reaction to it and a justification of Hare's own actions and those of the wider bodies of police involved with the Kelly affair. To the extent that the Commission is quoted, it is done so selectively, to *support* Hare's self-justifications, and is not explicitly contradicted in favour of them. Hare also conspicuously omits from his narrative certain police actions that were heavily censured by the Commission. The report therefore becomes fragmented and certain of those fragments are selected and incorporated to support the authority of the memoir, whilst others are ignored or glossed over.

Fragments of press coverage, from the time of the Kelly events of around 1880, are also incorporated into the book. Towards the end of

Hare's narrative, when representing the final showdown at Glenrowen, the author explains that he can no longer recount from his own memory what happened at the scene, having been forced to retire with an injury. Instead he incorporates press coverage of the events, taken from *The Age*. Two whole chapters of the memoir are extracted from the newspaper and synthesized with Hare's representation of his own experience in the rest of the book. Not only that, but, as Hare claims "A few errors have crept in, and these I have corrected in brackets; but on the whole, it is a very fair account of what took place" (273). An interesting relationship of authority takes place here: Hare invokes the authority of the newspaper to aid his narrative, but simultaneously stamps the paper with the authority of his own memory. The incorporation of large quantities of press coverage in combination with the occasional bracketed correction effects a hierarchical relationship between the genres of memoir and press, one based on the temporal immediacy and status of the press as the "fourth estate" and the other based on lived, embodied experience, in which the press is subordinate, in terms of authority, to the police memoir.

However, during his earlier narration of the gang's bank robbery in Jerilderie, Hare comments "I am indebted to the newspapers of the day for refreshing my recollection of the facts that took place after the robbery, as I did not like to trust to my memory as to the numerous incidents that occurred during that exciting time" (157). This sentence acknowledges the failure of autobiographic memory and the need for another textual genre—the press—to take the place of the memoir. Hare thus fragments press coverage from the time of the events and the Police Commission report from shortly afterwards, and integrates the fragments with the representation of his memory, synthesizing three powerful modes of communication into his book. The materiality of the book-object contains and totalizes the outcome of this synthesis, in an attempt to produce one authoritative and authentic, stabilized and solid version of events.

The relationships between the institutions of the press, the Police Commission and the police, though contradictory and often fraught, were fundamentally harmonious. However, *The Last of the Bushrangers* also references another mode of representation, used by participants on the other side of the binary opposition set up initially by the press: the letters written by members of the gang and their sympathizers. At the time of this memoir's publication Ned's now famous "Jerilderie letter" and other documents, had still not been published in full, due to government censorship. The letters are Kelly's own representations of his life and of the persecution he had faced at the hands of the police. Hare makes reference to the Jerilderie letter in the following passage: "with regard to the documents Ned Kelly left with Mr. Living for Mr. Gill to publish, it was sent to the Government of Victoria, and I read it. It was a tissue of lies from beginning to end, a wandering narrative full of insinuations and complaints against the police, and of the type familiar to all who have had experience of tales which men of the criminal stamp are in the habit of telling; it is as impossible to prevent these men lying as it is from stealing" (154). Hare then goes on to paraphrase certain sections of the letter, mainly in fact to exonerate the very police action that Kelly attempts to expose. Of Kelly's rendition of the police murders at Stringybark Creek, Hare writes "An account is given in this statement of Ned Kelly's of the terrible tragedy at Mansfield, but it is obviously a string of falsehoods, and it would be quite improper to have it published, but he admitted that the police were not in any way the aggressors at the Wombat, but were surprised and shot down in cold blood" (155-6). (If the letter that Hare is referencing is the same as the one now published in full, it says nothing of the sort.) Here Hare tries to undermine completely the authority of Ned's own memoir, whilst simultaneously lending it authority in order to vindicate the police and to indict its author years after his judicial execution. The letter is fragmented and paraphrased, and turned against itself in the process. The battle that had already been invested *within* the memory site of Ned Kelly by the press is thereby mirrored in the authority-battle between media products that sustain and develop it.

The point is that *The Last of the Bushrangers*, as with almost all the Kelly texts from this period, is marked by its will to authenticity; each attempt at veracity involves the incorporation of other texts, for the purposes either of appropriation or destabilization of the authority of the other. A battle for authority and authenticity is carried out *between* these texts, which is also manifested *within* each text. In this sense of conflict, the production process of this stage in the development of the memory site is parallel to the content of the Kelly story itself, which, since its initial construction by the press, has been anchored in an opposition and conflict between forces (the forces of "the Kellys" on one side and of "law and order" on the other). The battles present in and between the media items that reproduce and develop the memory site reinvest the sensation of struggle and opposition back into this stage of the site, thereby fuelling its continuation. Here we see the "internal proliferation of meaning" of the "vortex" that is the memory site, whereby, through dogged insistence upon their own veracity, the Kelly texts that contribute to its development interact with each other to perpetuate a sense of contestation, controversy and division. These sensations, caused by the production processes of the site, are furthered by the text's receptions, especially in terms of government or police censorship (as in the case of the film, below). The incorporation enlisted in such textual battles leads to constant narrative repetition and layering in more and more arenas of cultural production, embedding the site vertically and horizontally further into the culture.

There were at least three films made on the subject of the Kellys during the period 1890-1930. *The Story of the Kelly Gang* was made in 1906 by the Tait brothers, and is arguably the world's first narrative feature-length secular film. It plays a central role in the remembrance both of Ned Kelly and Australian cinema. This movie is considered to have spawned the Australian bushranger film trend, which flourished until 1912, when screenings of many bushranger films were banned by the police (who actually had responsibility for film censorship in certain areas). This film was itself banned, and only a few minutes of footage remain today. The governments and police saw the films as glorifying criminals and encouraging young people to take to a life of crime. I will consider *The Story of the Kelly Gang* with regard to its incorporation of and relationships with other texts, in terms of its bid for veracity.

In 1906 the Taits claimed at least partial authenticity for their film, writing in a booklet that accompanied the film screenings, "We might state that we have scoured the country to give as faithful a representation as was possible, and we trust that our endeavours to please the public are appreciated." (Stetson). At that time, what is now our conventional film grammar had not yet been established, so the filmic authenticity now associated with "realism" could not be relied upon. In this picture there were no close ups, limited camera movement (to the right or left—to reframe the action), rudimentary acting, no real editing and no intertitles. The producers and exhibitors therefore had to incorporate other media to provide an "authentic" experience. There was an on-stage lecturer, who also filled in the time occupied by reel changes, and live sound effects.

More important for my purposes is the booklet which accompanied the film, sold in the venues for 6d. This pamphlet is comprised of a synopsis explicating the six scenes of the film, and a lengthy newspaper report from the *Australasian Sketcher* of 17 July 1880. The article is entitled "Destruction of the Kellys" and is followed by the newspaper's retrospective of the gang's career. Interspersed in the pages of the newspaper report is a selection of stills from the film itself.

Integrated into the booklet, then, is a newspaper report; incorporated into that is an eyewitness account from somebody (almost definitely a press representative) who was on the special train that went to the final siege at Glenrowen. The authenticity that comes with the "I" of the eyewitness account is even more pronounced when the journalist foregrounds his proximity and interaction with Ned Kelly himself: "I had several conversations with him, and he told me he was sick of his life, as he was hunted like a dog and could get no rest" (Stetson). The film thus incorporates the genre of the printed booklet, to aid in the provision of an authentic experience, which film alone could not produce at that time. The booklet borrows two forms of immediacy associated with the press— truth status and temporal immediacy—and the press article integrates the immediate authority of the personal narrative. There is therefore a layering of three genres of the *print* medium and the authority or authenticity that attaches to each, which is inserted into the one *filmic* experience.

The film thus incorporates the press into itself. But it may also be said that it incorporates itself into the press, likewise in its claim to authenticity. As mentioned, dispersed throughout the newspaper article in the accompanying booklet are stills from the very film that the audience is watching. These stills are illustrations of the text of the synopsis and article, which are themselves illustrations and explanations of the moving picture. One of the stills is captioned: "the actual armour as worn by Ned Kelly". This complicated and complete fusion of the film and the press effectively makes the press part of the film and the film part of the press; the film stills merge with the press article to give the impression that they were "there" with the journalist providing his first person narrative. The film creates a symbiotic relationship between itself and the press, with the effect of integrating multiple layers of media authenticity into itself simultaneously.

In the 1906 film's incorporation of the press, we see that the particular article used was selected very carefully. It manages to appropriate the immediacy and truth status of the press without appropriating its strong anti-Kelly bias. Whether the film intentionally supports and glorifies the gang is difficult to say—there is little in the remaining fragments or in the booklet that directly exposes it as pro-Kelly. With the film, the product does not in itself struggle with the texts it integrates, and does not replicate in its production process the sensation of conflict present within the Kelly story. Instead it was the police reaction of a ban that located the film as a significant "pro-Kelly" text, pulling the film-experience onto one side of the Kelly divide. It would appear that it is, therefore, in its reception rather than its production that the film enacts its battles.

In terms of the workings of the media dispositif that formulates the Ned Kelly memory site at this time, we can conclude the following: the individual media products that together develop the site in this phase constantly assert their authority and bid for authenticity. In doing so, they also always incorporate each other, either to requisition the authoritative or authentic status of the other, or in a hostile attempt to usurp the other. The effects of this incorporation and struggle are two fold: firstly, the continuous repetition and layering of the story in ever-increasing spheres of cultural production advances the memory site both diachronically and synchronically. And secondly, the process reproduces and intensifies the fault-lines and tensions that were initially set up by the press, repeating and enhancing the themes of controversy, ambiguity, and the sense of societal or communal division that were already invested within the site, and thereby perpetuating the furtherance of the memory site.

4. Myth, Contestation, Temporality

In Deleuze's analysis he makes it clear that the relational lines within a dispositif are shifting and unstable, and can produce unexpected conse-quences. One such (at least superficially) surprising effect can be seen in an examination of the Kelly memory site in the phase 1890-1930: in their incorporation of other texts and their bids for veracity, *myth-making* effects are simultaneously emitted by these Kelly representations. While the texts are clamouring for authenticity they are also, paradoxically, producing or developing a myth of Ned Kelly. In this sense the texts' statements of proximity to reality are also their detachment from it. The myth-making process takes place in two ways. Firstly, as mentioned above, the textual battles serve to reinforce the tensions and divisions that are integrated into the site, intensifying the controversy and heat which enable it to grow, transforming Kelly from a man into a legend and enabling the mythologi-cal. Contestation appears to be an important element in the maintenance of the memory site, arising out of a preoccupation with veracity, but stimulating the production of myth. The myth-making effects can be seen almost as a by-product of the struggle for veracity, whereby the creation of myth is an effect of the "internal proliferation of meaning".

Secondly, this contradictory state in which the Kelly texts' statements of proximity to reality are simultaneously their estrangement from it is related to and extended by an equally contradictory relationship the texts develop with *time*. Indeed one of the most striking features of the compila-tion of Kelly materials in this phase is the obvious foregrounding of the themes of time and memory, and the *temporal relationships* they produce between the text and its consumer.[2] Many of the texts from the period effect a number of different temporal relationships, sometimes all at once. I will use a few sentences from *The Last of the Bushrangers* to illustrate this confusing tendency.

In his memoir, Hare sets out his reason for wanting to textualize his memories: "when narrating to friendly audiences my experiences in the early days of the Colony of Victoria in what may be termed the 'gold era', and some of the various incidents which occurred during my connection with the Victorian police, I have often been asked to give the records of them a more permanent form" (1). In his concluding remarks he discusses the relationship of that past of the "gold era" with the present in which he is writing: "under the altered conditions which now exist, and the progress of the settlement, there is no likelihood of another Kelly episode in the history of the colony"; "the habitual criminal in Australia has been taught that, however romantic and exciting the career of the bushranger may appear, as a trade bushranging 'does not pay'"; "while the criminal classes have been shown that the Government of the colony is not to be played with…and that no considerations of economy, no saving of trouble, no sacrifice of time, energy or even life will be allowed to stand in the way when the law has to be upheld by the Executive. To the wisdom of such a policy let this fact bear witness—The execution of the last of the Kelly gang destroyed the 'Last of the Bushrangers'" (326). In these passages a rupture is manufactured between the Kelly past and the text's present. This is accomplished firstly in the assertion that conditions are so different "now" from what they were "then", as to make another bushranger outbreak inconceivable. Secondly, in these sections Hare imbibes romantic sentiment into the past in which the Kellys lived. This can be seen in the first instance in his use of the phrase "gold era" to describe the Kelly period. This era was already being mythologized and written into the narrative of Australia in nostalgic and sentimental terms, and Hare's use of it repeats that nostalgic vision of the past. The very fact that the term is placed in inverted commas demonstrates its mythologized nature. Indeed, the Kelly affray took place only at the very tail end of the "gold era", if it can be located there at all. The life of the bushranger, associated with a past time, is also described here using expressions such as "romantic" and "exciting". This romanticization of the past distances the reader from it and generates the sensation of a disjuncture between past and present (even though those expressions are used negatively the romantic effect is nevertheless produced). However, the temporal rupture is simultaneously effaced in those same passages of writing, in Hare's use of the present perfect tense—"the habitual criminal in Australia has been taught . . . the criminal classes have been shown". This grammatical choice provides a continuum between past and present—the criminal classes that were there in 1880 are still there in 1892. Lastly, the final line of the book—"The execution of the last of the Kelly gang destroyed the 'Last of the Bushrangers'". does not either create or efface a disjuncture between past and present. Instead it stops time, discontinues temporal movement, in effect rendering the Kellys "timeless".

A brief example from the 1906 film illustrates one of the many interesting temporal relationships it forges. Its accompanying booklet, which incorporates a newspaper article, contains the following sentence: "the…incidents of the terrible tragedy [the Stringybark Creek murders] are events of which the public still have a vivid recollection. The shock created a panic throughout the colony". This sentence is from the article's retrospective of the gang, which follows its personal account of the Glenrowen showdown. The sentence was written in 1880, referring to a key incident in the Kelly narrative that occurred in 1878, which is why it uses the past tense. However, it was being read at the film screenings that commenced in 1906, twenty-six years after the article was first written. The film projects onto its present audience the experiences that were already memories in 1880; the "public" of 1880 that "still have a vivid recollection" of the 1878 Stringybark Creek murders, thus becomes the public of the 1906 film-going audience. *The Story of the Kelly Gang* takes the present back into the past, whilst simultaneously retaining the force of "vivid recollection". At the same time the narrative moving picture attempts to transport the spectator spatially and temporally into the events themselves, allowing for the power both of recollection and of simulated embodied experience.

We have established that these Kelly texts develop multiple, contradictory and simultaneous temporal relationships. The claims of authority often rest on the author having "been there", or on the incorporation of a text or medium that "had been there". This assertion creates the sensation of being firmly lodged in time—in the particular time of the Kelly gang's escapades. However, the romantic or mythological features of those texts are also correlated to a dislocation of the media consumer from our temporal positioning. Sometimes the romanticism is related to a kind of temporal universality or "timelessness". On other occasions the historical period of the Kelly outbreak is conflated with a time which preceded it; this produces an enhanced sense of "pastness" that feeds back into the romantic or myth-making techniques that fashion it. In yet other instances the Kelly period touches or merges with the present of the texts that describe it; far from providing a sense of historical continuity, however, in these cases such a meeting refuses to allow us to locate ourselves entirely in either the texts' present or the Kelly past, as it is in conflict with those other concomitant relationships. This temporal duality, whereby the texts both claim to historicize and refuse historicization, recalls Claude Lévi-

Strauss's study of myth. Lévi-Strauss asserts that a myth consists simultaneously of "reversible time" and "non-reversible time" (209); it is at once historical and ahistorical, timeless. In claiming historicity, therefore, the texts are also producing myth. It might even be argued that it is this very claim that leads to myth, as without the "reversible time" aspect, myth would not be generated. The overall outcome of the temporal relationships that the texts engender, both individually and in combination, is an intense temporal confusion, strengthening the mythical or legendary aspects of the site and distancing us from the real by proscribing any temporal orientation to it.

The two sections above describe and analyze how the constellation of various Kelly texts, media and genres in this period interact with each other to develop the memory site and the effects of this: they battle with each other for veracity and they incorporate each other to this end. The effects are to produce a contested and fraught site of memory (which stimulates its continuation), and to develop the legendary or mythical aspects of the site, furthered by the cumulative production of confusing temporal relationships. "Truth" and "myth" are therefore both part of the same medial processes, and, paradoxically, the media work *together* to produce a *contested* site of memory.

5. Conclusion

Media representations are probably the most important elements in the formulation and maintenance of sites of memory. Therefore, this article has focussed specifically on the idea of a *media* dispositif and its role in the composition of a memory site at a particular moment. However, texts are obviously never produced or received in isolation, and media products also always interact with other areas of a culture and society to manufacture memory. Foucault's dispositif consists of "discourses, institutions, architectural forms, regulatory decisions, laws, administrative measures, scientific statements, philosophical, moral and philanthropic propositions", and the system of relations established between these elements (Foucault 194). The "primary" media representations that together help develop the Ned Kelly memory site are always in dialogue with far wider cultural, political and socio-economic processes (which of course also have relationships with each other), be they other discursive practices, institutions such as the police or judiciary, or government policies, to channel cultural recollections and apprehensions in particular directions and form what might be called a *memory dispositif*. Getting to grips with the idea of a memory dispositif would entail identifying the constituent elements within it at a given historical moment, the system of relations between them and, not least, its "dominant strategic function". This conceptualization would add another dimension to the theorization of the memory site, which describes a historical self-perpetuating "vortex", as it were, sucking assorted memories into itself to form "layers" of memory. The dispositif would enable us to locate the precise relations by which this vortex is formed, develops, and functions over time. It could provide new insights into how and why a culture remembers, and the nature of the important and intricate relationships between memory, identity and power.

References

"About Ned Kelly." *Ironoutlaw*. N.p.: n.d. Web. 14 Dec. 2007. <http://www.ironoutlaw.com/html/history_01.html>.

Brigg, Morgan. 2001. "Empowering NGOs: The Microcredit Movement through Foucault's Notion of *Dispositif*." *Alternatives: Global, Local, Political* 26.3 (2001): 233-58.

Chomley, C.H. *The True Story of the Kelly Gang of Bushrangers*. Melbourne: Fraser and Jenkinson, 1907.

Cookson, B.W. "The Kelly Gang from Within." *The Sydney Sun* 27 Aug. 1911.

Deleuze, Gilles. "What is a *Dispositif?*" *Michel Foucault Philosopher: Essays*. Ed. and trans. Timothy J. Armstrong. New York: Routledge, 1992. 159-68.

Elliott, William. "The Kelly Raid on Jerilderie by One Who Was There." *The Jerilderie Herald and Urana Advertiser* 4 July 1913.

Foucault, Michel. *Power/Knowledge: Selected Interviews and Other Writings, 1972-1977*. Ed. and trans. Colin Gordon. New York: Pantheon, 1980.

Hare, Francis Augustus. *The Last of the Bushrangers*. London, 1892. Facsim. ed. East Sussex: Naval & Military, 2006.

Kenneally, J.J. *The Complete Inner History of the Kelly Gang and Their Pursuers*. 1900. 8th ed. Moe: Kelly Gang Pub., 1969.

Kessler, Frank. Home page. *Notes on* Dispositif. Faculty of the Humanities, Utrecht U, May 2006. Web. 14 Dec. 2007. <www.let.uu.nl/~Frank.Kessler/personal/notes%20on%20dispositif. PDF>.

Lévi-Strauss, Claude. *Structural Anthropology*. New York: Basic, 1963.

Nora, Pierre. "Between Memory and History: 'Les Lieux de Mémoire'." *Memory and Counter-Memory.* Ed. Natalie Zemon Davis and Randolph Starn. Spec. issue of *Representations* 26 (1989): 7-24.

---, ed. *Les lieux de mémoire.* 3 vols. 1984-1992. New ed. Paris: Gallimard, 1997.

Rigney, Ann. "Plenitude, Scarcity and the Circulation of Cultural Memory." *Journal of European Studies* 35.1 (2005): 11-28.

Stetson. F.S., ed. *The Story of the Kelly Gang.* N.p.: n.p., 1906. National Film and Sound Archive. Sydney. Web. 10 Dec. 2007. <http://colsearch.nfsa.afc.gov.au>.

The Story of the Kelly Gang. Dir. John Tait and Nevin Tait. 1906. National Film and Sound Archive, 2007. DVD.

Winter, Jay. *Sites of Memory, Sites of Mourning: The Great War in European Cultural History.* Cambridge: Cambridge UP, 1995.

Notes

[1] The preparation of this article was made financially possible by The Netherlands Organisation for Scientific Research (NWO).

[2] Of course, it is not possible for me to know how a media consumer from 1890-1930 would have responded to the texts in terms of these temporal relationships. All I can do is extrapolate from my own experiences of this temporal positioning as a consumer from 2008, reading a text from, say, 1900, about persons and events that came to an end in 1880.

Remediation as a Moral Obligation: Authenticity, Memory, and Morality in Representations of Anne Frank[1]

DAVID WERTHEIM

In October 1997 *The New Yorker* published a provocative article on the diary of Anne Frank in which American writer Cynthia Ozick protests against what she believed had been a continuous misuse of the diary throughout the history of its representation. At the very end of the article, she returned to the beginning of Anne Frank's afterlife: the historic moment in 1944 in which one of the helpers of the Frank family, Miep Gies, found the papers of the diary scattered on the floor of the secret annex. She describes how Gies, respecting Anne Frank's privacy and hoping eventually to return the diary to its author after the war, saved the document unread. She also reports how Gies later admitted that, had she indeed read it, she would most probably have burned it, as in the wrong hands the diary could have endangered many of the people it mentioned.

By the time Ozick wrote her article, this anecdote had been brought up many times to underline the miraculous coincidence that stands at the basis of Anne Frank's iconicity. This time, however, Ozick turns the common interpretation of the story on its head, writing:

> It may be shocking to think this (I am shocked as I think it), but one can imagine a still more salvational outcome: Anne Frank's diary burned, vanished, lost—saved from a world that made of it all things, some of them true, while floating lightly over the heavier truth of named and inhabited evil. (120)

Ozick based her scandalous wish that the diary had been burned upon her revulsion at the way the diary, since its first publication, had been "bowdlerized, distorted, transmuted, traduced, reduced . . . infantilized, Americanized, homogenized, sentimentalised, falsified, kitschified, and, in fact, blatantly and arrogantly denied." In her eyes, "Almost every hand that has approached the diary with the well meaning intention of publicizing . . . contributed to the subversion of history" (103-4).

Ozick's wish that the diary had been burned was only the most extreme manifestation of unhappiness with the image of Anne Frank as it
developed during the second half of the twentieth century. Many have
chronicled the various faces Anne Frank has been given since her diary
first appeared and worried about their historical accuracy. Few authors
have gone so far as to imagine a better world without the diary of Anne
Frank, but in different ways many have complained about what they considered to be unhistorical uses of the diary.[2]

Their worries were based upon the diary's use for various political
purposes, and they argued that the process by which Anne Frank had
become a symbol for human tolerance and the inner goodness of man had
come together with a disregard for historical truth. They feared that Anne
Frank would become separated from reality; in the words of Ozick, a
"distant fable–no different from tales, say, of Attila the Hun" (119).

The observation that Anne Frank's public image has taken her away
from her historical reality parallels developments in the rise of memory
studies. Here the rise of interest in why and how people want to evoke the
past has gone hand in hand with scepticism over the truth-claims of the
historicist method. As Jeffrey K. Olick and Joyce Robbins phrase it, "history's 'epistemological claim'" has been "devalued in favor of memory's
meaningfulness" (110).

This has led students of memory to focus on the social, economical,
psychological, or anthropological processes involved in collective remembrance. Critics of Anne Frank's reception have pointed to the working of
a number of these processes in that particular case. Whereas in memory
studies authors such as Yosef Hayim Yerushalmi, Avishai Margalit and Jan
Assmann have pointed to the close connections between religion and
memory (Assmann; Margalit 108; Yerushalmi), a common complaint of
critics of Anne Frank's remembrance has been her sanctification. Much of
the reception of the diary of Anne Frank indeed has religious overtones.
She has become a source of moral and religious values—of meaning—and
has sometimes literally been described as a saint (Schnabel 10).

Ozick regrets the "uplift and transcendence" Anne Frank has come to
represent; Lawrence L. Langer has criticized the conclusion of the play
made out of the diary as "a benediction assuring grace after momentary
gloom"; Alvin A. Rosenfeld rejects the making of a "saintly figure"; and
Ian Buruma describes Anne Frank as a "symbool van de heilige onschuld"
("a symbol of holy innocence") (Ozick 120; Langer 199; Rosenfeld 261;
Buruma 158). The problem according to these authors is that this sacralization has come at the cost of historical truth. As Alvin A. Rosenfeld

writes, "As for her historical substance, after so much had been diffused into the gathering legend of a secular saint, little was left" (Rosenfeld 261).

Another factor in shaping memory that is relevant to the reception of Anne Frank is the way in which her story has been mediatized. Whereas the sole focus of historiography is on writing, memory studies also deals with alternative (mass) media such as audiovisual media, museums, monuments, and the internet. These media are regarded not only as reflecting the past but also as constituting an integral part of this reflection. As Wulf Kansteiner argues, "'media of memory' . . . neither simply reflect nor determine collective memory but are inextricably involved in its construction and evolution" (Kansteiner 195).[3] This seems relevant for the afterlife of Anne Frank, since one of the remarkable elements of that afterlife is that it is so highly mediatized. The memory of Anne Frank has remained alive in public consciousness, not only because of the availability of her diary in print but also because of the many adaptations of the diary in various media such as film, theatre, museums, documentaries, and the internet.

A factor related to the mass media is the economic interest in remembering. Newspapers, books, and tickets for museums, films, and theatres have to be sold. To that end, memory may be exploited and needs to be presented in a way that takes the market into account (Cole 23-47).[4] Some criticism of Anne Frank's public image has focused on this aspect. Especially the movie and the play made of her diary have frequently been criticized for being kitsch or Americanized. Such accusations involve the idea that economic factors have distorted Anne Frank's true history. They presume that the wish to make Anne Frank bankable cannot but result in sentimentalizing or romanticizing her "real" experiences as without such "kitschification" too few people would be willing to spend their money on her history.

On the face of it, then, Anne Frank's afterlife seems to confirm the idea that "memory's meaningfulness" prevails over what used to be history's "epistemological claim". I would, however, like to argue here that a different picture arises if we take a closer look at the way Anne Frank has become an icon engraved in our cultural memory. We then see that epistemological claims regarding the reality of her history and the most accurate representation of that truth have always been present in the background. They are constantly at hand to justify each renewal of Anne Frank's remembrance. We should, therefore, be careful in arguing that the economic exploitation, mediatization and particularly the sacralization and politicization of the diary of Anne Frank grate against the search for the most authentic representation of her history. Instead, my argument will be that these processes are at least partly caused by a desire to represent the past as authentically as possible; that they have hardly ever originated without that desire; and, most importantly, that they should be understood as the result of efforts to represent the truth.

To understand this we need to take a closer look at some of the adaptations of Anne Frank's diary that, through the media attention they generated, have become key factors in her memory's remaining in public consciousness, paying particular attention to how they have claimed to be an improvement on existing mediatizations of Anne Frank's history. We may start with the translation of the diary into German, published in 1950 (Schütz). The first German translator of the diary, Anneliese Schütz, made significant changes. She toned down specific wordings which a German audience might have considered offensive. For example, a sentence in which Anne Frank described the brutality of the German occupation as "the Gestapo simply puts five hostages or so against the wall" became "they then have a reason to shoot a number of these hostages"; and when Anne Frank wrote that there was no greater enmity between two peoples than that between Germans and Jews, Schütz added the word "these", so the sentence became: "there is no greater enmity in the world than between these Germans and Jews".[5] It may seem obvious that this was done to keep the diary from hurting the feelings of its German readers too harshly, and critics of the reception of Anne Frank have certainly viewed it that way (Lefevre 66, 68). This was not, however, why Anne Frank's father, Otto Frank, consented to these changes and justified them. Otto Frank instead argued that the changed version was how Anne Frank truly thought things were. He believed his daughter had been careless in some of her phrases and he was certain she would have agreed to these changes as well (Lee 189-93). In other words, Otto Frank not only permitted these changes; he wanted them in the name of historical truth.

Another example is the mediatization of Anne Frank into a play and a movie that made Anne Frank famous all over the world. These have been heavily castigated by Rosenfeld, Bruno Bettelheim, and others for obscuring historical truth by—in an attempt to be accessible to large audiences—neglecting the tragic ending of her life, and also because of the optimistic ending, in which Anne Frank expresses the goodness of mankind. It would be a mistake to deny, however, that the play and the movie did strive for a truthful representation of the history of Anne Frank. To understand this, it needs to be recognized that such a claim to truthful representation was made through the choice of new kinds of media which each time entailed an attempt to improve the representation of Anne Frank's history in new ways.

What we see in the adaptation of the diary into other media is what Jay David Bolter and Richard Grusin have called "remediation": the transference of one medium into another with the aim of obtaining a more direct connection with reality. In this case, it was the transference of the medium of diary into that of theatre and film. The idea is that people watching the play or movie do not experience the story through the barrier of written language but directly, because they hear and see the events on stage with their ears and eyes. The departures from the precise details described in the book are therefore compensated for by an experience which pretends to be more real as it is more direct, or in Bolter and Grusin's vocabulary of remediation: more "immediate" (30-31).

That this was the reason for adapting the diary is confirmed in the arguments with which the play and movie were motivated, the way they were made, and the way they were reviewed. We see that constant emphasis was put upon the opportunities staging and filming offered to convey the reality of the historical events that were their subject.

One of the first to call for an adaptation of the diary of Anne Frank into a play was the Jewish-American author Meyer Levin. During the Second World War, Levin had been a reporter with the allied forces and had been one of the first reporters to see the liberated concentration camps (Graver 7). That experience had an enormous impact on the writer: it left him with a life-long drive to make sure the world would learn what had happened to the Jews during the war. When he read the diary of Anne Frank, he believed it to have the potential to fulfil his mission but also that it could do so best if it were translated into other media. He wrote, "Anne Frank's Diary should be a play and a film: it should be on television and on radio" ("At Long Last"). Later he explained: "It is on the stage that she may be reincarnated, and her words, directly heard, can influence a larger audience than the book itself" and, therefore, "a play and film would even more universally bring home the reality" (*Anne Frank* 12). Thus, the desire to convey the reality of history was at the heart of Anne Frank's adaptation into theatre and film.

Levin believed that the authors who ended up writing the play and the movie script, Frances Goodrich and Albert Hackett, failed in this task as he did not find them realistic enough.[6] But it should be recognized that, in their own way, they did much to make sure the play would be as true to history as possible. They felt they had to acquire knowledge about Amsterdam in the war years, even if they did not make use of it in the play. For this purpose Goodrich, Hackett, and Garson Kanin, the director of the play, travelled to Amsterdam and talked to people who had known Anne Frank, including Otto Frank. They also visited the secret annex in

Prinsengracht 263 to see and feel the hiding place for themselves. A photographer spent two days photographing every detail of the annex, from the stairs to the doorknobs. They also recorded authentic sounds from Amsterdam, such as street organs and the *Westertoren* ("West Tower") carillon (Goodrich and Hackett). The information gathered during this Amsterdam trip was then used for the stage design and the sound effects used during the play. Kanin started rehearsal, underlining the importance attached to the historical nature of the play by giving a speech in which he said, "This is not a play in which you are going to make individual hits. You are real people, living a thing that really happened" (Goodrich and Hackett). For the movie a similar trip was made to shoot on location and make further use of authentic information and props.

Levin had been correct in predicting that a play based upon the diary of Anne Frank would have an effect on audiences that the book did not have. The play was frequently lauded for the degree to which it succeeded in convincing its audience that it had accurately represented the historical events. Reviewers praised the fact that the play showed reality so well because, for them, this improved the moral impact of the play. As one reviewer in New York wrote, "There is an authoritative quality to the play that makes it absorbing: one has the feeling that this is not theatre, this is real" (McClain); while another wrote: "There is a shattering sense of reality about 'The Diary of Anne Frank'. Frances Goodrich and Albert Hackett have made the only too-true story deeply moving in its unadorned veracity. Last night's opening at the Cort Theatre provided a sense of truth that is unusual in playgoing". For this same reviewer, the ability of the play to provide such a "sense of truth" overshadowed the fact that as a play he thought it mediocre. He conceded that there have been "finer plays from a critical viewpoint in recent years" but then added that it was rare in having "combined so complete a sense of reality with such overwhelming emotion." Therefore, he concluded, "'The Diary of Anne Frank' is not only a play but an experience" (Watts).

The movie received similar reviews: the *New York Times* wrote that the director had "done a superb job of putting upon the screen the basic drama and shivering authenticity of the Frances Goodrich-Albert Hackett play" (Crowther). *Variety* published a review that praised the movie for combining humor, suspense, and romance with "an achingly accurate account of persecution", emphasizing that Goodrich and Hackett had used the movie only to "add authenticity" ("Diary"). The *New York Herald Tribune* noted: "The stress on authenticity has been carried through to the smallest detail" (Wood). In all these examples the drive to accurately represent the history of Anne Frank translated into attempts to heighten the directness and emotional impact this history had on audiences.

A very different form of representation, revealing the same drive for a true representation of the history of Anne Frank, was the publication of the critical edition of her diary. The making of this edition was the direct result of Holocaust deniers' attempts to dispute the authenticity of the diary. The Netherlands Institute for War Documentation ("Nederlands Instituut voor Oorlogsdocumentatie") published this edition in 1986 to refute the deniers' fantastic claims that the diary was a hoax and to establish once and for all that it was an authentic document about events that had actually happened. This edition may, however, also be seen as a reaction against the play, the film, and other existing media representations of the diary, by returning to the down-to-earth philology of the diary manuscripts themselves.

On almost every page the critical edition exuded the desire to represent the definitive version of the diary, establishing once and for all that it was an authentic document which recounted a history that really had happened. The critical edition showed that the manuscript of the diary consisted of two different versions. The first version was what Anne Frank had initially written in the annex (version A), and a second version was Anne Frank's own edited version of version A, made in hiding in the hope of having her diary published after the war (version B). These were shown together with the edition Otto Frank had published in 1947 (version C), which was a combination of versions A and B but omitted certain sections Otto Frank believed inappropriate for publication for reasons of privacy ("Otto Frank"). The main body of the critical edition consisted of these three versions of the diary, one underneath the other. Apart from that there were a number of introductory chapters on the biography of Anne Frank which underlined that the diaries were documents about an important historical episode. At the end of this section, a graphic photograph of corpses in Bergen Belsen was deliberately used as an illustration to underscore the gruesomeness and reality of this biography (Barnouw, Paape and van der Stroom vii). Then there were a number of chapters on the reception of the diary, including a separate chapter on the "attacks on the authenticity of the diary", discussing the accusations the authors set out to deny. Finally, the critical edition included a summary of the report on the authenticity of the diary by the Netherlands Forensic Institute. Here, the will to get to the bottom of things was stretched to the limit. Thirty-five pages (the original report was 270 pages) were devoted to discussions of the ink, the paper, and the glue of the diary as well as the handwriting.

Thus the critical edition of the diary was yet another attempt to determine the truth about Anne Frank, this time using the classic method of historical and philological criticism. But the cost of this edition was exactly what previous representations of the diary had attempted to avoid. Precise as it was, the critical edition failed in representing past events in light of their emotional impact. Scholarly perfectionism made the critical edition into a work that took considerable intellectual effort for a reader to truly engage with. It meant constantly comparing three different versions, reading footnotes and complicated chapters on graphology.

It should therefore not come as a surprise that, in the wake of the critical edition, more accessible works on Anne Frank were created and managed to draw much attention by using more accessible media than philological scholarship. The remembrance of Anne Frank was carried on, in particular by two prize-winning documentaries. Both claimed that the medium of the documentary was the best way to bring people closer to the actual facts of Anne Frank's history. In 1988 Willy Lindwer made the documentary *The Last Seven Months of Anne Frank,* which won an Emmy Award. It aspired to show "the girl behind the symbol" and attempted to do so by focusing entirely on the history of Anne Frank after her betrayal. Lindwer firmly believed that his shift of focus away from the diary to the persecution and death of Anne Frank in the camps was necessary to do justice to the reality of Anne Frank. He aimed at a "cleane, zuivere beschrijving, zonder vals sentiment" ("a clean, pure description, without false sentimentality") (Benima 13).

The other documentary was made by the British documentary-maker Jon Blair and premiered in 1995, winning not only an Emmy Award but also an Oscar. It was called *Anne Frank Remembered.* In a press release, the producers of the film explained, referring to the filmed interviews characteristic of a documentary, that "to comprehend fully the events in the life of Anne Frank, one must listen to the voices of those who were there" (Disney Channel).

Blair's biggest trump card was his discovery and acquisition of a seven-second film fragment which had been believed lost and which showed unique moving images of Anne Frank. Despite all the representations of Anne Frank, there had never been the possibility of seeing the real Anne Frank—not an actress—filmed directly. Blair therefore invested heavily in these seven seconds of film. The press release, issued with the opening of the documentary, pointed out that film restorers "cleaned and treated each frame of the footage and brought it back to compelling life". Blair made the fragment the climax of the documentary. He showed it almost at the end, when the entire biography of Anne Frank had already been treated. It came right after a short overview of the iconization of Anne Frank through the play, movie, and the Anne Frank House. This particular placement of the fragment fully exploited its potential to convey the reality of "the woman behind the symbol".[7] It made clear the message, one final time, that Anne Frank had once been a real living child. It worked well for the reviewer for the *New York Times*, who called this part of the documentary, "an image that stands as a rebuke against all attempts to turn Anne Frank into an icon" (Rothstein).

A final example of the remediation of Anne Frank was a new book version of the diary itself. The Anne Frank Fund deemed it necessary to publish a new "reading edition" that would make use of all the newly discovered pages of the diary that had been incorporated in the critical edition. In doing so, it again revealed its dissatisfaction with the potential of a critical edition to convey the history of Anne Frank. Mirjam Pressler, who compiled the new edition, decided to make this edition thirty percent larger than the original version C and also made sure that it included certain passages that had been left out by Otto Frank due to their explicitness.[8] It did not mean, though, that no parts of the original manuscript would be left out. That would have made this "reading edition" still too difficult to read. This was just a new "edition" of the manuscripts, a new selection. The Anne Frank Fund, however, believed that Pressler's selection was an improvement as in it readers would meet "an Anne more real, more human and more vital than ever" (Frank and Pressler, back cover), promising audiences yet again that they could come closer to the absolute truth about Anne Frank.

This so called "definitive edition" may finally also help us understand the problem with the argument that the politicization and sacralization of Anne Frank would grate against the accurateness of her representation. This new edition saw the edition of version C go out of print. That means that anyone who would like to read the text that brought about such a shock in the years after the Second World War and in which so many people had found a source for their ideals can now only be found in antiquarian bookshops or concealed within the critical edition. The Anne Frank Fund, which instigated this edition, however, argued that the new editorial changes did not amount to a rejection of the editorial work done by Otto Frank and, moreover, that it did not diminish the political significance the diary had acquired over the years. As the introduction stated, "This new edition in no way affects the integrity of the old one originally edited by Otto Frank, which brought the diary and its message to millions of people" (Frank and Pressler, ix).

The fact that the Anne Frank Fund did not see this as a problem reflected a belief which helped to inspire the whole chain of representations of the diary of Anne Frank described here: the conviction that the normative value of the diary was based upon the history it revealed. Each mediatization had its own particular claim to superior representation of this history, be it the immediacy of theatre and film, the exactness of scholarship, or the footage of live witnesses. But they all reflected the conviction that the better the representation of this history, the more pronounced its message would be.

In other words, the call for new mediatizations of the diary was motivated by the argument that, to fully comprehend the diary's moral lessons, there exists a moral obligation to know the entire and precise truth about Anne Frank. This also balances the claim that such mediatizations were motivated by economic interests. In some cases, publishers, producers and institutions may have had such motivations or may at least have used Anne Frank simply as a means to attract attention. But even if this were in fact the case—and it is difficult, if not impossible, to establish whether people's motives are sincere—these examples show that, for mediatizations of the diary to "work" to find their audiences, and be a source of moral inspiration to them, the claim of a more truthful representation had to be made.

The length of this article only allows for the consideration of but a few of the existing representations of Anne Frank's history. A similar argument could, however, be made about exhibitions and museums about her history, other films that have been made, and biographies that have been published. In each case we see that Anne Frank's memory was renewed not so much through the availability of the diary but through a continuous stream of adaptations of it in different media, while each media representation justified its existence as an improvement over previous media used to represent the diary. They constantly claimed to offer a more accurate representation of Anne Frank's history by virtue of their being free from the limitations of previous media representations. As a result, it was argued that a play conveyed history more directly than a book; that a critical edition contained more accurate information than a book or a play; that a documentary was the best way to represent the past accurately; and that a book based upon a critical edition was more accessible than a critical edition and more accurate than a book not based upon a critical edition, and so forth.

It is for this reason that I would like to argue against the idea that the iconization of Anne Frank entailed a "subversion of history", based upon a lack of interest in the historical Anne Frank. I am not concerned here with Ozick's question of whether remembering Anne Frank has been a good thing. I would just like to argue that it cannot be denied that this remembrance has focused on the disclosure of the historical truth about her life.

It should finally be noted that the continuous quest for the true Anne Frank gained its impetus from the fact that those who attempted to transmit her history were convinced that they were fulfilling a moral obligation. All the media representations not only intended to represent the diary as authentically as possible, but the very process was constantly justified by idealist motives. This was based upon a strong belief that only an accurate representation of Anne Frank gave her the moral authority that in some cases could lead to some kind of sacralization. It assumed a connection between discovering the truth about Anne Frank and the lessons she was believed to teach. Indeed, it is doubtful whether Anne Frank's memory would have remained so prominently in the public consciousness over such a long period of time, had it not been for this assumption that ultimately propelled the constant remediation of her history. The "many faces of Anne Frank" (van der Stroom)[9] should not be understood as evidence that reality has become irrelevant in the memory of Anne Frank. It should, rather, be understood as the result of the interaction between on the one hand the differing limitations and capabilities in representing reality inherent in each kind of medium and on the other hand the moral necessity to represent reality.

The case of Anne Frank thus makes clear that there are instances in which some of the key elements in the construction of memory are motivated by the desire for truth. It shows that mediatization, politicization and sacralization cannot simply be reduced to fabrication, but that, on the contrary, they may reflect a desire and conviction that actual history can and must be uncovered. It also shows that this desire may be a key to understanding why memory in some cases stays "alive", since such a desire forces memory to renew itself. The classical distinction between historiography and other (popular) forms of remembering therefore not only misses the point because historiography, like memory, can be politicized and instrumentalized, but also because in some cases memory reflects the desire to convey the truth of the past, just as much as classical historiography.

References

Arendt, Hannah. Letter. *Midstream: A Monthly Jewish Review* 8.3 (1962): 85-87.

Assmann, Jan. "Invisible Religion and Cultural Memory." *Religion and Cultural Memory: Ten Studies*. By Assmann. Trans. Rodney Livingstone. Stanford: Stanford UP, 2006. 31-64.

Barnouw, David. *Anne Frank voor beginners en gevorderden*. Den Haag: Sdu, 1998.

Barnouw, David, Harry Paape, and Gerrold van der Stroom, eds. *De dagboeken van Anne Frank*. By Anne Frank. Met een samenvatting van het rapport van het Gerechtelijk Laboratorium, opgesteld door H.J.J. Hardy. 1986. 5th rev. and exp. ed. Amsterdam: Nederlands Instituut voor Oorlogsdocumentatie, 2001.

Benima, Tamarah. "Filmer Willy Lindwer is kundig maker van joodse documentaires." *Nieuw Israelitisch Weekblad* 31 Aug. 1990: 13.

Bettelheim, Bruno. "The Ignored Lesson of Anne Frank." Enzer and Solotaroff-Enzer 185-91.

Bolter, Jay David, and Richard Grusin. *Remediation: Understanding New Media*. Cambridge: MIT Press, 1999.

Burke, Peter. "History as Social Memory." *Memory: History, Culture and the Mind*. Ed. Thomas Butler. Oxford: Blackwell, 1989. 97-110.

Buruma, Ian. "Anne Frank als bijbelles (1995)." van der Stroom 158-60.

Cole, Tim. *Selling the Holocaust: From Auschwitz to Schindler: How History is Bought, Packaged, and Sold*. New York: Routledge, 2000.

Crowther, Bosley. "The Diary of Anne Frank (1959)." *New York Times* 19 Mar. 1959: 40.

"The Diary of Anne Frank." Collection Anne Frank Stichting, Amsterdam. [*Variety* 18 Apr. 1959].

The Disney Channel. *Anne Frank Remembered*. 1995. Collection Anne Frank Stichting, Amsterdam.

Enzer, Hyman Aaron and Sandra Solotaroff-Enzer, eds. *Anne Frank: Reflections on Her Life and Legacy*. Urbana: U of Illinois P, 2000.

Finkenstein, Norman G. *The Holocaust Industry: Reflections on the Exploitation of Jewish Suffering*. London: Verso, 2000.

Frank, Otto, and Mirjam Pressler, eds. *The Diary of a Young Girl: The Definitive Edition*. By Anne Frank. Trans. Susan Massotty. 1995. New York: Bantam, 1997.

Goodrich, Frances, and Albert Hackett. "Diary of 'The Diary of Anne Frank'." *New York Times* 30 Sept. 1956: 1+.

Graver, Lawrence. *An Obsession with Anne Frank: Meyer Levin and the Diary.* Berkeley: U of California P, 1995.

Kansteiner, Wulf. "Finding Meaning in Memory: A Methodological Critique of Collective Memory Studies." *History and Theory* 41.2 (2002): 179-97.

Langer, Lawrence L. "The Uses—and Misuses—of a Young Girl's Diary: 'If Anne Frank Could Return from among the Murdered, She Would Be Appalled.'" Enzer and Solotaroff-Enzer 203-05.

Lee, Carol Ann. *The Hidden Life of Otto Frank.* 2002. London: Penguin, 2003.

Lefevere, André. "Translation: Ideology: On the Construction of Different Anne Franks." *Translation, Rewriting, and the Manipulation of Literary Fame.* By Lefevere. London: Routledge, 1992. 59-72.

Levin, Meyer. *Anne Frank: A Play.* N.p.: M. Levin, [1967?].

---. "At Long Last We Have a Real Story of Jews Under Nazism." Collection Anne Frank Stichting, Amsterdam. [*National Jewish Post* 30 June 1952].

Margalit, Avishai. *The Ethics of Memory.* Cambridge: Harvard UP, 2002.

McClain, John. "Stark Study of Terror." Collection Anne Frank Stichting, Amsterdam. [*New York Journal American* 6 Oct. 1955].

Olick, Jeffrey K., and Joyce Robbins. "Social Memory Studies: From 'Collective Memory' to the Historical Sociology of Mnemonic Practices." *Annual Review of Sociology* 24.1 (1998): 105-40.

"Otto Frank liet uit Annes dagboek groot gedeelte weg." Collection Anne Frank Stichting, Amsterdam. [*Trouw* 30 Jan. 1981].

Ozick, Cynthia. "Who Owns Anne Frank?" *A Scholarly Look at The Diary of Anne Frank.* Ed. Harold Bloom. Philadelphia: Chelsea House, 1999. 101-20.

Rosenfeld, Alvin A. "Popularization and Memory: The Case of Anne Frank." *Lessons and Legacies.* Ed. Peter Hayes. Evanston: Northwestern UP, 1991. 243-78.

Rothstein, Edward. "Anne Frank: The Girl and the Icon." *New York Times* 25 Feb. 1996: 1+.

Schnabel, Ernst. *Anne Frank: Spur eines Kindes: Ein Bericht.* 1958. Frankfurt am Main: Fischer, 1997.

Schütz, Anneliese, trans. *Das Tagebuch der Anne Frank: 14. Juni 1942 – 1. August 1944.* By Anne Frank. Heidelberg: Schneider, 1950.

Stroom, Gerrold van der, ed. *De vele gezichten van Anne Frank: Visies op een fenomeen.* Amsterdam: de Prom, 2003.

Watts, Richard, Jr. "The Stage's Tribute to Anne Frank." *New York Post* 23 Oct. 1955: 13.

Wood, Thomas. "'Anne Frank' Offers Realism on Screen." Collection
    Anne Frank Stichting, Amsterdam. [*New York Herald Tribune* July
    1958: 3+].
Yerushalmi, Yosef Hayim. *Zakhor: Jewish History and Jewish Memory*. 1982.
    New York: Schocken, 1989.

Notes

[1] The preparation of this article was made financially possible by The
Netherlands Organisation for Scientific Research (NWO).

[2] For examples, see Arendt; Barnouw; Bettelheim; Buruma; Rosenfeld;
Langer.

[3] For a discussion on the importance of media in the study of memory,
see Burke.

[4] For a similar argument on the memory of the Holocaust in general, see
Finkenstein.

[5] "[E]r bestaat geen groter vijandschap op de wereld dan tussen Duitsers
en Joden" became "eine grössere Feindschaft als zwischen *diesen*
Deutschen und den Juden gibt es nicht auf der Welt"; and "zet de
Gestapo doodgewoon een stuk of 5 gijzelaars tegen de muur" became
"dann hat man einen Grund, eine Anzahl dieser Geiseln zu erschiessen"
(Lefevere 66, 68).

[6] On this controversy, see Graver.

[7] See Graver.

[8] These were mostly passages in which Anne Frank discussed sexual matters, or the problems with her mother.

[9] I have used Van der Stroom's phrase "the many faces of Anne Frank",
but it should be noted that he does not make the assertion that this means
that reality is irrelevant when it comes to Anne Frank.

III. The Public Arena

Performances, Souvenirs, and Music:
The Diamond Jubilee of Queen Victoria 1897

MEIKE HÖLSCHER

The Jubilee of 1897 was invented as a memorial day in order to commemorate 60 years of Queen Victoria's reign, but also, and more importantly, to celebrate the just recent history and success-story of her imperial reign as "Empress of India", a title which was bestowed on her in 1877 through the Royal Titles Bill. It represented the end and at the same time the zenith of a process which Ansgar and Vera Nünning strikingly call the "Turning of a Domestic Queen into a familiar and idealized icon of the British Empire" (Nünning and Nünning 108). In their diachronic analysis of a selection of poetic and journalistic representations of Queen Victoria's Jubilees of 1887 and 1897, they make a strong claim for the constructive power of metaphors and fictions in the "making of imperial mentalities" (Mangan). Metaphors and narratives of the Queen as a mother to her people and of the Empire as family served to create and support the perceptual and ideological fictions that "formed the conceptual matrix of imperialism" (Nünning and Nünning 108) and as such, functioned as efficient tools in the propagation and justification of an imperialist ideology.

In my article, I will analyze selected media-offerings like performances, souvenirs and music and discuss their potentials as media of collective remembering in a very specific (media-)historical situation, which has been outlined by David Cannadine as follows:

> So in mugs and medals, as in music and magnificence, the last quarter of the nineteenth century and the first decade of the twentieth was a golden age of 'invented traditions', as the appeal of the monarchy to the mass of people in an industrialized society was broadened in a matter unattainable only half a century before. ("Context" 137-38)

The "invented tradition" of the Diamond Jubilee of 1897, the transnational celebrations, their medial representations as well as their materializations not only served the purpose of increasing the "appeal of the monarchy", but, and this is my main argument, proved successful in increasing the appeal of the British Empire, to generate the impression of imperial *communitas* (V. Turner) based on a largely fictive or mythic account of the history of the British Empire. I will argue that changing media and cultural practices played an important role in the process which can also be termed "imperialistic self-fashioning". In the first part of this article, I will reflect on the media-historical situation around the time of the Diamond Jubilee taking into account new concepts of the interplay between media and the dynamics of collective remembering. In the second part, I will try to delineate certain aspects of this dynamic interplay in the process of imperialistic self-fashioning, namely 1) the Empire as *mise en scène*; 2) the Commodification of Empire and 3) music and memory.

1. Dynamics of Collective Remembering: Imperialistic Self-fashioning at the End of the Nineteenth Century

On 22 June 1897, the popularity of Queen Victoria with her 320 million subjects was at its peak: "Throughout the Empire, [her Diamond] Jubilee was the occasion of holidays and public performances" (Filewod 13). Victoria even made use of new media technologies and sent a special telegraph message across the Empire reading: "From my heart I thank my beloved people. God bless them!" (qtd. in Plunkett 240). The main Jubilee parade in London was filmed by more than a dozen filmmakers including the brothers Lumière and the celebrations around the globe were extensively covered and broadcasted by the press in such an effective way that the Diamond Jubilee turned into an outstandingly memorable "transnational media-event", as Nünning and Rupp ("Königin Victorias Thronjubiläen") have demonstrated convincingly.

In the last part of the nineteenth century, the modes of media production, distribution and circulation changed rapidly and new media offerings also changed the processes and politics of remembering. John Plunkett points out that "Victoria's endless materialization [was] so important because it was a bridge between individual experience and the type of mass-collectivity created by industrialism". He continues to argue that "[i]t was the individual and collective experience provided by the different media. The wealth of newspapers, prints and photographs offered Victoria's subjects an intimate and personal interaction with the monarchy"— and the Empire (Plunkett 7).

In order to provide an adequate background for the analysis of this specific stage in the process of imperialistic self-fashioning it is necessary to take into account new approaches in cultural memory and media studies and apply them to a very specific historic situation, namely the late nineteenth century. These new approaches in cultural memory studies stress the fact that collective remembering is a constructive, media-bound process which highly depends on "memory-workers" (Rigney). Scholars like Astrid Erll and Martin Zierold (402-05) suggest a more complex view of "the media" in such processes. In Erll's model of the functions of media in processes of collective remembrance (*Kollektives Gedächtnis* 130-42), both the material and the social components of media are included. Semiotic instruments of communication, media technologies and media offerings form the material part of media, whereas the social dimension is constituted by the contexts of production and distribution on the one hand and the reception of a media offering on the other hand. Both aspects need to be included in an analysis of collective memory, which Ann Rigney defines as an "ongoing result of public communication and of the circulation of memories in mediated form . . ." (17). She argues that the analytical focus must shift towards an exploration of the "memorial practices, mnemonic technologies and the cultural processes by which shared memories are produced". Thus, collective memory is neither static nor simply a product of certain media, but "[something which is] continuously *performed* by individuals and groups as they recollect the past selectively through various media and become *involved in various forms of memorial activity* . . ." (ibid.; emphasis added).

An analysis of the processes of collective or imperial remembrance at the end of the nineteenth century must therefore include the performative aspects, the active involvement of the populace in the Jubilee celebrations. However significant the social contexts of production and reception might be, one must also pay attention to the material dimension of the media offerings involved in the dissemination of an imperial ideology. Amongst other scholars, Ansgar Nünning and Jan Rupp ("The Dissemination of Values" 255) show that metaphors of Empire worked as "conceptual tools" and "[imparted] some sort of structure to an amorphous geographical and political entity, thus serving as unifying devices". Rather than considering metaphors and narratives as mere conceptual models, they stress their power to "impose structure [and] serve as important means of fostering and maintaining loyalty" which is especially due to their emotional function. Nünning and Rupp also highlight the constructive force of narratives (266). According to them, it is necessary to take an analytical look at the "metaphors of Empire, which impacted on a wide range of genres and media from political speeches to poetry and even cultural performance" in order to "illuminate how the British Empire was

conceptualized not only politically . . . but also in terms of certain value
. . ." (258).

By taking into account the contexts of both production and reception
as well as the material and symbolic dimension of the process of the
emergence of an imperial remembrance culture, it is possible to offer a
more complex and a more dynamic view on how the Jubilee and its representations and performances transformed the way the Empire was remembered in the last part of the nineteenth century. From a methodological perspective it is, of course, difficult to trace back the vividness, the
emotional appeal and the community-building potential of the media offerings and cultural performances in question. Since the eye-witnesses
have long since died it is difficult to draw a complete picture of how the
celebrations were perceived (all over the world) and to determine whether
they were regarded as an imperial event. David Cannadine, who studied
the dynamics of royal rituals and practices at the end of the nineteenth
century, emphasizes these methodological difficulties:

> Ceremonial occasions, [like the Diamond Jubilee], can only be understood by at-
> tempting to recover the historical context within which they actually happened,
> by looking at the participants in the ceremonial (or conflict) and by investigating
> the conditions in which the ceremonial (or conflict) took place. (Cannadine and
> Hammerton 184)

The changing facets of media production, distribution and reception
formed an integral part of the imperial "enterprise". John MacKenzie's
influential series "Studies in Imperialism" consistently highlights the functions of popular medial forms in the making of "imperial mentalities". He
makes a very strong claim for "escaping the literary obsession and . . .
consider[ing] the relationships among different cultural forms, both elite
and popular in character" (xiv).

The shift in focus from a very static idea of "cultural memory" towards a more complex view of the processes of collective remembering
forms the theoretical basis of my analysis of the dynamics of "imperialistic
self-fashioning". The way in which the celebrations and the medial representations of the Diamond Jubilee contributed to the process of imperialistic self-fashioning, the way in which they fueled and shaped the dynamics of collective remembering will now be analyzed more closely in the
next part of my article by paying specific attention to the context of production, the very form and the interplay of selected media offerings, as
well as to the modes of reception.

2. Empire as *Mise en Scène*:
Jubilee Processions and Celebrations

Before commenting on the actual events, I will discuss some of the organizational aspects of the Jubilee celebrations and, therefore, focus on the context of the production of media offerings. In a letter to the mayor of London a few weeks before the actual event, the imperial "design" is expressed by the Prince of Wales:

> I have ascertained that a public memorial which would illustrate the progress her Empire has made during her Reign would be more gratifying to Her Majesty than any personal or private tribute; and that the form which the Queen would most wish such a memorial should take would be an institution illustrative of the Arts, Manufactures and Commerce of Her Majesty's Colonial and Imperial Empire. (qtd. in J. Richards 122)

Both the main celebrations in London and the local celebrations were carefully planned and organized as an imperial event. They started on 19 June 1897, but the meticulous preparations and the pre-press coverage started much earlier. Schedules of the Jubilee events were available on leaflets and published in the local as well as in the national dailies. The main parades, the unveilings of monuments and the thanksgiving services were planned by the "Office of Works" and "the routes of the Jubilee processions were published weeks in advance to ensure maximum attendance and maximum order" (Schneider 59). The press invited the public to actively contribute to the preparations and local organization committees were founded. The press supported the acclaimed "imperial enterprise" and devoted lots of space to the coverage of the preparations. The campaigns proved successful and on 23 July 1897, more than 2 million people holding flags and banners lined the procession route in London. The brothers Lumière, amongst others, filmed what Alan Filewod (*Performing Canada*) termed a "Mise en Scène of Empire – A Nation on Parade."[1] In the commentary of Joseph Chamberlain, the Colonial Secretary who was in charge of organizing and planning the main festivities in London, the imperial dimension of the celebrations becomes manifest:

> [I]n wave after wave of glittering ranks came the living evidence of the vast Empire: Giant Maoris, New Zealand Mounted Troops, The Jamaica Artillery, The Royal Nigerian Constabulary, Negroes from the West Indies, British Guiana and Sierra Leone, the Cape Mounted Rifles, New South Wales Lancers, the Trinidad Light Horse and Zaptiehs from Cyprus, the Borneo Dyak Police, 'upstanding Sikhs, tiny little Malays, Chinese with a white basin turned upside down on their

heads', grinning Houssa's from the Gold Coast and perhaps best of all, the tur-
banned and bearded Lancers of the Indian Empire 'terrible and beautiful to be-
hold'. (qtd. in Chapman and Raben 44)

Carefully rehearsed in advance, an allegory of the "vast Empire", "embodied" by representatives from every colony, paraded through London with
Queen Victoria at the head of the procession. The Empire was put on
display not only in London, but also throughout the world in equally cho-
reographed processions and parades. Mark Twain was amongst the audience as a spectator, watching the big Jubilee procession in London on 20
June 1897. His description of the scenery can be regarded as representative of the many "eye-witness"-accounts of the proceedings in London
and the colonies. He describes his subjective impressions at length:

> It took me a while to determine that this procession *could not be described.* . . . It was
> a spectacle for *the Kodak*, not the pen. . . . All the nations seemed to be filing by.
> They all seemed to be represented . . . The procession was the *human race on exhi-
> bition*, a spectacle curious and interesting and worth travelling far to see. . . . The
> Queen Empress was come. She was received with great enthusiasm. It was realiz-
> able that *she was the procession herself*, that all the rest was mere embroidery; that in
> her, the public saw the British Empire itself. (197-98, emphasis added)

Even for a renowned writer and journalist like Mark Twain it was difficult
to put the astounding experience of this unique procession into words. To
him it seemed as if only the photographic image ("the Kodak") was able
to capture the presumably overwhelming scenery, which he describes as
"the human race on exhibition". The iconic power of this big "state pag-
eant" (*sensu* Filewod) becomes even more evident in his observations on
the role of Queen Victoria in this procession. The Empress and the representatives from every nation of the Empire seemed to symbolize the vast
British Empire and therefore represented the "invented" homogeneity of
an imperial remembrance culture. The long-lasting commemorative effects of the festivities and especially the Jubilee-procession in London are
described by Twain as follows: "It was a memorable display and must live
in history" (198).

Concepts of "culture as performance" or, as Milton Singer terms it,
"cultural performances", stress the notions of theatricalization and spec-
tacularization in the process of creating a sense of communality. Obviously, these performances lack the material and medial qualities traditionally ascribed to popular media, but, as the Jubilee celebrations show, they
can serve as powerful mnemonic vehicles because "they leave no room
for critical negotiations, they offer a parade of icons that progressively

accumulate as a narrative [and iconic] embodiment of the (presumably) consensual ideology shared by the audience" (Filewod 13).

Millions of British subjects played an active role in that "cultural performance" as co-actors and collectively and creatively re-invented an imperial past. In an article in *The Times*, published two days after the main celebrations in London, the long history of the Queen's reign is rhetorically combined with the much shorter history of the Empire:

> To-day the eyes of the whole Empire, and of millions of men beyond its pale, will be fixed upon London, and up on the great and inspiring ceremony in which we celebrate the sixty years of the Queen's reign. . . . Since the Queen first made a like State progress, as she passed to her coronation in 1838, what transformations! These Colonies, who form perhaps the most applauded section of her escort, have travelled thousands of miles to be here. . . .They have come representing not a few small, scattered communities, but millions of men, brave, intelligent, wealthy, and loyal. These Indians, too, children of 'the unchanging East', are changed. They are proud Princes tracing their descent back for many centuries; and yet they have become faithful vassals of the Queen. They are a sign and symbol of the British Peace which now, after many a struggle and one heroic episode, prevails from Ceylon to the Himalayas. (qtd. in Chapman and Raben 42)

The author of this newspaper article not only enthusiastically comments on the transnational dimension and reception of the Jubilee processions in London ("the eyes of the whole Empire, and of millions of men beyond its pale, will be fixed upon London"), but also successfully combines Victoria's long reign with the success-story of the Empire ("symbol of the British Peace").

While the main celebrations in London were taking place, similar and also carefully rehearsed processions, thanksgiving services and unveilings of monuments were being held in all big cities of the Empire. The pictures of the London ceremonies reached Bombay only two days after the celebration and were presented to the public in the form of filmic presentations. Perspectives "from the crowd" were published in the illustrated magazines and thus represented a change of perspective: the audience played an active role in the course of the construction of this event and the personal memories written down in diaries are a good source for proving the enthusiastic reception of the festivities and the memory politics at work.

3. Commodification of Empire

In the context of a growing commodity culture and advertising industry in Britain between 1870 and 1900 the role of Jubilee items and souvenirs cannot be underestimated in the processes of imperialist self-fashioning. The studies of Ralph Schneider and Thomas Richards have successfully traced the linkage between Queen Victoria's image and the growing commodity culture.

The Diamond Jubilee was not only a media event, but a big commercial event as well. Even before the official celebrations started, the growing advertising and souvenir industry sold millions of Jubilee items and advertised them in large campaigns in local and national dailies. Queen Victoria's image (as Empress) was not only impressed on domestic household goods like commemorative plates, mugs, terra-cotta, spoons, stamps, medals, brooches, rugs and toys, but also on colonial goods like tea, tobacco and coffee.

The Empire was made visible—and purchasable—in the form of texts, images and a series of familiar objects, which were labelled "available throughout the Empire". The image of Queen Victoria appeared on "biscuit tins, commemorative plates, and souvenir artifacts of every description. It was engraved for most of the illustrated periodicals and exported throughout the Empire" (Plunkett 197).

"What began with the charisma of a single personality ended with the charisma of a thousand manufactured objects", writes Thomas Richards, who analyzed the "Image of Queen Victoria" at the time of her Golden Jubilee and concludes that her image became a "commodity" (13). With Jubileeana, "the Empire was seen not through a sampling of strange relics, but rather through a complete line of familiar objects representing all aspects of everyday English life: toys, cutlery, household decorations" (21).

"The Jubilee campaigns succeeded in transforming the commodity [the image of the Queen-Empress] into something which Baudrillard calls "a total medium, a system of communication administering all social exchange" (qtd. in Th. Richards 29). The image of the mother of an imaginary unit, the Empire, was also created through objects.

These Jubilee souvenirs formed productive alliances as they were integrated into festive celebrations such as the Children's Jubilees, which were celebrated even in small towns in Britain and the colonies. The imperial remembrance culture was therefore not only on display, but could also be "purchased" through a range of objects. At the time of the actual celebrations, every household in Britain and in the colonies possessed at least one Jubilee item, which ensured a long-lasting commemorative effect. The

Jubilee items served as material reminders of the big state occasion and can be regarded as medial cues for the "imperial experience". It was also through objects, and in this special case, Jubilee items, that the British and the colonial subjects "saw" their Empire.

4. Music and Memory:
The Mnemonic Function of Anthems and Hymns

Music, especially hymns and anthems, was performed not only on the occasion of the Jubilee, but was an important part of everyday life. Jeffrey Richards reminds us that during the 1890s, music, and especially national music, was industrialized and commercialized and national hit songs and hit music were produced. In the months before the major events, the production of anthems, hymns and odes to the Queen boomed. These combinations of textual and musical reminiscences of the Queen's long reign were not only published in national dailies and local newspapers, but they were also available on leaflets which circulated in the streets of London and the big cities of the colonies:

> Deeply conscious of his inability to succeed to the honoured Patrician Laureate's Chair, it is nevertheless hoped these simple verses may (in the absence of severe criticism) be deemed sufficiently interesting to secure a wide circulation; be counted worthy a place in every Christian home, and an echo in every loyal heart. The Author. (*A Collection of verses referring to the Jubilee*, 1887, n.p.)

Competitions were launched for the best anthems or odes to the "Empress of India" and people were encouraged to perform them collectively in public. Furthermore, hymns and anthems were not only specifically written for the occasion, but also integrated into cultural performances like the unveiling of monuments, street parades and church services.

In his original study on *Imperialism and Music* Jeffrey Richards persuasively argues that hymns and anthems, written specifically for the Diamond Jubilee events, played a major part in fostering an emotional attachment and commitment to the Empire:

> With its unique capacity to stimulate the emotions and to create mental images, music was used to dramatize, illustrate and reinforce the components of the ideological cluster that constituted British imperialism in its heyday. . . . Music was written specifically to promote the idea of Empire . . . . (525)

His study draws attention to one of the major vehicles for fostering imperial sentiment and attaching it to a popular sense of national identity. The
music discussed by Richards reflects the fact that the Empire received a
positive response from Britons at home and abroad. The "Empire
Hymn", composed by Edgar Elgar, was the smash hit of the Diamond
Jubilee and another Jubilee hymn "O Kings of Kings" with music by Sir
Arthur Sullivan and lyrics by the late Bishop of Wakefield were selected
for use in all churches and chapels throughout the Empire on that day.

The "Sons of England", an association of British living in exile, organized a church service on the day of the Jubilee "to be held in continuous succession throughout the British colonies around the World". The
service was planned carefully to ensure that congregations in every colony
would sing "God Save the Queen" at 4 p.m. local time. Along with the
text of the service a chart of local starting times for the anthems was distributed, set aside "Time of the Empire—Windsor Castle". The service
started in Fiji at 4:20 p.m. GMT and moved around the globe: "The zenith of the British dream of a world Empire can be identified to the exact
minute, but the time of that minute moved with the rotation of the earth
. . . For the duration of that day, someone, somewhere, was always singing
the royal anthem" (Filewod 22).

But how did contemporaries, like Sir Arthur Sullivan, one of the major British composers of the nineteenth century, assess the effects of
popular media products like hymns and anthems in the process of fostering a sentiment of imperial unity? Sullivan, commenting on the effects of
his own composition, expresses a very optimistic view:

> Amongst our own people, no one who has visited the Greater Britain beyond the
> seas but must be alive to the depth of feeling stirred by the first bar of *God Save
> the Queen*. It is not too much to say that this air has done more than any other
> single agency to consolidate the national sentiment which forms the basis of our
> world-Empire. (qtd. in J. Richards 95)

Sir Arthur Sullivan highlights the community-building potential of anthems, and especially national anthems, focusing on the emotional appeal,
the "depth of feeling", which a national anthem can stir in those who
collectively perform it.

Recent studies push this optimistic view of the mnemonic function of
music and musical performances even further:

> Musical culture and its products, both live and inanimate, can be sponsored in
> order to establish community identity, fix power relations between its members,
> demonstrate taste and purchasing power and, above all, stave out boredom that

comes with isolation in an outpost far from familial and community supports at 'home' . . . . Musical sounds, like smells, can be desperately evocative of memories and feelings associated with them, but unlike smells (other than commercial perfume) can be taken along, reproduced for this purpose at will, and employed to occupy the time that geographical distance may cause to hang heavy. (Banfield 63)

Due to its performative and emotional qualities music was able to bridge the geographical gap between Britain and the colonies and create the idea of an "imperial unity" more than any textual representation could have done. Popular media like music, as Simon Frith has suggested, have primarily social functions, providing ways of managing the relationships between public and private emotional lives.

5. Conclusion

In 1897, the Empire was no longer a negatively connoted political construct, but entered the every-day life of British and colonial subjects via new medial forms, settings and practices. The "imperial idea" of an imperial family with Queen Victoria at its head was represented, as well as constructed as such *across* the media and *in* performances in very specific ways. The growing commodity culture, new media technologies and the late Victorian festivity culture, the interplay of different popular media, their integration into civic rituals as memory performances and the active participation of the populace, enhanced the feeling of belonging to an imperial community with Queen Victoria as both symbol and narrative kernel. First and foremost, the invention of an *occasion* to remember, namely the invention of a commemorative day to remember the history of the Queen's reign and the recent history of the Empire was essential in the process of "imperial self-fashioning".

Secondly, the narratives and metaphors of popular imperialism, the conceptualization of the "Empire as a big, happy and harmonious family" played an important part in this process as they were distributed *across* the media which resulted in "a maximum possible exposure" (Th. Richards 12). The fact that the Jubilee was embedded into a newly emerging commodity culture perpetuated the synchronic circulation of an imperial ideology, by domesticating as well as spreading commemorative objects around the globe. Finally, the populace's active participation as "memory-workers" (*sensu* Rigney) contributed to the imagination of an "imperial family" with a shared past, and to the expansion of the imperial image of Queen Victoria as Empress. The imaginary union with an invented history was put on display and was made experienceable through spectacular displays, public performances, Jubilee items and anthems: "The Empire staged itself"—and the audience, the British and colonial subjects, acted as co-performers in the affirmation and creation of the "presumable consensual ideology". Cultural performances were media of self-fashioning which not only appealed to the masses and generated a certain feeling of belonging, but also fuelled the process of constituting an imperial remembrance culture. Popular media like music and souvenirs encouraged and facilitated transnational communication and the synchronic processes of collective remembering. Static media, material objects and cultural performances formed productive alliances in this dynamic process of collective remembering. In the end I would argue that it is mainly due to the wide range of performative settings as well as popular medial forms which were available and appropriated by the public, that the Diamond Jubilee of Queen Victoria can be described as a key event in the process of imperialistic self-fashioning.

However, David Cannadine points out that not everybody joined this big imperial party and he provides examples of conflicts which arose before, during and around the Jubilee and its celebrations: "In the Empire, therefore, the responses to the Diamond Jubilee ranged from enthusiastic support and participation via studied indifference and cold, inarticulate hostility, to the full flowering of anti-ritual" ("Context", 114). This delineates a clear focus for future research and raises the question, whether these non-consensual reactions had an influence on the processes of imperialistic self-fashioning. Rather than treating memory as the manipulative action of the powerful to narrate the past to suit their particular interests, a fuller account might follow Samuel who suggests that one "might think of the invention of tradition as a process rather than an event, and memory, even in its silences, as something which people made for themselves" (Samuel 17).

References

Anderson, Benedict. *Imagined Communities: Reflections on the Origin and Spread of Nationalism.* London: Verso, 1983.

Banfield, Stephen. "Towards a History of Music in the British Empire: Three Export Studies." *Britishness Abroad: Transnational Movements and Imperial Cultures.* Eds. Kate Darian-Smith, Patricia Grimshaw and Stuart Macintyre. Melbourne: Melbourne UP, 2007. 63-89.

Cannadine, David. "The Context, Performance and Meaning of Ritual: The British Monarchy and the 'Invention of Tradition', c. 1820-1977." Hobsbawm and Ranger 101-64.

---. *Ornamentalism: How the British Saw their Empire.* Oxford: Oxford UP, 2001.

Cannadine, David, and Elizabeth Hammerton. "Conflict and Consensus on a Ceremonial Occasion: The Diamond Jubilee in Cambridge in 1897." *The Historical Journal* 24.1 (1981): 111-46.

Chapman, Caroline, and Paul Raben. *Debrett's Queen Victoria's Jubilees 1887 & 1897.* London: Debrett's Peerage; New York: Arco, 1977.

Erll, Astrid. *Kollektives Gedächtnis und Erinnerungskulturen: Eine Einführung.* Stuttgart: Metzler, 2005.

---. *Prämediation—Remediation: Repräsentationen des indischen Aufstands in imperialen und post-kolonialen Medienkulturen (von 1857 bis zur Gegenwart).* Trier: WVT, 2007.

Erll, Astrid, and Ansgar Nünning, eds. *Medien des kollektiven Gedächtnisses: Konstruktivität—Historizität—Kulturspezifität.* Berlin: de Gruyter, 2004.

Filewod, Alan. *Performing Canada: The Nation Enacted in the Imagined Theatre.* Kamloops: U Coll. of the Kariboo, 2002.

Harlow, Barbara and Mia Carter, eds. *Imperialism and Orientalism: A Documentary Sourcebook.* Malden: Blackwell, 1999.

Hobsbawm, Eric, and Terence Ranger, eds. *The Invention of Tradition.* 1983. Cambridge: Cambridge UP, 1992.

Jansohn, Christa, ed. *In the Footsteps of Queen Victoria: Wege zum viktorianischen Zeitalter.* Münster: LIT, 2003. Studien zur Englischen Literatur 15.

MacKenzie, John. *Orientalism: History, Theory, and the Arts.* Manchester: Manchester UP, 1995.

Mangan, J.A., ed. *The Making of Imperial Mentalities: Socialisation and British Imperialism.* Manchester: Manchester UP, 1990.

Nünning, Vera, and Ansgar Nünning. "The Invention of an Empress: Factions and Fictions of Queen Victoria's Jubilees of 1887 and 1897 as a Paradigm for the Study of Cultural Memories." Jansohn 83-112.

Nünning, Ansgar. "Metaphors of Empire: Victorian Literature and Culture, and the Making of Imperialist Mentalities." *Anglistentag 1997 Giessen.* Eds. Raimund Borgmeier, Herbert Grabes and Andreas H. Jucker. Trier: WVT, 1998. 347-67.

Nünning, Ansgar and Jan Rupp. "Königin Viktorias Thronjubiläen 1887 und 1897: Konstitutive Medienereignisse einer imperialen Erinnerungskultur." *Medienereignisse der Moderne.* Eds. Friedrich Lenger and Ansgar Nünning. Darmstadt: Wissenschaftliche Buchgesellschaft, 2008. 61-78.

---. "The Dissemination of Values in Late Victorian Literature and Other Media." *Ethics in Culture. The Dissemination of Values through Literature and Other Media.* Eds. Astrid Erll, Herbert Grabes & Ansgar Nünning. Berlin: de Gruyter, 2008. 255-78.

Plunkett, John. *Queen Victoria: The First Media Monarch.* Oxford: Oxford UP, 2003.

Rigney, Ann. "Plenitude, Scarcity and the Circulation of Cultural Memory." *Journal of European Studies* 35.1 (2005): 209-26.

Richards, Jeffrey. *Imperialism and Music: Britain 1876-1953.* Manchester: Manchester UP, 2002.

Richards, Thomas. "The Image of Victoria in the Year of the Jubilee." *Victorian Studies* 31.1 (1987): 7-32.

Schneider, Ralph. "Consuming Monarchy: The Changing Public Images of Queen Victoria." Jansohn 41-66.

Singer, Milton, ed. *Traditional India: Structure and Change.* Philadelphia: American Folklore Society, 1959.

Thompson, John B. *The Media and Modernity: A Social Theory of the Media.* 1995. Cambridge: Polity, 2003.

Turner, Victor. *The Ritual Process: Structure and Anti-Structure.* Chicago: Aldine, 1969.

Twain, Mark. "Queen Victoria's Jubilee (1897)." *The Complete Essays of Mark Twain.* Ed. Charles Neider. Garden City: Doubleday, 1963. 189–199.

Zierold, Martin. "Memory and Media Cultures." *Cultural Memory Studies: An International and Interdisciplinary Handbook.* Eds. Ansgar Nünning and Astrid Erll, in collaboration with Sara B. Young. Berlin: de Gruyter, 2008. 399-408.

Notes

[1] Another big pageantry was what Alan Filewod describes as: "Perhaps the greatest peagant of all time . . . the Diamond Jubilee Naval Review at Spithead, . . . [i]n which the entire Home Fleet of the Royal Navy performed itself with a procession of 21 battleships, 53 cruisers, 30 destroyers, and 24 torpedo boats" (14).

News Media and Historical Remembrance: Reporting on the Expulsion of Germans in Polish and German Magazines

Maren Röger

On 4 February 2002, the German magazine *Der Spiegel* carried the headline "The German Titanic", referring to Günter Grass's most recent novel *Im Krebsgang* (*Crabwalk*). Grass's novel deals with the history of the *Wilhelm Gustloff*, a ship that sank on 30 January 1945 after being attacked by a Soviet submarine, leading to the death of about 9,000 people, most of them German refugees from East Prussia. It was a tragedy, a "suppressed tragedy" as the magazine claimed in its subtitle and as was repeated several times in the review by Volker Hage that followed. Hage maintained that "the bloody history of the flight from the East" was a "topic omitted by German literature". Grass, according to Hage, had dared to deal with a "taboo issue of German post-war history and literature" (184).

Only a few weeks later, the issue of the expulsion of Germans from the pre-1945 eastern territories of the German Reich dominated once again the cover of *Der Spiegel*, the most widely read cultural and current affairs magazine in Germany.[1] On 25 March, it started a series about this historical event that had affected 10 to 12 million Germans and claimed about two million victims.[2] "Only now" could one mention this topic, wrote an editorial journalist who had lived through that era in the "*Hausmitteilung*", a kind of editorial about the current issue. Once again, the coverage was staged as breaking a taboo (*Der Spiegel*, 25 Mar. 2002: 3).

Much of the German mass media argued in spring 2002 that the forced migration of the Germans during and after World War II had been omitted from reporting about the war. While dedicating their energies to revealing the alleged taboo, most of them forgot that they in fact never had forgotten to cover the topic. A glimpse at the column "50 years ago" that reviews the key topics reported on in *Der Spiegel* half a century earlier shows how present the subject of flight and expulsion had been, particularly in the first decades after World War II (see Moeller). One of the first cover pictures of *Der Spiegel* showed an expellee from the former German city Breslau in Silesia (*Spiegel* 27 Jan. 1997: 9; originally published 25 Jan 1947).

On the one hand *Der Spiegel* covers flight and expulsion from 1947 on; on the other hand the magazine claims in 2002 that remembering this historical event is a taboo— paradoxically, it seems. But a closer look leads us to a crucial question concerning the contemporary memory boom of flight and expulsion and concerning present cultural memory studies: what role do mass media play in cultural memory and, specifically, in the cultural remembrance of flight and expulsion?

This article examines how German and Polish news media have remembered the expulsion of Germans since 1989.[3] By alternating empirical results and theoretical approaches, it seeks to offer some new insights into the functions and actions of mass media in regard to "collective memory". Firstly, I will give a brief overview of the research conducted on the connection between mass media and cultural memory. Against the background of those studies I develop the (theoretical) assumptions of the article. Secondly, two important aspects of news media remembrance will be discussed. One will deal with the "occasions for remembering" in Polish and German magazines; this is a fundamental question about what type of events inspire magazines that focus on current affairs to choose a historical event as a central theme. The second part compares the different agendas as regards content, that is, the different topical "foci of remembrance" that are sometimes well-established memory sites *sensu* Pierre Nora.

1. Mass Media and Cultural Remembrance: The Current State of Research

Both cultural memory studies and research into the remembrance of flight and expulsion have paid far too little attention to the role of mass media. Central to the German academic debate on cultural memory are the studies of Jan and Aleida Assmann and therefore their concept of media has greatly influenced this field of study. Firstly, they use a very broad definition of media that includes symbols and rituals as well as audiovisual media, i.e., modern mass media. Secondly, they tend to conceptualize media one-dimensionally and reduce their role to that of mere storage (for a critical review of, among other things, the Assmanns' media concepts, see Zierold 91-96).

Though new differentiated approaches have been published in recent years, mass media and especially news media are still rather neglected. Astrid Erll recently developed an interesting model to distinguish among different groups of media and how they relate to cultural remembrance (130-37). She differentiates between products of the (mass) media— interpreted as media offerings for cultural memory—and media of remembrance (*"Gedächtnismedien"*) that influence memory processes. The latter can not only encompass almost everything—Erll lists grandparents and literature as well as stones and rivers, so that she ends up with a broad media concept (135)—but also seem to be more relevant for cultural memory studies. They are socially relevant while mass media mainly (and only?) circulate "contents of the collective memory" (139) and disappear very quickly.

In this article I argue that it is worthwhile to study the everyday action of mass media, their daily contribution to cultural remembrance. Although a single newspaper article, for example, disappears quickly and is seldom remembered in collective memory, as Erll correctly claims, it nevertheless re-writes or affirms our ideas of a historical event. Hence, mass media products do not only (passively) spread contents of the collective memory, they have to be understood as (collective) actors: by the way they screen issues they set the agenda of their readers; by repeating pictures and interpretations they create and/or perpetuate icons and historical narratives.

Regarding flight and expulsion we have surveys at our disposal that show the agenda-setting influence of mass media on remembrance. People interviewed in Germany stated that their interest in the issue was mainly aroused by media: by documentary films, by Grass's new book *Crabwalk* and by the previously cited series in the magazine *Der Spiegel* (Schäfer 86).

Ulrike Klein, in her book *Das internationale Medienereignis D-Day: Presse und kollektives Erinnern nach 50 Jahren* ("The international media event D-Day: The press and collective memory 50 years later"), suggests calling this role of the media "collective-memory setting" (196). Her study deals mainly with the question of whether print media can also create/perform a "media event". So far this term has been limited to extraordinary events on television (Dayan and Katz 4-9). But as Klein selects the fiftieth anniversary of D-Day as her case study, she also deals with the relationship between cultural remembrance and print media. She points out that there is a severe gap in our knowledge regarding the interpretation of history by mass media and their potential influence, leading her to call for a combination of media theories and studies in the field of cultural remembrance.

Only at the very end of her book does she touch on the term "collective-memory setting" and suggest it should be established as a branch of the research into "agenda-setting theory" (196). This theory, which is widely accepted and acknowledged in media studies, describes mass media as influential actors: what kind of issues are reported and how they are presented by the mass media intensively affects the public. It is not a matter of the audience all having the same perception of issues; the agenda-setting theory instead emphasizes that the media can successfully tell the public what issues to think about (not necessarily what to think about them). Therefore agenda-setting has to be understood as a political process with a high relevance for society (see McCombs and Shaw).

In the following, this article relies on Klein's attempt to combine theoretical approaches and tries to apply insights into the role of mass media in agenda-setting processes to our understanding of their role in cultural remembrance. Still, what follows is not an elaboration of media theory, specifically the agenda-setting theory, but can be understood as the theoretical background information on which the analysis is built.

2. Collective-Memory Setting I: What Inspires Polish and German Magazines to Remember the Expulsion after 1989?

Before 1989, the expulsion of Germans was rarely and not openly discussed among the Polish public.[4] With the political changes, the official censorship and thus also the prescribed terminology regarding the expulsion was abolished and new media were founded. In this article I will focus on two Polish publications that already existed during the Communist era: the magazines *Polityka* (Politics) and *Wprost* (meaning "outspoken", "direct"). While *Wprost* was founded in 1982, *Polityka* has a longer tradition. It was introduced in 1957 as one of the official party organs, but offered rather non-conformist and critical views. Now it is the most widely read magazine in Poland and is considered to be an intellectually leading publication. For Germany I selected *Der Spiegel*, also the most widely read magazine and furthermore one of the key media, meaning that opinion-makers rely on this magazine.

What are the occasions for remembering flight and expulsion for these German and Polish magazines after 1989? Which kind of events inspires German and Polish magazines dealing with current affairs to put the expulsion—an historical event—on their agenda? After all, it is more than fifty years in the past.

Jürgen Wilke, a German media studies scholar, points out that one of the crucial functions of mass media regarding history is to "re-thematize" (*"rethematisieren"*) ("Massenmedien" 24). According to him, history generally appears on the media agenda when there is an anniversary (on the general role of anniversaries in cultural remembrance, see Zerubavel)—an assumption which is supported by a study by Karin Böhme-Dürr analyzing the coverage of the Shoah in German and American magazines (248).

In the case of flight and expulsion other "occasions for remembering" besides the anniversaries can be observed. The main causes for reporting about this issue are political events connected to the historical event. *Der Spiegel*, for instance, covered thoroughly the German-Czech negotiations on a "reconciliation treaty" between 1995 and 1997. One of the controversial subjects of the bilateral agreement was the forced migration of the Sudeten Germans. In this period, the magazine published numerous articles about the issue and conducted interviews with Czech politicians, authors and historians. In 1996 alone nine articles and five interviews were published.

Although magazines are considered to be a kind of meta-news medium—Knut Hickethier, for instance, talks about their "rewriting" function, meaning that they summarize stories, focus some events under a new perspective and create new backgrounds for news (13)—it is striking that they are very closely bound to political events. But in addition to political events, artistic works or scholarly publications often also gain media coverage. *Der Spiegel* reported during the whole period under consideration here on numerous documentary films and works of fiction that deal with flight and expulsion. In 1991, for example, the magazine dedicated a three-page article to a documentary by Eberhard Fechner, a well-known German documentary filmmaker, which tells the stories of children who became orphans while they were fleeing East Prussia (*Spiegel* 25 Mar 1991: 291-293). The fate of the orphans, the so called "wolf-children" ("Wolfskinder") was also researched by the German historian Ruth Kibelka. Her book was reviewed in *Der Spiegel* (15 Jan 1996: 62-68) as well, one of the few scholarly books about flight and expulsion discussed in this magazine at all. The magazine thus concentrates more on literary criticism. In this field, many new books were reviewed. While Nobel prize-winner Grass's novel warranted a whole cover story, books by Christoph Hein, Reinhard Jirgl or Tanja Dückers were discussed in only one or two pages. One year before her book *Himmelskörper* ("Heavenly Bodies") was released, *Der Spiegel* published an interview with Dückers, even though she was still an up-and-coming author and not one of the established German writers. Since her planned novel dealt with the maritime disaster of the refugee ship *Wilhelm Gustloff*, which is also the subject of Grass' novel *Crabwalk*, she was interviewed shortly after the cover story about *Crabwalk* was published (*Spiegel* 11 Mar 2002: 236). Here we can observe a phenomenon in news media that was analyzed by (among others) the German media studies scholar Hans Matthias Kepplinger: when a mass medium declares something to be a crucial event—here the release of *Crabwalk*—it then looks for subsequent events ("*Folgeereignisse*") to extend the initial issue (125-26). Interestingly, the case of the Dückers interview shows that even a non-event in the normal logic of mass media (an unfinished, unpublished book) can become news.

As shown, besides political events, new artistic publications such as novels, films, etc. also cause the remembrance of flight and expulsion in Germany. In Poland, the academic world seems to be more inspiring for the magazines. The first article in *Wprost* that highlighted flight and expulsion as a central theme was even written by an academic. Andrzej Sakson, at that time head of a renowned research institute in Poland, presented in this article results of a "memory competition" about forced migrations during and as a result of World War II (*Wprost* 10 July 1994: 59-60). The first *Wprost* article, not published until 2000, that speaks openly about Polish guilt regarding the expulsion of Germans was also influenced by an academic publication. It was a—somewhat delayed—reaction to the anthology *Kompleks wypędzenia* ("Expulsion Complex", see Borodziej and Hajnicz) that was published in 1998 (*Wprost* 30 July 2000: 28-30).

Comparing *Wprost* and *Polityka* with regard to the "occasions for remembering", the character of *Polityka* here reveals itself to be an intellectual project as well. Particularly in the early 1990s, its journalists attended important academic conferences and reported also in these contexts about flight and expulsion. *Polityka*'s coverage of the forced migration of Germans has been greatly influenced by Adam Krzemiński, the most important member of the editorial staff of the magazine concerning this topic. Krzemiński is considered to be one of the experts on Germany and Polish-German relations and is further one of the most influential Polish intellectuals pleading for Polish-German reconciliation. Krzemiński not only follows the academic debates for *Polityka* but also, with his background in German studies, reviews German fiction as well. *Polityka* does not leave out any book by Günter Grass that deals with the historical or current German-Polish relationship. Krzemiński reviewed the 1992 publication *The Call of the Toad* (*Unkenrufe*) that sketches an ironic setting of Polish and German wheeling and dealing with former expellees after the breakdown of Communism, and he discusses *Crabwalk* as well (*Polityka* 30

May 1992: 9; and 23 Feb 2002: 56)—to name the two novels that addressed flight and expulsion as their central theme.

What can we gain from this information as regards "cultural remembrance"? Firstly and very basically, it is obvious that news media still report on flight and expulsion and its aftermath. Secondly, it is striking that the coverage is always connected with a more or less current "event": no magazine reports simply for the sake of a "conversation" on the topic. They seem to need an occasion to legitimize historical reporting. Hence, the coverage of flight and expulsion is activated by real and recent events, by political events, by book releases, by academic conferences, etc. Only in a few cases do magazines not rely on such a "real event"; in these cases they argue with a "societal event", for instance with an alleged societal need to discuss flight and expulsion right now, as many German media did in spring 2002. Regarding the (false) claim that the forced migration had been a taboo, the idea almost suggests itself that some media not only legitimize their coverage this way but also stage their own coverage as an event: if there is a taboo, it can be broken, and the very coverage itself can become an event this way. What happened in those months in German media can only be understood as a "collective media speech act": by constantly repeating that there had been a taboo, they created it and that way created a new status in cultural memory for the topic of flight and expulsion.

Nevertheless, it is true that Grass's book triggered the debate; it is often the case that works of fiction influence processes of remembrance (see Prinz). But the interactions between news media and "cultural/artistic media" should also be analyzed the other way round. On the one hand, there is the important circulation function of news media that Erll mentioned: they announce new works of fiction, documentaries, etc. (139). For instance, the publisher's press release regarding Reinhard Jirgl's book *Die Unvollendeten* ("The Unfinished"), which also addresses the expulsion of Sudeten Germans as a central theme, comprises a dozen reviews published in the most important German newspapers and magazines.[5] But on the other hand, their selection is influenced by the previous remembrance discourse, as the example of the interview with the author Dückers has shown. Remembrance events (may) lead to presence in and the attention of mass media—one of the most valuable goods in times of the "economy of attendance" in terms of Georg Franck. In fact, I would like to argue that without considering the logic of mass media cultural memory studies cannot convincingly explain waves of remembrance.

3. Collective-Memory Setting II: What Are the "Foci of Remembrance" in Polish and German Magazines?

While the first section of this article revealed the kind of events—political, literary, academic—that make the issue of flight and expulsion appear on the agenda, this part compares the German and Polish media agendas with regard to content. The article traces the different aspects of the "Expulsion Complex", which the magazines focus on from 1989 to 2000 and asks which issues of the "Expulsion Complex" they put on their agendas. Some of these different "foci of remembrance" could also be called "sites of memory", to use Pierre Nora's term.

The term "Expulsion complex" means not only the relationships between all forced migrations during and after World War II, but also the aftermath of the expulsion of Germans (regarding the aftermath in Poland, see Borodziej and Hajnicz). This includes the Germans who remained in the former eastern territories that became Polish (and Russian) territories after 1945. A basic element of the aftermath is also the "League of Expellees", a group representing the interests of expellees and their descendants (on the history of this organisation, see Ahonen).[6]

One of the important issues in the coverage of flight and expulsion in all three magazines is the German minority in Poland that "re-appeared" after the mid-1980s. During Communist rule, its existence was denied and only with the breakdown of the People's Republic of Poland could they rebuild organizations and become visible within Polish society (for an overview, see Fleming). For many Poles this "return" of the Germans was "a huge shock", as reported in *Wprost* in 1990. Numerous Poles could not believe that about half a million Germans were living in the region of Upper Silesia, writes the journalist Jerzy Przyłucki. He continues with an ironic tone: "Certainly, they endure a million Negroes [sic!], even with some thousand Eskimos, but why that many Germans?" (*Wprost* 7 Oct.1990: 22+).

The German minority inspired the Polish magazines to cover the flight and expulsion of the Germans mainly because of two aspects. One connection was the aspect of migration. Many of the "new Polish Germans" tried to emigrate to the Federal Republic of Germany (FRG), which inspired *Wprost* in particular to publish some articles offering an overview of Polish migration to Germany. These often tacitly presented the post-war expulsion of Germans as simply one of the numerous emigration waves—the compulsory nature of this migration thus being lost (see *Wprost* 12 Mar. 1989: 12-14). The other connection was the logical question about the prehistory and led directly to post-war evacuation. *Polityka* published already in 1989 numerous articles by German and Polish academics and authors who focused on the expulsion of Germans as a central theme in their work. Here we can already observe that the same event—the re-appearance of the German minority in Poland—leads to different kinds of coverage, to different perspectives on the topic in different magazines.

Both Polish magazines started to discuss in this context the internment system during the forced migration of Germans (see the definitive studies by Nowak). Regarding cultural memory studies it is striking that the media debate concentrates on one of the internment camps, the camp Lamsdorf / Łambinowice. Lamsdorf had become a memory site for both Poles and Germans, but a controversial one. It served from 1870 on as a German internment camp for war prisoners. During World War II mainly Soviets and Poles were detained there; among the prisoners were also participants in the Warsaw uprising. Hence, Lamsdorf became in Polish collective memory a symbol—but not a central one—for Polish suffering. Parts of German post-war society tried also to establish Lamsdorf as a memory site for German suffering, as it served as an internment camp for Germans in Upper Silesia from summer 1945 to autumn 1946. Especially the "League of Expellees" in the FRG tried to establish Lamsdorf as a symbol for Polish cruelty during the post-war expulsion. The group published a text by Heinz Esser, a former prisoner and doctor in the camp; the first edition was in 1968 and it later went through several editions with significant print runs. Esser made severe accusations about the number of deaths and the way the prisoners had been treated. Polish communists brushed off Esser's charges as mere propaganda and used the book as part of a campaign against the so-called revisionists, not only in the "League of Expellees", but in the whole FRG. The internment camp for Germans at Lamsdorf/ Łambinowice was hence not simply a taboo in communist Poland, but was defended against German attempts to define its meaning.[7]

With the political changes, however, the internment camps were set on the public agenda, not least by *Polityka* and *Wprost*, which published some articles on the topic in the early 1990s. One reason for the magazines to put the camp on the agenda was that representatives of the German minority often mentioned (amongst other things) Lamsdorf / Łambinowice (see, e.g., *Polityka* 24 Jun 1989: 5). As for the coverage of *Wprost* we can speak about a stimulus-response pattern at this point: a representative of the German minority chooses Lamsdorf as a central theme and *Wprost* directly reacts with an article that points out Germany's "primal guilt". To illustrate this: in 1990 a representative of the German minority—who is not further specified—says on the Polish television program "Spór o przeszłości" ("Controversies About History") that Lamsdorf is a German place of remembrance of Polish crimes against Germans. *Wprost* author Przyłucki protested vigorously against this statement. It is only a "fragment"—so the heading—of the truth to say that Lamsdorf is a place where Poles committed crimes against Germans. In the article's introduction he runs through the camp's history, starting non-chronologically with the period of World War II, when Lamsdorf was one of the biggest German prisoner-of-war camps. Thus also in the structure of the text, on a symbolic level, the "correct order" is restored (*Wprost*, 21 Jan 1990: 14-15).

Two aspects regarding medial remembrance seem to be crucial here. First, news media take an active part in remembering memory sites such as Lamsdorf. By putting this issue on their agenda they preserve their existence as a memory site. It is striking that they perpetuate the concentration on one camp—a controversial, but well-established memory site—even though there was a whole system of internment camps. This condensation is typical of cultural remembrance processes (see Rigney 18-19). As the Lamsdorf example shows, the news media advance this concentration further. Second, they are actively shaping memory sites even decades after the historical event took place. *Wprost,* for instance, is still fighting the German interpretation of the controversial memory site Lamsdorf in the early 1990s.

Lamsdorf / Łambinowice is also mentioned in *Der Spiegel* but it is not a focus of remembrance. This can mainly be explained by the fact that *Der Spiegel* mistrusts the "League of Expellees", which was one of the main forces trying to install Lamsdorf as a memory site of German suffering and Polish cruelty. This organization has quite often played a problematic role in post-war history: it fought aggressively against the *Ostpolitik* of Willy Brandt[8] and opposed still in 1989 and 1990 the Polish-German border treaty that was finally signed on November 14, 1990. *Der Spiegel* developed a merciless attitude towards the "League of Expellees" which is quite obvious in the post-1989 articles. They referred to its members mainly as "professional expellees" or "professional refugees" (*"Berufsvertriebene"* or *"Berufsflüchtlinge"*). In a commentary, Rudolf Augstein, the founder of *Der Spiegel* and its editor for decades, came up with a new name for the president of the Territorial Association of Silesia (*"Landsmannschaft Schlesien"*): he called him a "professional Silesian" and a few sentences later he characterized all of the leaders as "upright revisionists" (*"aufrechte Revisionisten"*) (*Spiegel* 17 July 1989: 22). This example was not an exception. In this period, *Der Spiegel* took a firm stand and the "League of Expellees" is depicted only in negative contexts. Not only, but also because the organized expellees cooperated with the "new Germans" in Poland, the German minority was also critically observed by the leading German magazine. In the November 1989 issue of *Der Spiegel*, Erich Wiedemann reports about one of the first minority organizations. He describes the discrimination they suffer(ed) but makes also clear that "they have to be taken with a pinch of salt" (*Spiegel* 20 Nov 1989: 196-197).

Interestingly, German media criticized the "League of Expellees" in the early 1990s almost more severely than the Polish did. After decades of Communist propaganda that presented the "League of Expellees" as a cruel organization and stereotyped their leaders as bugbears, Polish media tried to form their own image of the organization. Especially *Wprost* mentions the propagandistic distortions in many articles (see *Wprost* 18 Nov. 1990: 17-19). And the magazine opened up to the representatives of the organization: they were interviewed by *Wprost* journalists and published articles as outside contributors. The opportunity of groups to speak for themselves is interpreted in numerous discourse-analysis studies as an indicator of openness and transparency (see van Dijk). Thus, *Wprost* seems to act almost ideally. But a closer look shows that the magazine is in fact quite ambivalent because it strengthens stereotypes by the way the articles or interviews are arranged. One of the most obvious examples is an interview in 1991 with Herbert Hupka, at that time vice-president of the League and the epitome of German revisionism in Poland. The discussion dealt with Hupka's national or ethnic opinions, his explanations for the League's unpopularity in Poland and its attitude towards the German-Polish treaty—an opportunity to exchange different views on history. *Wprost*, however, chose a sensationalist title and foiled the possibility of rapprochement immediately. Above the interview text and a relatively large photograph of a grim-looking Hupka, *Wprost* placed the bold-printed headline "I don't eat Poles"—a quote from the discussion taken out of context (*Wprost* 9 June 1991: 32).

To summarize: in the first period after 1989, *Der Spiegel*, *Wprost* and *Polityka* had quite similar "foci of remembrance": regarding the content, the German minority caused the coverage of flight and expulsion and the League of Expellees was often a central theme. In 1993 and 1994, the (national) media discourses drifted away from this topic. *Der Spiegel* was no longer interested in the German minority in Poland and their interactions with the "League of Expellees". They started to focus on the German-Czech discussions about flight and expulsion. Furthermore, it is interesting that in 1993 the magazine reported on a "post-war tragedy", namely the deportation of East Prussians from Königsberg in 1948 by the new occupying power, the Soviet Union. With empathy the author describes the people´s destiny and ends with the statement that this deportation was an "ethnic cleansing" (*Spiegel* 28 June 1993: 168). In February 1995, *Der Spiegel* covered the bombing of Dresden (*Spiegel* 6 Feb. 1995: 44+), in July of that year the "children of shame", children of German women raped by members of the occupying forces (*Spiegel* 10 July 1995: 56+). Expulsion, the bombing war, rape—topics that five years later are all declared to be taboos, not least by *Der Spiegel*. The magazine seems to have a rather short memory.

Polityka kept the coverage at a high level during the entire period analyzed here. From 1989 on, the magazine offered reflective comments and pluralistic interpretations of the expulsion. Many authors, academics and politicians—from Poland and Germany—published guest articles about the issue. In 1993, *Polityka* published an article by Maria Podlasek about the forced migration (*Polityka* 15 May 1993: 17-22) which helped initiate a groundbreaking debate in Poland about the expulsion of the Germans. This debate was the first public discussion about the expulsion after 1945. Before 1989, the issue was not completely taboo but any (media) coverage was dominated by prescribed terminology. In spite of the importance of this debate it was rarely noticed by German media. In *Der Spiegel* not a single article was published about the Polish debate—a significant oversight for such a key publication, one could argue. *Wprost*, in contrast to *Polityka*, reduced its reporting about the expulsion complex in 1994 and took no part in the groundbreaking debate. Although the first article about forced migration was published in the magazine in 1994, they omitted the topic afterwards. Only in 1997 did they slowly recommence with a harsh article about the "League of Expellees" (*Wprost* 20 July 1997: 74)— the prelude for a campaign against the organization. From 1997 and 1998 on, *Wprost* did not merely focus on this lobby group in its coverage of flight and expulsion, it was downright fixated on it (see Röger 87-88).

What can we gain from this information with regard to "cultural remembrance"? By tracing the coverage of *Der Spiegel*, *Wprost* and *Polityka* between 1989 and 2000 it becomes clear that "foci of remembrance" constantly change, that the remembrance of flight and expulsion is in constant flux. For instance, attitudes towards the League of Expellees change—for the better in *Der Spiegel*, for the worse in *Wprost*. This reveals furthermore how different the "collective-memory agendas" of magazines are. This shows again that media are influential actors in the way they choose and deal with historical issues. We can observe German-Polish differences—as exemplified by the controversy over the internment camp Lamsdorf—but also discrepancies on a national level. *Polityka* and *Wprost* not only choose to focus on other issues at different points, they also present and evaluate the matter differently. This comparison shows how pluralistic the cultural memory of flight and expulsion in Poland is so that we should speak about cultural memories in the plural. Individual media outlets, such as magazines, shape our memories and support different memory communities. *Polityka* serves in the Polish discourse not least as a discussion forum where problematic historical issues such as the forced migration of the Germans are discussed.

4. Conclusion and Perspectives for Future Research

The aim of this article was to show the "historical" role of mass media that I called—following Ulrike Klein—"collective-memory setting". The main idea of the concept of "collective-memory setting" is to understand news media as important actors in shaping memory cultures. This article pointed out this function by researching the different agendas, contents, and evaluations of the magazines examined. Summarized, the results show clearly that the cultural memory of flight and expulsion is in constant flux in Poland as well as in Germany and furthermore is not homogeneous at all in either country. Hence, we should rather speak of "media remembrance" to stress the process and of "cultural memories" in the plural. And mass media should be conceptualized as one of the most important moving forces in cultural memories. They constantly affirm or change them by new coverage, by new inscriptions. After the breakdown of Communism the prescribed terminology ceased to officially exist—*Polityka*, for instance, offered its readers new perspectives on the forced migration of the Germans and also *Wprost* reported on the League of Expellees more openly than before. Hence, "transitory" news articles also have an important role in cultural memory as they contribute to the constant flux.

Therefore there is an urgent need to examine media activities with regard to cultural memory in more detail. In particular the remembrance of flight and expulsion should be analyzed in this respect since only a few studies have dealt with this subject. The role of the media is omitted by the majority or only superficially analyzed and most of the research concentrates on the German perspective. Only one study that I am aware of has examined media action in Poland and Germany with regard to the discussion about the "Centre against Expulsions" (Łada). Without integrating media theories into our accounts, I want to conclude at this point, neither German nor Polish cultural memories of the flight and expulsion of the Germans nor the recent bilateral debates about the topic can be explained.

References

Ahonen, Pertti. *After the Expulsion: West Germany and Eastern Europe, 1945-1990*. Oxford: Oxford UP, 2003.

Böhme-Dürr, Karin. "Wie vergangen ist die Vergangenheit? Holocaust-Erinnerungen in amerikanischen und deutschen Nachrichtenmagazinen." Wilke, *Massenmedien* 247-259.

Borodziej, Włodzimierz, and Artur Hajnicz, eds. *Kompleks wypędzenia*. Kraków: Znak, 1998.

Dayan, Daniel, and Elihu Katz. *Media Events: The Live Broadcasting of History*. Cambridge: Harvard UP, 1992.

van Dijk, Teun A. "Elite Discourse and the Reproduction of Racism". *Hate Speech,*. Eds. Rita Kirk Whillock and David Slayden. Newbury Park: Sage, 1995. 1-27.

Dückers, Tanja. *Himmelskörper*. 2003. 2nd ed. Berlin: Aufbau, 2003.

Erll, Astrid. *Kollektives Gedächtnis und Erinnerungskulturen: Eine Einführung*. Stuttgart: Metzler, 2005.

Esser, Heinz. *Die Hölle von Lamsdorf: Dokumentation über ein polnisches Vernichtungslager*. 1969. 2nd ed. Bonn: Landsmannschaft der Oberschlesier, 1971.

Fleming, Michael. "The Limits of the German Minority Project in Post-communist Poland: Scale, Space and Democratic Deliberation." *Nationalities Papers* 31.4 (2003): 391-412.

Franck, Georg. *Ökonomie der Aufmerksamkeit: Ein Entwurf*. 1998. München: Hanser, 2004.

Grass, Günter. *Crabwalk*. Trans. Krishna Winston. Orlando: Harcourt, 2002. Trans. of *Im Krebsgang: Eine Novelle*. Göttingen: Steidl, 2002.

---. *The Call of the Toad*. Trans. Ralph Manheim. New York: Harcourt, 1992. Trans. of *Unkenrufe: Eine Erzählung*. Göttingen: Steidl, 1992.

Handro, Saskia. "'Ein Tabuthema' oder 'Die andere Geschichte.' Zum öffentlichen Umgang mit 'Flucht und Vertreibung' in der SBZ und DDR." *Migration und Fremdverstehen: Geschichtsunterricht und Geschichtskultur in der multiethnischen Gesellschaft*. Eds. Bettina Alavi and Gerhard Henke-Bockschatz. Idstein: Schulz-Kirchner, 2004. 177-92. Schriften zur Geschichtsdidaktik 16.

Hickethier, Knut. "Das Erzählen der Welt in den Fernsehnachrichten: Überlegungen zu einer Narrationstheorie der Nachricht." *Rundfunk und Fernsehen* 45.1 (1997): 5-18.

Jirgl, Reinhard. *Die Unvollendeten.* München: Hanser, 2003.

Kepplinger, Hans Matthias. "Der Ereignisbegriff in der Publizistikwissenschaft." *Publizistik: Zeitschrift für die Wissenschaft von Presse, Rundfunk, Film, Rhetorik, Öffentlichkeitsarbeit, Werbung und Meinungsbildung* 46.2 (2001): 117-139.

Kibelka, Ruth. *Wolfskinder: Grenzgänger an der Memel.* 1996. 3rd ed. Berlin: BasisDruck, 1999.

Klein, Ulrike. *Das internationale Medienereignis D-Day. Presse und kollektives Erinnern nach 50 Jahren.* Bochum: Brockmeyer, 1996.

Kraft, Claudia. "Die aktuelle Diskussion über Flucht und Vertreibung in der polnischen Historiographie und Öffentlichkeit." *Zeitgeschichte-online.* Zentrum für Zeithistorische Forschung and Staatsbibliothek zu Berlin—Preussischer Kulturbesitz, Jan. 2004. Web. 11 Jan. 2006. <http://www.zeitgeschichte-online.de/md=Vertreibung-Kraft>.

Łada, Agnieszka. "Podobieństwa i różnice w sposobie prowadzenia debaty publicznej na temat powstania Centrum przeciw Wypędzeniom w prestiżowych dziennikach w Polsce i Niemczech." *Studia Medioznawcze* 25.2 (2006): 63-103.

McCombs, Maxwell E., and Shaw, Donald L.: "The agenda-setting function of the mass media." *Public Opinion Quarterly* 36.2 (1972): 176-85.

Moeller, Robert G. *War Stories: The Search for a Usable Past in the Federal Republic of Germany.* 2001. Berkeley: U of California P, 2003.

Nora, Pierre, dir. *Symbols: The Construction of the French Past.* Ed. Lawrence D. Kritzman. Trans. Arthur Goldhammer. New York: Columbia UP, 1998. Vol. 3 of *Realms of Memory.* 3 vols. 1996-1998.

Nowak, Edmund. *Schatten von Łambinowice: Versuch einer Rekonstruktion der Geschichte des Arbeitslagers in Łambinowice in den Jahren 1945-1946.* Opole: Centralne Muzeum Jeńców Wojennych w Łambinowicach-Opolu, 1994.

---. *Lager im Oppelner Schlesien im System der Nachkriegslager in Polen (1945-1950): Geschichte und Implikationen.* Opole: Zentrales Kriegsgefangenenmuseum Łambinowice, 2003.

Overmann, Rüdiger. "Personelle Verluste der deutschen Bevölkerung durch Flucht und Vertreibung." *Dzieje najnowsze* 26.2 (1994): 51-65.

Prinz, Kirsten. "'Mochte doch keiner was davon hören'—Günter Grass' *Im Krebsgang* und das Feuilleton im Kontext aktueller Erinnerungsverhandlungen." *Medien des kollektiven Gedächtnisses: Konstruktivität—*

Historizität—Kulturspezifität. Eds. Astrid Erll and Ansgar Nünning. Berlin: de Gruyter, 2004. 179-94.

Rigney, Ann. "Plenitude, Scarcity and the Circulation of Cultural Memory." *Journal of European Studies* 35.1 (2005): 11-28.

Röger, Maren. "Medien als diskursive Akteure: Die polnischen Nachrichtenmagazine 'Wprost' und 'Polityka' über den 'Vertreibungskomplex' 1989-2003." *Diskurse über Zwangsmigrationen in Zentraleuropa: Geschichtspolitik, Fachdebatten, literarisches und lokales Erinnern seit 1989*. Eds. Peter Haslinger, K. Erik Franzen and Martin Schulze Wessel. München: Oldenbourg, 2008. 77-91.

Schäfer, Hermann. "Zur musealen Auseinandersetzung mit der Vertreibung in Europa: Ein Projekt der Stiftung Haus der Geschichte der Bundesrepublik Deutschland." *Zwangsmigration und Vertreibung: Europa im 20. Jahrhundert*. Ed. Anja Kruke. Bonn: Dietz, 2006. 83-95.

Ther, Philipp. *Deutsche und polnische Vertriebene: Gesellschaft und Vertriebenenpolitik in der SBZ/DDR und in Polen 1945-1956*. Göttingen: Vandenhoeck, 1998. Kritische Studien zur Geschichtswissenschaft 127.

Wilke, Jürgen, ed. *Massenmedien und Zeitgeschichte*. Konstanz: UVK, 1999. Schriftenreihe der Deutschen Gesellschaft für Publizistik- und Kommunikationswissenschaft 26.

Wilke, Jürgen. "Massenmedien und Zeitgeschichte aus der Sicht der Publizistikwissenschaft." Wilke, *Massenmedien* 19-31.

Zerubavel, Eviatar. *Time Maps: Collective Memory and the Social Shape of the Past*. Chicago: U of Chicago P, 2003.

Zierold, Martin. *Gesellschaftliche Erinnerung: Eine medienkulturwissenschaftliche Perspektive*. Berlin: de Gruyter, 2006. Media and cultural memory 5.

Notes

[1] In the paper the terms "flight and expulsion", "expulsion" and "forced migration" are used as synonyms, a generally accepted convention in history writing today. On the long debate about the appropriate terms in Germany, Poland and between the countries, see Ther (88-95).

[2] In the field of history, the total number of twelve million as well as the figure of two million victims is still considered to be controversial (see Overmann).

[3] Before 1989, Polish and Eastern German media coverage of the forced migration of Germans after World War II was dominated by prescribed

terminology (regarding Poland, see Kraft; regarding the GDR, see Handro).

[4] See endnote 3.

[5] I would like to once again thank the press department of the publisher Hanser.

[6] According to the "Bundesvertriebenengesetz" the descendants of an expellee are also to be treated as if they were expellees themselves, regardless of whether they themselves were displaced persons.

[7] In the 1950s the camp commander was put on trial in Poland, but found not guilty (see Nowak).

[8] The term *Ostpolitik*, ("Eastern Politics"), describes the foreign policy of the Federal Republic of Germany under the Social Democratic Chancellor Willy Brandt. It aimed at normalizing West Germany's relationships with Eastern European nations, including Poland. In the Polish-(West) German case *Ostpolitik* comprised the recognition of Poland's western border and hence the loss of the former eastern provinces of the German Reich.

Restitution and the Dynamics of Memory: A Neglected Trans-Generational Perspective

NICOLE L. IMMLER

"History catches up with you." (Robert I.)[1]

After the Second World War, victims of National Socialism had widely different experiences with regard to the restitution of property and monetary compensation for losses.[2] In 1959, one woman wrote in a letter to the German chancellor Adenauer:

> I firmly believed that the reparation which had been offered voluntarily would be carried out with human understanding and with goodness. Instead, not only do they require the most detailed descriptions of the inhumane treatment suffered, but also one has to search through, stir up one's memories, letting this anguish once experienced come to life again, be conjured up. And then, once conjured, witnesses have to corroborate the agonies presented. Is such treatment humane? *I do not want to beg for reparation that has been offered to me* and I wish to be trusted when I testify under oath!!![3]

In 1970, an exiled German, by then an American journalist, wrote about the day he received compensation payments from Germany in a letter to the Bavarian Compensation Office: it was "an important day in my life, a day of personal satisfaction and joy". It was then that he recognized "that Germany has nothing in common anymore with the Germany of Hitler" (qtd. in Winstel 384).[4]

Since the 1960s compensation programmes have been surrounded by controversial debates: some describe them as a "second persecution" (Helga Fischer-Hübner) or "continued persecution" (Milton Kestenberg) and even demand a "reparation for the reparation" (Kurt Eissler). Others perceive them as "negotiated justice" (Elazar Barkan) or, a little less emphatically, as "imperfect justice" (Stuart E. Eizenstat). These phrases illustrate the opposing poles of a debate which was reintroduced towards the end of the 1980s, when the "forgotten victims" (such as Roma and Sintis) were "re-discovered". One of the major negotiators of restitution in Ger-

many, Walter Schwarz, concluded in 1986 that after four decades the restitution was "practically finished" (Schwarz 33), but for some groups of
victims and minorities, compensation had just begun in the late 1990s,
particularly in Austria.

In the last fourteen years, three different funds for the victims of National Socialism have been initiated by the Federal Government in Austria.
Soon these measures of property restitution and monetary compensation
will be concluded. The history and political impact of these measures have
already been broadly discussed and documented.[5] However, we know
little about the consequences of this repeated confrontation with the past
for those people involved and their families. In this article, I present first
impressions from a three-generation interview-study, exploring the impact
of restitution and compensation on people who claimed losses in their
own name or in the name of their parents or grandparents, focusing on
the consequences for the generation of survivors, the families and the
relationships between the generations.[6] This article reflects particularly
upon the meaning of restitution for the individual experience of having
been a victim of National Socialism, and its consequences for the family
and the collective memory (in interplay with memory politics). I will argue
that, firstly, the role of the media—the way it reports or neglects the issue—is key to restitution affairs, and that, secondly, restitution itself is a
"medium", a kind of mediator between the family memory and the collective memory, because it affects a specific form of recollection, either providing a bridge or deepening a gap between individual and collective
memory. I want to suggest that research on restitution could learn from
cultural memory studies (having even some practical implications), and,
vice versa, that memory studies could profit by looking at the long-lasting
effects of restitution. As Milton Kestenberg stated in the 1980s: the compensation programme influenced the life of a whole generation of survivors and their children, whether they received restitution or not (76).

I will give an overview of the historical context of restitution and outline some general problems using the example of Austria, before focusing
on the role of the mass media in influencing the public perception of restitution by looking at the discourse on "victims" in recent decades. Finally,
some examples from my interviews should show why the representation
of restitution in the media and the dynamics of family memory deserve
more attention.

1. Restitution in Austria: An Historical Overview

With the end of the Cold War, when long-suppressed memories erupted and access to documents became possible, historical commissions were established worldwide to investigate what kind of compensation had already been made to the victims of the Second World War and what still needed to be done. These commissions uncovered the huge scale of the property transfer implemented by the Nazis in conjunction with businesses, banks and insurance companies. They delivered facts, figures and percentages, thereby forming the basis for new political action. Although there had been restitution measures after the war in all West European countries, the regulations differed from country to country, were partially incomplete, and limited by deadlines. The definition of who was a "victim of National Socialism" also changed, along with the social and political context. In the atmosphere of the Cold War, it was difficult for communists, for example, to receive acknowledgement for their suffering in the Nazi camps. Especially in the former Soviet countries of Eastern Europe only a few measures were taken. It was not until the 1990s that forced labourers and concentration camp prisoners from Eastern Europe received some compensation on a larger scale. Other groups also had to wait a long time to be recognized as victims: Roma and Sintis, Jehovah's Witnesses and (only since 2005 in Austria) victims of "euthanasia" and sterilization, homosexuals and deserters from the German *Wehrmacht*.

Various events drew new attention to this matter: the discussion about the looted gold and the discovery of former Jewish bank accounts in Switzerland (as in Austria), the pressure of class action suits (*Sammelklagen*) in the US against German and Austrian firms, and the public attention to cases of art theft, for example the affair linked to the Klimt paintings. This created the impression that there was still a need to do something for the victims of National Socialism and their descendents. One particular reason for that was a changed view of the past since the mid 1980s; Austrians no longer saw themselves as the first victims of Hitler, which they had done until then, based on his aggression against Austria and its annexation (*Anschluss*) to Hitler's Germany in 1938. This self-perception, the so-called *Opfer-These*, was linked to a hesitant and reluctant attitude towards compensation: confronting themselves directly with the "real victims" would have demolished their constructed belief of being themselves victims (Walzer and Templ 24). Instead of taking "responsibility for the victims" as was done in Germany, in Austria compensation was long regarded as voluntary rather than as a matter of moral obligation (only restitution was seen as a legal obligation). Only after the Germans declared in 1952 that they would not pay for the Austrian victims, did Austria enter into the compensation negotiations, as was also demanded by the occupying powers, mainly by the US. This externalization of guilt annoyed even Adenauer at the time, who called the Austrians a stubborn people ("unbelehrbares Volk"), as reported by Bruno Kreisky in his memoirs.[7] In the end, Austria passed seven laws for restitution (1946-49) and a law, amended twelve times, providing for the welfare of victims (*Opferfürsorgegesetz*). But still the US demanded further obligations: the Austrian state treaty, the declaration of independence in the year 1955, had implemented Article 26, obliging Austria to administer property without heirs via Collection Agencies (*Sammelstellen*), selling heirless properties to pay lump sums to the survivors; it also established a fund (*Hilfsfonds*) to support those who were no longer living in Austria. These measures were supplemented by other laws regarding personal belongings (*Kriegs- und Verfolgungssachschädengesetz* 1957), life insurance policies or wrongfully collected discriminatory taxes (*Abgeltungsfonds* 1961). This is just a short summary of what had happened in the post-war decades.

It was only in the 1990s that, for the aforementioned global reasons, a revision of Austrian wartime history and its attitude towards restitution came about. One particular reason was also the need of the right-wing government in 2000 to improve its public standing and to show its credentials in being able to deal properly with the past. The former FPÖ delegate Eduard Mainoni called it a "win-win-situation".[8] To what extent these measures were also initiated by a change in the national consciousness since the mid 1980s is still being debated; whether this consciousness was affected, for example, by the commotion surrounding the case of Kurt Waldheim, former Secretary General of the UN and president of Austria from 1986, who tried to hide his controversial past; by the fiftieth anniversary of the "annexation"; or by Chancellor Franz Vranitzky's promise in 1991 to take "historical responsibility", repeated by President Thomas Klestil in 1994 in Israel. Parallel to the fiftieth anniversary of the founding of the Second Republic in 1995, the National Fund of the Republic of Austria for Victims of National Socialism was established, providing a lump-sum payment of 5,000 euros to all victims of Austrian origin, later supplemented by an additional 6,000 euros for lost household goods. Six years later, as a result of the work of the Historical Commission (1998), the Reconciliation Fund (for former forced laborers) and the General Settlement Fund (GSF), specific losses were calculated on an individual basis, and compensation was provided for losses which had been ignored over the last six decades.

2. The Ambivalent History/Nature of Restitution

Reports about current claims before the GSF show how applicants, often for decades, had already fought for restitution or compensation. Many people had already tried to get their property back during the post-war years but they often failed, because of restrictive laws or the unsystematic and restrictive application procedure. As the final report of the Historical Commission states: the restitution laws often had short deadlines, were not systematic and were bewildering owing to the many different contact points and several extensions at short notice, and the procedures took disproportionately long (Jabloner et al.). These delays meant that people often had to stay in camps until the 1950s before receiving any help. Because the authorities applied a limited interpretation of inheritance law, many properties were not returned. Often in restitution procedures people were asked to pay to get their property back. In many cases, especially when living abroad, they accepted certain payments (settlements) as compensation for the property. For all these reasons it can be said that the restitution helped to return some of the property and there was some help regarding the welfare of victims, but that many people felt they were treated unjustly, as they had to ask for what was rightfully theirs and prove their case. There were also many survivors who never applied for compensation, because they did not want to negotiate anything with the Germans or Austrians, often feeling shame or anger at the thought of taking money from the perpetrators.

Some issues were totally neglected: in Vienna alone approximately 59,000 flats were confiscated, including furnishings and all private belongings. However, only recently were people able to claim financial compensation. One successful case is Rosa Weinberger: after 60 years, she received compensation for her father's flat, which was confiscated during the Nazi era. She also got back parts of the real estate that he had owned, but only because that property was by then owned by the Republic of Austria (Lessing, Meissner and Bjalek 247ff.). In such cases, where no measures had been taken after the war, there is still the possibility of returning the real estate. In cases where properties are under private ownership today, monetary compensation is provided. However, only about 15% of its value is paid out in compensation. As the GSF only has 210 million US dollars, the whole amount has to be proportionately distributed. This procedure is not only difficult to understand, but even harder to accept. Peter Phillips, chairman of the Austrian Restitution Group in Britain, writes in an article in the *Jewish Chronicle,* entitled "My Holocaust compensation is an insult": "to be given only 15% of what is owned, after so many years, is the final insult" (33). What does it mean to see all your losses listed in detail and calculated to be worth a certain amount and to then receive just a percentage of the former value? Here even a very complex procedure seems not always to serve the greatest possible justice. This example shows the ambivalent and unjust nature of restitution. It is a rare accident that some of the properties claimed are now publicly owned and can therefore be given back. However, it must be noted that there had in fact already been many cases of restitution procedures after the war, so that about 70% of the confiscated real estate in Vienna was restituted, about 20% was part of settlements, and about 10% was not claimed and without heirs (Jabloner et al. 318-19). Many of these procedures were either forgotten or not acknowledged as such. To explain this loss or re-writing of memory, I will refer to a few examples which could offer some explanation.

It can be seen from the application forms for compensation from the GSF that knowledge of family history and what happened after 1945 is often limited because documents were lost and the war generation was unwilling to speak or its childhood memories were clouded by nostalgia. A child's imagination often misinterprets what is meant when parents say the family was "well-off". For example, instead of receiving compensation for an apartment house or a summer villa, one is confronted with the information that the family had "just" a rented flat or a rented place to spend the summer. "False" memories like these are often also shaped by present circumstances. People living in the US today can hardly imagine that most people in Vienna in the 1930s lived in rented flats. And the family itself is an important social framework of memory, which, according to Maurice Halbwachs, means that only certain things can be remembered (Halbwachs). As Halbwachs says, family memory is always symbolic and variable, concentrating only on certain aspects, events and people, and consequently reveals less about historical details than about the present and its view of the past. This is particularly obvious when children, for example, do not really try to find out about their parents' past, but rely on long-imagined pictures and attempt to have them confirmed. From this perspective, compensation procedures are sometimes disappointing, be-cause they do not correspond to certain expectations, and they also chal-lenge the family memory. This family memory seems particularly restric-tive regarding the post-war procedures of restitution. Why? To explain this, it helps to take a closer look at the construction of the narratives regarding restitution.

Gerald Aalders, an expert on Dutch restitution, made an interesting observation with respect to family memory and restitution, which I will take as the starting point for my research on the perception within family memory of the Austrian restitution measures. At a conference in Israel, at the end of the 1990s, he described the system of restitution in the Netherlands in the 1950s, admitting that the system had had its shortcomings (long legal procedures without compensation measures or emotional support), but emphasizing that the restitution had not failed and was "by no means a disgrace" (Aalders, "A Disgrace?" 402). Many people in the audience were upset, because they perceived things differently: for the public, there was no doubt that the restitution procedure was a disgrace. Additionally, they could not accept his way of using statistics and numbers to prove the restitution of about 90% of the material value. Consequently they tried to make him change his mind, ignoring the issue that his results were matters of fact and not a question of morality (Aalders, *Berooid* 9-12). Aalders tries to explain this widespread negative view of restitution today in terms of its negative image in the post-war media: in the 1950s sad stories and complaints about the issue of restitution were more "newsworthy" and represented in the newspapers, which may well have influenced private memory. But this example shows further that the whole debate seems based less upon facts than on morals. It almost seems as if family memory insists that restitution in itself is always an unsatisfying and deficient procedure.

Before I discuss this phenomenon regarding Austria, I will follow this hypothesis and take a closer look at the role of the media in presenting and communicating the subject of restitution in public. This is possibly influential in the perception of the post-war restitutions and can probably help to understand its presence in family memory today.

Restitution affairs are directly linked to the broader discourse on National Socialism. By looking at the two extremes—ignoring victims of National Socialism in the 1950s and the "victimization" culture of the 1970s—it can be shown that the discourses current in society and in the media have a strong impact on people's self-perception. As the term "victim" is such a strong attribution, whether applied to a person by him- or herself or by an external source, this historical interaction between public discourse and individual stories provides a telling background.

3. "Being a Victim": Public Discourse and Individual Stories

In the post-war decade, people in Europe as well as those in exile abroad, were primarily focused on reconstruction, keeping their eyes and minds turned to the future. In this atmosphere, victims of National Socialism were not encouraged to tell their stories. This is clearly expressed in the application forms for restitution at that time, asking for a quantification of all losses, and providing categories for certain material aspects, but not any space for the retelling of personal experiences. This "material reductionism" to individual material aspects was enforced by the use of abstract and impersonal language as well as by the separation of the procedures concerning damages to life and to property, excluding any non-material losses regarding lifestyle or education. Nonetheless, some people added lengthy reports of their whole story of persecution, inserting their life story into the files (Bajohr 56). Whereas many survivors preferred not to talk about the past in order to start a new life, others wanted to tell their sad stories and wanted to confront the public. But the public did not want to listen. Some observers interpret this as an intentional denial of the past, others as behaviour which was instrumental in stabilizing the society at that time.

Only in the 1970s, after a "psychological turn", first in the field of medicine (the understanding that trauma was a consequence of the Holocaust), and then in society, a sudden awareness of the psychological dimension of the Holocaust grew, and this created a new interest in personal life stories, whether published as autobiography or broadcast, for example in the *Holocaust* series on TV (broadcast in the US in 1978, and in Germany and Austria in 1979). "Hollywood" conventions enabled new identifications with Jewish victims (Olick 102). As a consequence, the experiences of victims became a strong image in the public's mind as survivors started to talk about themselves in these stories. As a result, Ido de Haan has noted, the language describing persecution changed: "it was no longer told to exemplify the wickedness of the Nazis, but more and more to display the lasting physical, but more importantly, psychological damage the persecution had caused among its victims. . . . Jewish survivors had no option but to talk about their experience in the psychiatric vocabulary of mental suffering" (426, 431). A strong connection between memory, image and identity is evident, and it is clear that "neither memory, nor identity can be understood as a strictly private affair" (434). In this way, the media became a mediator between the collective and the individual memory in changing people's self-expression and self-perception.

This change enabled, for example in Holland, new forms of institutionalized help for victims of National Socialism, such as benefits in the welfare system or the establishment of institutions for mental health care, thus recognizing the social dimension of trauma. In Austria the TV series *Holocaust* transformed the focus of public memory: instead of concentrating on who was responsible for the *Anschluss* and on the political problems before 1938, anti-Semitism, the murder of the Jews and the fate of the victims became part of a new, emotional narration. Contemporary witnesses and psychologists were frequently interviewees in different media, and the question of guilt was no longer addressed to political parties, but to the "Wir-Gemeinschaft", the generations of the parents and grandparents (Uhl). Austrian society felt a new sense of responsibility for the victims, linked to a new interest in family histories.

In the 1980s, with the omnipresence of the Holocaust in mass media—the so called "Schindler-effect"[9]—Jewish identity became a "symbol of universal victimhood", resulting even in a "competition of victims" with other underprivileged groups in society, a development experienced all over Europe. These discourses of victimization were one pre-condition amongst others allowing for a resumption of political negotiations concerning compensation in the 1990s. At that time, a decade began which was marked by, to use Jeffrey Olick's term, the "politics of regret". Regret he sees not as a new emotion or phenomenon, but its "ubiquity and elevation to a general principle" and to an "emblem of our times" was a new element; it framed anew the dealings with the past (Olick 14). This atmosphere fed expectations and created the need to react: in France, despite having quite a successful restitution policy after the war, if measured in terms of the percentage of property restored, the state decided nevertheless on compensation payments in the 1990s (Andrieu). Members of governments regretting in public earlier mistakes in dealing with the past became a matter of course. In a similar way the restitution of Jewish property in former East Germany became "business as usual", having lost most of its moral drama and become a matter of mere rational and legal action (Goschler and Lillteicher, "'Arisierung'" 28). But as Dan Diner has emphasized, restitution is a *dialectical* process: it is the result of recovered memory, but it also effects a revival of memory (Diner 39-40). He describes restitution as both a catalyst and a consequence of memory. This puts the focus on the trans-generational perspective and on the effects of restitution on family memory as a kind of re-mediation of memory. I will now focus on the way in which the confrontation with restitution changes the dynamics of memory and the relationships between generations.

In the following pages I will report on some impressions from my interviews conducted in Vienna in 2007/2008, with representatives from three generations, who recalled their experiences of restitution and its effects on their families—at a time when some of them were receiving their first payments from the GSF. As the interviews show, the way survivors feel about compensation varies from absolute rejection to a kind of reconciliation—and depends on their personal experiences and their life situation at the moment of the interview. Some of them still vehemently refuse it; some take the money for the simple reason that they need it, others because they are entitled to receive it; for others it means an acknowledgment of their suffering and they see it as a symbol of recognition. I will try to generalize some individual experiences by concentrating on the trans-generational dimension of restitution.

4. Interviews: Restitution, the Media, and the Dynamics of Memory

As demonstrated already, the different discourses regarding victims in society were not only a pre-condition for re-negotiating compensation, they are also a certain mindset which today influences not only how restitution is perceived and judged, but also what particular life stories are expected. Many members of the Jewish community in Vienna had already been interviewed several times about their life story, for one of the many documentaries on the Holocaust, such as the one made by the Spielberg Foundation. Nevertheless some of them are willing to contribute to the issue, motivated by the emotions this topic evokes.

(a) The Need for Success Stories: Narrative Identity

Interviewing people about what "compensation" means to them—using the familiar German term *Wiedergutmachung*—leads directly to a chain of explanations about its deficiency, connected with a rather hostile attitude. From an academic point of view, the "so-called *Wiedergutmachung*" is a metaphor for a complex and diversified topic (Goschler "Die sogenannte Wiedergutmachung"). Yet for the people involved, the term is explicitly defined by its inadequacy and shortcomings, although when—as in recent debates—it is only referred to symbolically, it is associated with recompense, which is impossible, as this would require being able to calculate an exact figure. And for some people it symbolizes a too-easy shift from "guilt into debts" (Weigel); they often perceive it as "dirty money" and refuse it, as did the husband of my interviewee Susi N. This discussion about what term to use leads directly to the center of the emotional upheaval those involved experience.

The compensation procedure in Austria started in 1995 with public campaigns: advertisements in newspapers and magazines titled "Who was a victim of National Socialism?" invited claims. The application is in itself a confrontation with a medium and its specific rhetoric: it is a sheet of questions (like that of the GSF), asking for losses in different categories (education, bank accounts, insurance policies, immovable property and movable property). For many people it meant talking about their experiences and recalling all these little details of their private belongings, how they had lost them and how they have been treated. Does this possibly advance the narrative of a failed biography or of "being a victim" instead of advancing a story of success, as generally presented by memoirs and autobiographies ("made it in spite of everything")? How is family memory influenced when confronted again with details of loss and persecution 60 years after the war? Has not each form of restitution some danger of reproducing the role of "being a victim", as this attribution is not only thereby officially acknowledged but possibly also manifested and perpetuated?

As the application form for receiving compensation is focused on losses, one could expect that to talk about restitution means to talk about losses. Yet although the interviewees knew that the topic was restitution and its effects, most of them told me the whole story of persecution, focusing on little success stories—how they managed—, a story they are more or less used to talking about. Talking about restitution is something unexpected and would mean remodeling their narrative, at least for the occasion. That also seems to be the reason why some people refused to be more specific in terms of their losses and their experiences with compensation procedures. One interviewee, Kurt Z., said: "I don't want to talk about it, because I can't live with that", and kept on talking about himself as a boy ("echter Lausbub"), a story he is used to telling. This shows an essential need for people to focus on the positive moments of life, also as a mechanism of self-protection. Here it becomes apparent how, via a narrative, a certain identity is created. Telling a story is not primarily a self-reflexive act, but is directed at an audience, at listeners, such as the fictive imagination of the "other I" ("anderen Ich"). As Jerome S. Bruner stresses, "stories are not only created to report experiences, but also and firstly to shape them" (52). Here, in the context of a narrated success story, the issue of restitution is associated with bad memories, but also with anger, as when Kurt Z. called the compensation payments " a pittance" ("Almosen"). He wants society to focus on the present and to improve the current relationships between different groups in society through knowledge and mediation, not past events and debts. In this respect he is involved in the trans-Jewish dialogue, which he sees as harmed rather than helped by compensation procedures, as it revitalizes old anti-Semitic stereotypes. Other interviewees also criticized the publicity given to restitution on television and in the newspapers, because they felt it feeds wrong ideas. Politicians, talking for years about compensation payments, give both the public and the victims wrong impressions about the amounts involved. This could also contribute to revitalizing certain stereotypes as well as certain segmentations within society, leading to the recipients' feeling once again that they are different from those around them. Accordingly some wish the procedure of compensation to be carried out in silence, not as a political act of generosity, accompanied by attention-catching speeches.

Indeed, media and restitution seem to be a difficult and ambivalent alliance. Until recently the media had never paid such attention to the issue or promoted restitution in such a concerted way. The mediatization of the Holocaust in America since the 1980s contributed to this change. One might think that a strong presence of restitution procedures in public would help show more clearly the legacy of the Nazi era and the necessity of dealing with it still today. But in my interviews I could see a certain gap between the generations. Members of the first generation seem somewhat sceptical about this particular publicity (emphasized, for example, by their near absence from media reports about restitution), while the second generation seems rather to appreciate this attention, arguing as Robert L. does that only a public discourse has the power to communicate restitution as a social process and to acknowledge its legitimacy.

(b) Restitution in the Austrian Newspapers

Reading the newspapers in Austria, how is the topic of restitution represented? In general, looking at the reports of recent years, documentation and commentary seem to be well balanced, reporting successes as well as disappointed and critical voices, but generally portraying it in a positive light.[10] Only recently, owing to the start of the commemorative year 2008, have the compensation payments received negative front-page headlines in *Die Presse* (18 January 2007), because at this point still only about half of the applicants have received any payment, after seven years of waiting for their claims to be processed. Voices calling for deadlines and for finality (*Schlussstrich*) are hardly present in the general public, mainly just in letters to the editors or in postings in internet forums. Even the tabloid *Krone* prefers to ignore most of the debates. The topic seems to be taken for granted, based upon such a consensus, to the extent that politically there seems to be nothing to win, no political profile to gain by discussing it. This does not mean that there are no negative feelings in society, which could be instrumentalized easily, as happens in cases involving the restitution of artwork, such as the Klimt case, provoking a debate about art and national identity. But in general the issue is handled seriously, without concessions to the boulevard press (cases of art restitution are an exception) but rather reflecting certain moral values and attitudes by communicating a specific picture of history. Thus, many reports in the media contrast the need for new measures with the failures of the past: they describe the property confiscations by the Nazis and then the recent measures in Austria, mostly neglecting the restitution procedures after the war. There is a certain resistance in the media to acknowledging the whole history of restitution. This raises the question: were the former measures too insignificant to become part of the collective memory? And secondly: does this abbreviated narrative in the media possibly back the common public view that nothing had happened after the war, and does this reduced perception, now reanimated and retold by the media, fix and support the view of "late justice"?

As the interviews show, the restitution procedures after the war are not very present in family memory. Few people know or recall details about their application; mostly they describe it as a disappointing experience, receiving little or nothing at all. But even those who succeeded in getting their property back often experienced it as a failed procedure, highlighting the years it took, or using summary descriptions like "we got it back, but had to sell it". For example, an elderly lady remembers very well that although the house of her parents was restored to her, she was forced to pay back the purchase price which she had supposedly received. Obviously the lawyer presumed that it was legitimately purchased from her family in the late 1930s. However, it was often the case that people had never received this money owing to enforced taxes and the reality of frozen accounts, which meant that many people had to re-buy their own property (or at least pay part of the purchase costs, reflecting the inflation rate of about 500% between 1938-50), and many could not afford it, like my interviewee Sophie R.. She was only in her twenties and had neither the knowledge nor the money to be able to keep the house and signed a settlement. The son Paul R. adds more losses: besides the house, there was also a flat, a business, and all the furniture and private belongings. His story could be summarized with his first phrase: "my family received nothing".

The lack of compensatory measures seems particularly to strengthen people's feeling that nothing had happened after the war. My interviewee Sophie R. remembers well, and has kept the letters from the administration, being confronted with "outrageous reasons" ("*haarsträubend*") why she supposedly had no right to compensation, even though she had lost her parents in the concentration camps. Her son kept the letter from the governor of Vienna from the year 1957, in which his father's application for compensation for his parents' time in a concentration camp was turned down, on the grounds that the conditions of *that* concentration camp did not correspond to those of a prison. Paul R. resumes bitterly: "they were *just* in a concentration camp, not in prison." Again, these kinds of stories, of which there are many, contribute to the perception that "nothing" had happened after the war. And if something was done, it was "half-hearted, not favorable and not recognizing one's mistake" (Robert I.).

It was less the war than the way people were treated *after* the war which was so hard to cope with. There were some restitution laws, and there were some announcements in the Austrian newspapers, but who of the scattered refugees read the Viennese newspapers, who knew what was going on at home? The government made little effort to communicate these procedures, instead it installed deadlines. Survivors remember unsuccessful letters, unfair deals, and long procedures often with no result. These individual experiences were painful, but also the post-war atmosphere was hurtful: not having been invited to come back after the war, not getting substantial support for the reconstruction or help dealing with the restitution procedures, having to deal with institutions and officials that were not long ago responsible for the "Aryanisation". Restitution was seen as a generous gesture on the part of the government, and not as a right of the victims, and was communicated in this manner by politicians and institutions. As Gustav Jellinek, negotiator for restitution on behalf of the Jewish community in Vienna (as board member of the Committee for Jewish Claims on Austria), has remarked: the people in Vienna and the Austrian press were almost without exception against restitution and many regarded the estimation of the lost properties as exaggerated (399). There were also rumors in the media about influential Jewish pressure groups in America or "Jewish capital", anti-Semitic stereotypes people believed in and which shaped the discussion. Arguments like these also indicate that the whole issue of restitution was mainly discussed along political lines, by representatives of the government or political functionaries demanding *Wiedergutmachung* for their political clientele. The conservative party (ÖVP) often insulted the exiled Jews, labeling them poor patriots, and called on them to moderate their claims, likening payments to the Jewish victims to payments to repatriates (which was also the main issue of the right-wing party VdU, demanding compensation for repatriates and for "Aryanisers", who were forced to give back property). The communist (KPÖ) and the socialist (SPÖ) parties demanded restitution and compensation especially for poor victims, rejecting them for the wealthy (Jarosch 28). With headlines accusing the upper class of having their castles restored while thousands of workers waited in vain, the communists possibly also created a discourse which again supports the individual's feeling of having lost out twice ("doppelte Verlierer"), during *and* after the war.

The discussion after the war was, in general, limited: restricted to political and Jewish victims, hardly mentioning any other groups, and very impersonal. You could mainly find reports about the restitution laws in the media; only in some party newspapers were there brief accounts of the life stories of NS victims. Perpetrators or the normal fellow citizen as an "Aryaniser" are hardly named. They are more criticized in general headlines such as "Housing Office Legalized Aryanisations"[11], an article about the poor living conditions of the Jewish victims after the war, a major issue in the media.

This social and media context seems at least as important as the question to what extent lawyers tried their best to help the survivors to reclaim their property. In face of this, people apparently often forgot what was possible in spite of this hesitant and often hostile attitude.

In this way it became manifested in family memory that the restitution had failed and was a very unsatisfying procedure, especially when compared to Germany: my interviewees often express their envy towards the neighboring country, which had acknowledged its responsibility in various ways. This dialectical perception, in all generations, is mentioned in nearly every interview. It shows how collective memory patterns such as the "victim theory" influence people's perceptions of the restitution measures, because filling in an application form for compensation does not only mean searching for historical documents to provide the exact dates of an individual or family past, but also remembering all the past struggles regarding compensation. In this respect, it means confronting private memory with the former official memory of Austria as the "first victim of Hitler", in which position it did not feel obliged to make compensatory payments. Consequently restitution itself is not part of the collective memory. This may also have contributed to the fact that the procedures after the war were often not acknowledged as such.

Here it would be interesting to know whether—in contrast to the 1950s—a strong positive picture of restitution in society and in the mass media, as it is (mainly) featured today, could aid a perception of the measures in general as positive, regardless of negative personal experiences or individual disappointments. It seems that the media and collective memory patterns have the power to influence family memory in that way.

(c) Generational Effects

What is quite striking is that to some extent restitution seems to be even more important for the second than for the first generation. One interviewee, Robert I., told me, emphasizing that this was typical for his generation (and it was repeated by others as well), that he wanted his parents to ask for restitution because they are entitled to do so. He was always criticizing the way his parents hide their Jewish identity and their defensive behaviour in general. For him restitution means giving them back some empowerment and self-confidence, because they have to be active, make a claim, confess to being Jewish. They have a certain life story and the right to ask for something. To that extent, it seems that the procedure of restitution could help to reformulate a conflict between the generations. To return to the older generation a sense of agency which they had lacked for many decades could improve communication with their children and bring the generations closer to each other. In this view, asking for restitution does not confirm the status of being a victim, but instead signals emancipation and empowerment.

This is confirmed by historical studies. They show the problems in families after the war, when, after fighting for decades, the claims for compensation were not successful. Then people often felt degraded, especially in front of their children. Their suffering was not acknowledged and because of that the family history was not officially legitimated. That often caused the children to doubt the credibility of their parents (Kestenberg 79).

This fact could explain why the second generation is often so much more emotional, demanding and argumentative about the matter of restitution. Whereas their parents sometimes even tend to see the faults of restitution within themselves (like having been too young and stupid to manage these affairs better), or explain them in terms of the unfortunate circumstances of the post-war situation, their children blame the state. Like others, Robert I. sees the post-war measures as a plain "second Aryanization". He thinks that his parents were treated with cynicism. Although he is very critical about the recent restitution—the sum is too small, "just a joke", given not from the heart but again owing only to international pressure—he sees it as a success for his parents, and as an occasion to remember what occurred.

Memory itself is an interactive and intergenerational process as later generations always take part in intra-familial communication concerning the past.[12] This can be seen, for example, in the way members of the third generation reflect upon their family past: in precise language, thoughtful explanations, with a specific political or social consciousness and a great awareness of being part of a minority. An interviewee in her mid-twenties called this the "hyper sensibility of our generation" (Linda I.). She sees a trend in her generation of going back to religion and back to their roots, explaining that it is not just important to know *who* you are, but also *where* you are living ("Es ist immer gut zu wissen wo man lebt!"). In this respect the issue of restitution means for her an opportunity to confront the public with Jewish history and the existence of the Jewish community in Austria. In general she sees restitution as important and subordinate at the same time: important for the grandmother, because she has been waiting for an official acknowledgement, and important because something is being done. Also, as for many old people, it gives her the chance to tell her story and to talk about it with official authorities. That is an opportunity that many survivors appreciate, especially when they had never told their stories within the family. But the granddaughter is also skeptical, because if one looks at the process in detail, very little is being done: the gesture is too small, giving evidence of the mindset of the politicians. Also the compensation is being paid too late and too slowly, so that many survivors do not receive the money during their lifetime. In this respect she calls it a "lose-lose situation". Also she sees a lack of seriousness; she compares filing a claim for compensation with playing some kind of lottery ("*irgendeiner Ausschreibung mitzumachen*"): "it is like a game, if you are lucky you win" (Linda I.). Another interviewee in his mid-twenties said: "one has to be honest with oneself . . . . Call it what it is: it is neither a *Wiedergutmachung* nor a compensation, only simple payments." And then he started telling the story of a thief who had been sentenced under Jewish law not to lose his hand, but to pay back twice what he had stolen: this is a painful sentence. It was similar in Germany, which had paid so much that it hurt the state tremendously and this was accepted by the victims. And he finishes: "I do not see this will in Austria." He, like many others, sees the compensation plans purely as the result of a contract which forces Austria to pay, as an obligation initiated by the American class-action suits and by international force, and not as something done out of free will.

Both young adults presented themselves—as did other members of the third generation I spoke with—as self-confident and proud of their Jewish identity and describe themselves as interested in, but not moved or disappointed by the issue; they are instead rather disillusioned, signaling no need for this acknowledgement personally. But this may be only half true. Linda's father described the measures as important for him, giving back some empowerment to his parents' generation. But for both it seems to be important that the survivors receive the money during their lifetime, so that members of the following generations can accept it as a sufficient gesture. This stresses the political dimension of these measures, independent of individual disappointments.

5. Extending the Debate on Restitution towards Memory and Media Studies

The discussion in history on the effects of restitution is rather ambivalent. According to Gerald Feldmann, the task of recompense becomes more complex and even insuperable the more we know and the more time passes by. He calls it a paradox that there is no direct relationship between the results of historical research and the ability to enact fair and effective measurements, rather the reverse (225). Lutz Niethammer, adviser to the German government on questions of compensation for forced laborers, emphasized that compensation is always only symbolic, containing elements of weak solidarity but also of insufficient recognition. He sees its importance in the sense of entering into a relationship and starting to communicate eye-to-eye (100-01). With the notion that money can only be an interim and symbolic element, he points to the danger of a "monetary valuation of memory", referring to repeated criticism leveled against the Historical Commissions that their focus was on material compensation. This criticism was taken into account on the last page of the final report of the Historical Commission in Austria, which pointed out that while there is a fundamental need for material compensation for the victims of National Socialism, the interest in converting "guilt into debts" is possibly also initiated by the desire to eliminate the guilt. They felt that one should not see restitution as a final act or as a settlement with the past (Jabloner et al. 457). However, the names of the funds already point to a difference; consider the tenor of the Austrian General Settlement Fund as compared to the German foundation "Remembrance, Responsibility and Future".

According to the literature, there is an urgent demand to reflect upon compensation *beyond* the question of money and its symbolic character. In this respect, I want to lead the debate beyond its focus on the first generation of survivors. As Margit Reiter puts it, there are no descendents in terms of memory (Reiter). What does this mean for the procedures of restitution? Amazingly the second and third generations are not really addressed in the debate (apart from having a right to make a claim), but the interviews show how involved they are in an indirect way. Consequently I would like to ask whether the thinking about restitution today is not focused too much on the first generation, and neglectful of the particular relationships in survivor families, influenced by the long-term effects of their experiences of persecution. This leads to certain sensibilities in the second, third and probably also fourth generations—although often in a very subtle form. Common to all generations seems to be the desire to see restitution as a social process, because when considered in detail, compensation often has to fail: "compensation always calls for a confrontation with the past", says applicant Robert L., "and this often makes a repetition of the victim-experience inevitable". But he sees an important civilizing effect "when a society proves that it has a memory", whether in giving back stolen property or in punishing perpetrators. Forming judgments about wrongdoings of the past he sees as an essential message for future generations: "it is an important experience for the younger generation that nothing is forgotten."

Many issues were mentioned by my interviewees that would belong to such an extended understanding of restitution and would need to imagine restitution in alternative ways, such as a serious prosecution of perpetrators, an open-minded debate about minorities and asylum seekers (like Jews from the East) or about the possibilities for descendents of persecuted families to obtain Austrian citizenship, to name just a few. I would think that a comprehensive debate about restitution and all its side-issues in the media and in society would give the affected people and their heirs the feeling of a change in society and that is what most of them would like to see—but hardly do. The media have a huge responsibility in the way they present restitution affairs, not just in their possible re-framing of the term "restitution", but also the term "victim". There are minorities in Austria like Corinthian Slovenes, partisans or deserters from the German *Wehrmacht* who were recognized officially as victims of National Socialism quite recently. But without any public campaign, this has presumably had little consequence for their family memory or for rehabilitation in public opinion, and as such nearly no effect on society as a whole. They and particularly their heirs could profit from an extended discussion which also integrates knowledge from memory studies. In this respect restitution can be seen as a medium for re-negotiating history.

References

Aalders, Gerard. *Berooid: De beroofde joden en het Nederlandse restitutiebeleid sinds 1945*. Amsterdam: Boom, 2001.

---. "A disgrace? Postwar Restitution of Looted Jewish Property in the Netherlands." Brasz and Kaplan 393-404.

Andrieu, Claire. "Zweierlei Entschädigungspolitik in Frankreich: Restitution und Reparation." Goschler and Ther 108-33.

Bailer-Galanda, Brigitte. "Die Rückstellungsproblematik in Österreich." Goschler and Lillteicher 161-188.

Bajohr, Frank. "'Arisierung' und Restitution: Eine Einschätzung." Goschler and Lillteicher 39-59.

Barkan, Elazar. *The Guilt of Nations: Restitution and Negotiating Historical Injustices.* New York: Norton, 2000.

Brasz, Chaya and Yosef Kaplan, eds. *Dutch Jews as Perceived by Themselves and by Others: Proceedings of the Eights International Symposium on the History of Jews in the Netherlands.* Leiden: Brill, 2001.

Bruner, Jerome S. "Vergangenheit und Gegenwart als narrative Konstruktionen." *Erzählung, Identität und historisches Bewusstsein: Die psychologische Konstruktion von Zeit und Geschichte: Erinnerung, Geschichte, Identität.* Ed. Jürgen Straub. Frankfurt am Main: Suhrkamp, 1998. 46-80.

Diner, Dan. "Restitution and Memory—The Holocaust in European Political Cultures." *New German Critique* 90 (2003): 36-44.

Diner, Dan and Gotthart Wunberg, eds. *Restitution and Memory: Material Restitution in Europe.* Oxford: Berghahn, 2007.

Eissler, Kurt. "Die Ermordung von wievielen seiner Kinder muß ein Mensch symptomfrei ertragen können, um eine normale Konstitution zu haben?" *Psyche* 17 (1963): 241-291.

Eizenstat, Stuart E. *Imperfect Justice: Looted Assets, Slave Labor, and the Unfinished Business of World War II.* New York: Public Affairs, 2003.

Feldmann, Gerald D. "Der Holocaust und der Raub an den Juden: Eine Zwischenbilanz der Restitution und Entschädigung." Goschler and Ther 225-237.

Fischer-Hübner, Helga. "Das Leiden an der 'Wiedergutmachung': Begegnungen mit Betroffenen." Fischer-Hübner and Fischer-Hübner 41-153.

Fischer-Hübner, Helga, and Hermann Fischer-Hübner, eds. *Die Kehrseite der 'Wiedergutmachung': Das Leiden von NS-Verfolgten in den Entschädigungsverfahren.* Gerlingen: Bleicher, 1990.

Forster, David. *'Wiedergutmachung' in Österreich und der BRD im Vergleich.* Innsbruck: Studien-verlag, 2001.

Goschler, Constantin. "Die sogenannte Wiedergutmachung: Deutschland und die Verfolgten des Nationalsozialismus." *Die Auschwitzleugner: 'Revisionistische' Geschichtslüge und historische Wahrheit.* Eds. Brigitte Bailer-Galanda, Wolfgan Benz and Wolfgang Neugebauer. Berlin: Elefanten, 1996. 273-296.

Goschler, Constantin and Jürgen Lillteicher, eds. *'Arisierung' und Restitution. Die Rückerstattung jüdischen Eigentums in Deutschland und Österreich nach 1945 und 1989*. Göttingen: Wallenstein, 2002.

Goschler, Constantin and Jürgen Lillteicher. "'Arisierung' und Restitution jüdischen Eigentums in Deutschland und Österreich: Einleitung." Goschler and Lillteicher 7-28.

Goschler, Constantin and Philipp Ther, eds. *Raub und Restitution: 'Arisierung' und Rückerstattung des jüdischen Eigentums in Europa*. Frankfurt am Main: Fischer, 2003.

de Haan, Ido. "The Postwar Community and the Memory of the Persecution in the Netherlands." Brasz and Kaplan 405-435.

Halbwachs, Maurice. *Les cadres sociaux de la mémoire*. 1925. Paris: Albin Michel, 1994.

Herbst, Ludolf and Constantin Goschler. *Wiedergutmachung in der Bundesrepublik Deutschland.*. München: Oldenbourg, 1989.

Holocaust. Screenplay by Gerald Green. Dir. Marvin J. Chomsky. NBC, 16-19 Apr. 1978. Television.

Jabloner, Clemens et al. *Schlussbericht der Historikerkommission der Republik Österreich: Vermögensentzug während der NS-Zeit sowie Rückstellungen und Entschädigungen seit 1945 in Österreich: Zusammenfassungen und Einschätzungen*. Wien: Oldenbourg, 2003. Vol. 1 of *Veröffentlichungen der Österreichischen Historikerkommission*.

Jarosch, Michaela. *Die Berichterstattung österreichischer Tageszeitungen zur Restitution von während der NS-Herrschaft entzogenem (jüdischen) Eigentum in den Zeiträumen 1945 bis 1948 und 1997 bis 2000*. Diplomarbeit U Wien, 2002.

Jellinek, Gustav. "Die Geschichte der österreichischen Wiedergutmachung". *The Jews of Austria: Essays on their Life, History and Destruction*. Ed. Josef Fraenkel. London: Vallentine, 1967. 395-426.

Kestenberg, Milton. "Diskriminierende Aspekte der deutschen Entschädigungspraxis: Eine Fortsetzung der Verfolgung". *Kinder der Opfer, Kinder der Täter: Psychoanalyse und Holocaust*. Eds. Martin S. Bergmann, Milton E. Jucovy and Judith S. Kestenberg. Frankfurt am Main: Fischer, 1995. 74-99.

Lessing, Hannah M., Renate S. Meissner and Nina Bjalek. "'Wir können nur anklopfen, wo die Tür offen ist'—Der lange Weg zu Anerkennung und Entschädigung." *Ausgeschlossen und entrechtet*. Ed. Verena Pawlowsky and Harald Wendelin. Wien: Mandelbaum, 2006. 241-274.

"Mainoni: 'Win-win-situation.'" *Der Standard* 22 Sept. 2006: 9.

Niethammer, Lutz. *Ego-Histoire? Und andere Erinnerungs-Versuche*. Wien: Böhlau, 2002.

Olick, Jeffrey K. *The Politics of Regret: On Collective Memory and Historical Responsibility*. New York: Routledge, 2007.

Phillips, Peter, "My Holocaust compensation is an insult." *Jewish Chronicle* 26 Oct. 2007: 33.

Pross, Christian. *Wiedergutmachung: Der Kleinkrieg gegen die Opfer*. Frankfurt am Main: Athenaeum, 1988.

Reiter, Margit. *Die Generation danach: Der Nationalsozialismus im Familiengedächtnis*. Innsbruck: Studien, 2006.

Rosenthal, Gabriele, ed. *Der Holocaust im Leben von drei Generationen: Familien von Überlebenden der Shoah und von Nazi-Tätern*. Giessen: Psychosozial, 1997.

Schwarz, Walter. "Die Wiedergutmachung nationalsozialistischen Unrechts durch die BRD." Herbst and Goschler 33-54.

Thonke, Christian. *Hitlers Langer Schatten: Der mühevolle Weg zur Entschädigung der NS-Opfer*. Wien: Böhlau, 2004.

Uhl, Heidemarie. "Von 'Endlösung' zu 'Holocaust': Die TV-Ausstrahlung von 'Holocaust' und die Transformation des österreichischen Gedächtnisses." *Zeitgeschichte-online*. Zentrum für Zeithistorische Forschung and Staatsbibliothek zu Berlin—Preussischer Kulturbesitz, n.d. Web. 18 Nov. 2008. <www.zeitgeschichte-online.de/Portals/_Rainbow/documents/pdf/uhl.pdf>.

Walzer, Tina and Stephan Templ. *Unser Wien: 'Arisierung' auf österreichisch*. Berlin: Aufbau, 2001.

Weigel, Sigrid. "Shylocks Wiederkehr: Die Verwandlung von Schuld in Schulden oder: Zum symbolischen Tausch der Wiedergutmachung." *Fünfzig Jahre danach: Zur Nachgeschichte des Nationalsozialismus*. Eds. Sigrid Weigel and Birgit R. Erdle, Zürich: Vdf, 1996. 165-192.

Welzer, Harald, Sabine Moller and Karoline Tschuggnall, eds. *"Opa war kein Nazi.": Nationalsozialismus und Holocaust im Familiengedächtnis*. Frankfurt am Main: Fischer, 2002.

Winstel, Tobias. *Verhandelte Gerechtigkeit: Rückerstattung und Entschädigung für jüdische NS-Opfer in Bayern und Westdeutschland*. München: Oldenbourg, 2006.

Notes

[1] I quote interviewees from my research project (see endnote 6) anonymously, to protect their privacy.

[2] In this text I will use the term "restitution" to refer to measures both of compensation (for losses) and restitution (of goods). The English term "restitution" has a comprehensive character (see: www.worldjewishcongress.org), similar to the German term "Wiedergutmachung", but is more neutral. "Wiedergutmachung" was commonly used for all such procedures after the Second World War.

[3] "Ich glaubte fest, dass die freiwillig angebotene Wiedergutmachung mit menschlichem Verständnis und Güte ausgeführt würde. Stattdessen verlangt man nicht nur bis ins Kleinste gehende Beschreibungen der erlittenen menschenunwürdigen Behandlung, man muss in seinen Erinnerungen suchen, wühlen, um diese erlittenen Qualen wieder aufleben zu lassen und sie beschwören. Aber einmal beschworen, müssen Augenzeugen die dargestellten Qualen bekräftigen. Ist eine solche Behandlung menschenwürdig? *Ich möchte nicht um die angebotene Wiedergutmachung betteln* und ich möchte, dass man mir glaubt, wenn ich an Eides statt aussage!!!" (qtd. in Pross 199).

[4] "Dies sei für ihn 'ein großer Tag im Leben, ein Tag der Freude und Genugtuung', da er erkenne 'dass die Deutsche Bundesrepublik nichts mehr mit Hitlerdeutschland gemein hat'" (Winstel 384).

[5] Since the 1980s much literature regarding restitution has been published from national and comparative perspectives. On Germany, see Fischer-Hübner and Fischer-Hübner; Goschler and Lillteicher; Herbst and Goschler; Pross; and Winstel. On Austria, see Bailer-Galanda et al. and Jabloner. See also Diner and Wunberg.

[6] This article is based upon the 25 interviews which I have conducted so far, carried out in Vienna in 2007 and 2008. The project is titled *The afterlife of restitution* and covers a case study in Austria with a sample of about five three-generational families, later extended to the Netherlands, England, the US, Argentina, Israel, Slovakia and Poland. Participants include both persons who claimed compensation from the General Settlement Fund (GSF), and also some who refused these measures. All are contacted through the Austrian embassies, the Jewish Communities or other institutions which deal indirectly with post-war effects. The qualitative interviews are biographically oriented, hence narrative but problem-oriented and guided, focusing on the experiences with restitution and compensation. My starting question is: "How were you confronted for the first time

with the topic of compensation?" People then tell me their experiences embedded in an initial overview of their family history. Further topics are communication concerning the past and how it is dealt with within the family, the meaning of public memory and the current attitude towards restitution.

See <http://www.oeaw.ac.at/kkt/projekte/odg/odg_r_e.html>.

[7] See Thonke 67. This comparison should not conceal the fact that there was also huge resistance in the German government and society to the *Wiedergutmachung*, as well as practical difficulties, for example the fragmentation of the measures caused by the existence of four occupying powers and different rules in each section. But whereas restitution in Germany was completed in the mid-1950s, in Austria thousands of cases were not yet dealt with, and often delegated to the courts. In addition, only a 25% reduction in ability to work due to the persecution was needed in order to receive a pension, while in Austria 50% or 70% was required. For more details, see Forster 222.

[8] Eduard Mainoni said to a journalist of *Der Standard*: "Wir konnten auf der einen Seite die politisch-moralische Verpflichtung einlösen—und auf der anderen Seite einem Ruf entgegensteuern, der uns Freiheitlichen angehaftet hat." In speaking to the political scientist Oliver Geden, he was even more precise: "Dass wir, besser als die Sozialdemokraten, die Wiedergutmachung an Zwangsarbeitern umgesetzt haben, fällt in diesen Bereich. Da haben wir uns eingekauft. . . . Damit haben wir im Prinzip auch den Rücken frei gehabt gegenüber den jüdischen Organisationen" ("Mainoni").

[9] Coined by Elan Steinberg, the executive director of World Jewish Congress, in an interview about the reasons for the revitalized debate about NS goods. See Thonke 153.

[10] The information is based upon an interview with Jürgen Schremser and Peter Stadlbauer, both media coordinators at the GSF, as well as on a survey of articles published in 2007 and 2008 in Austria.

[11] "Wohnungsamt legalisiert Arisierungen." *Arbeiterzeitung* 14 Jan. 1946. Qtd. in Jarosch 97.

[12] The framework for my research project is the current debate about "Familiengedächtnis". For the narratives of successors of victims and perpetrators from a three-generation perspective see particularly Rosenthal and the results of the project "Tradierung von Geschichtsbewusstsein" at the Center for Interdisciplinary Memory Research at the Institute for Cultural Science in Essen, including Welzer, Moller and Tschuggnall. See also the generation-studies of Dan Bar-On.

Literary Icons and the Religious Past in the Netherlands: Jan Wolkers and Gerard Reve

JESSEKA BATTEAU

Up until the 1950s, Christianity had in many ways dominated Dutch society. Like in other European countries, the influence of the church could be felt in many domains, ranging from the social to the political and cultural. Yet, during the 1960s and 1970s, the social function of religious practice diminished and church attendance dropped dramatically (Becker and Vink 11). In this period the Protestant and Catholic churches lost many of their members, and traditional Christian values were challenged time and again in the media, the arts, and the political arena. During these years, the autobiographical work of particular Dutch authors—who either portrayed the Christian past of their youth, or engaged with traditional Christian discourse in a novelistic manner—served as triggers and reference points for some of these debates.

Considering the dramatic social and cultural changes during the 1960s and 1970s, the question arises of how these literary engagements with a rapidly disappearing traditional religious culture have contributed to the collective memory of the religious past in the Netherlands. By looking closely at the work, reception, and reputation of two key Dutch authors, following them from their debut up to the present, I have tried to distinguish particular "patterns" within the complex relations between literary texts, artistic reputation, religious memory, and the dynamics of collective memory. As we shall see, the fact that both authors have become cultural icons in the Netherlands cannot be explained by the content of their literary work alone. It was the *reciprocal* relationship between the past represented in their work and the development of their public persona via (mass) media which led to their iconicity. Because of this, both have not only acquired a literary reputation but have come to represent a certain *era* in the Dutch religious past, as well as a certain *stance* vis-à-vis traditional religious practice.

1. Collective Memory and Religious Memory

Since I am interested in the way literary representations play a role in the collective memory of the religious past, I will first need to explain how these two domains can be defined in light of each other. First of all, religion, or religious culture, can be interpreted as *one specific form of collective memory*. The definition I use for traditional religious culture comes down to the following: it is made up of particular mnemonic communities which consider themselves to be part of a *lineage* of believers and which sustain this self-image through the repeated observance of rites and the material anchoring of religious belief in texts, artefacts, buildings, and holy sites.[1] Furthermore, these communities wish to distinguish themselves explicitly from the secular domain. They present themselves, and are experienced by those outside of the religious chain of memory, as separate, different from the secularized world.

Maurice Halbwachs explains that the essential difference between the sacred and the profane is realized in material surroundings. A believer will visit a sacred place or building because he knows that it is there that he will experience communality and will be able to reconstruct communal memories, as he has done many times before. The stabilizing function of memory sites seems to be especially important for religious groups, since these groups operate on the assumption that the essence of the group has stayed the same through the ages (*La mémoire* 162). However, the fact that religious tradition is anchored in the spatial and material creates the possibility for *others*, outside of these religious mnemonic communities, to encounter, contemplate, and reflect on these texts, artefacts, buildings, and holy sites. Since they do not adhere to the collective memory of a religious group, they are free to ascribe new meaning to these media and locations.

And here Pierre Nora's distinction between *lieux de mémoire* and *milieux de mémoire* is of use. *Milieux de mémoire*, in his understanding, are those environments where memory is "unselfconscious, commanding, all-powerful, spontaneously actualizing, a memory without a past that ceaselessly reinvents tradition, linking the history of its ancestors to the undifferentiated time of heroes, origins, and myth" (8). According to Nora, most "real" or "natural" environments of collective memory, which characterized archaic societies, have been eradicated by democratization, mass culture, and globalization. In modern times, instead of living "within" memory, we can at best simulate the experience by reflecting on or commemorating the past with the help of artificial and constructed sites of memory, that is: *lieux de mémoire*.

Now, contrary to Nora's suggestion, I am convinced that the communal experience of non-reflexive memory is still existent within religious communities in modern times. When one takes Halbwachs's analysis of religion into account, it could be argued that believers *do* live within memory, a memory which sustains their self-image as a group following in the footsteps of their forebears, and do *not* experience a distance between themselves and the past when contemplating religious texts, artefacts, and sites. The difference between *milieu* and *lieu* lies in the *function* and *experience* of the shared remembrance. For believers a church building or the Bible may (re-)establish a sense of continuity, but for others, non-believers, religious culture has become part of their cultural heritage; a past to be remembered, reflected upon (or forgotten) in various ways. For these people a church building, the Bible, rituals, and religious discourse can function as *lieux de mémoire*.

If traditional religious culture is described as a *form* of collective memory practice, it could be said that during the 1960s and 1970s this particular form of memory was under pressure in the Netherlands. Yet, this does not mean that those leaving or already outside of the Christian communities collectively suffered from religious amnesia. As I hope to show in what follows, the literary texts and the Dutch authors engaging with the religious past ensured that Christianity, albeit no longer functioning as a *milieu de mémoire*, was still collectively remembered as an integral part of the Dutch past and thus gained the status of *cultural heritage*.

2. Literary Texts and Artistic Reputation

Others working in the field of cultural memory have already established that literary texts can in various ways function as triggers, reference points, or as subjects of collective memory. Aleida Assmann's introduction of the notion of *kulturelle Texte* raised our awareness of the way canonical or founding texts can serve as media of the shared remembrance of a distant past (241). Astrid Erll in turn has pointed out that it is not only canonical literature which functions as a medium of collective remembrance, but that any fictional text circulating within society can potentially be actualized as a medium for collective remembrance of the past and thus function as a "collective text" (*Kollektives* 158). Ann Rigney calls attention to the dynamic and complex processes informing the interplay between literary texts and our collective dealings with the past. Not only do literary texts, as "display texts", have the capacity to be re-discovered by future generations, but they can also stabilize particular versions of the past;

recycle existing memories; or become objects of recollection in themselves, to name just a few of the possibilities ("Plenitude"; "Portable").

But what I would like to add to these insights is that the potentiality of
a literary text functioning as a medium of collective remembrance is
largely dependent on the reputation of the author and the medial exposure
of his person and work. The case studies of Jan Wolkers and Gerard Reve
reveal that the reputation of the author and his presence in the media
greatly influence whether or not his work is actualized as a medium of
collective memory. Public appearances on television and radio, interviews
in the press, articles, and prizes: all these instances ensure that his work
remains part of the public debate. One must therefore not only look at the
author's engagement with the past in his literary work and the reception of
this engagement by readers over time, but one must also reckon with the
fact that the author *himself* might become the subject, in more than one
way, of collective remembrance.

In other words, an author may not solely become an icon of a particular *literary* style, subject, or movement, but can function as a *figure of memory*
by representing a culturally relevant era or a particular social transformation. The term "figure of memory", or *Erinnerungfiguren*, was introduced by
Jan Assmann. Assmann's choice of the term "figure" (which he prefers to
Halbwachs's "memory images") calls attention to the fact that figures of
memory do not only have an iconic dimension, but that they can also
function in the formation of culturally shared narratives (38). It seems that
collective memory can also adhere to an *historical figure*, preserving his or
her name, as well as that which he or she represents.

Whether or not an author becomes a figure of memory or icon depends a great deal on the dynamics of reputation. Cultural sociologists
G.E. Lang and K. Lang distinguish between two forms or phases in an
artist's reputation. The first, recognition, has to do with the position of the
artist in his or her own field of art, be it painting, writing, cinema, etc: "the
esteem in which 'insiders' hold the artist". When an artist becomes known
and valued outside the boundaries of this domain, the authors speak of
"renown": "Renown represents a more cosmopolitan form of recognition,
measured by how well the artist is known beyond the network of professional peers" (6). This form of reputation, say Lang and Lang, lifts the
artist into the position of "lasting stardom" and is accompanied by the
formation of myths and legends. Interestingly, these authors describe
how, once an artist has become valuable property, "greatness begins to
feed on itself". In other words, the publicity surrounding his new work or
publication turns the artist into a persona until "anything touched by his
or her hand comes to have value for that reason alone" (7).

Still, renown, as described by these authors, does not account for the phenomenon that an artist's name comes to represent *more* than just his or her talent and work. My definition of a figure of memory or icon would rather entail *renown plus X*. To put it differently, the artist can start to stand for more than just him- or herself: his reputation moves *beyond* his artistic achievements and he comes to represent an era, ideology, or even a cultural transition. How long this remains "fixed" after his death is perhaps dependent on the factors mentioned by Lang and Lang: the amount of work that has been left to posterity, the accessibility of this work to the public, and the interest (be it artistic or economic) of those surviving in keeping his memory alive. Yet the survival of religious icons such as Reve and Wolkers also depends on the extent to which they continue to serve as ideological/symbolic reference points for contemporary culture.

3. The Christian *Milieux de Mémoire* in the Work of Jan Wolkers and Gerard Reve

The comparison between the authors I have selected as my examples, Jan Wolkers and Gerard Reve, is of interest for several reasons. First of all, they are of the same generation. Born in the early 1920s, both grew up in the 1930s and were adolescents during the Second World War. Both authors reached their pinnacle of renown in the late 1960s and 1970s and are to this day celebrated as accomplished artists in the Netherlands. In both cases, the religious dimension of their literary work was enforced by its remediation in other media, as well as by their own public appearances. Over time, both authors have become icons in more ways than one, representing not only a particular corpus of texts but also a certain *stance* vis-à-vis "traditional religiosity", as well as a certain *era* in the Dutch cultural and religious past.

Furthermore, the cases of Wolkers and Reve have shown that once an author starts to function as a figure of memory his literary texts can even become superfluous. The public might never have read a novel by the author in question yet still share in the collective memory of the past the author and his work represents. What makes the comparison between the two particularly interesting is the fact that both engage with the traditional religious *milieux de mémoire* in two fundamentally different ways.

(a) Jan Wolkers (1925-2007): Experiential Memory and Cultural Memory

In the first case, Jan Wolkers, we are dealing with an ex-protestant author who published quite a number of autobiographical stories and novels in the early 1960s about his orthodox childhood. As an adolescent, the author left the church, and his perspective on his past is that of someone traumatized by a repressed youth and by the fear of God and death installed in him by his father. These early stories were thought to be a bitter reckoning with a past which ceaselessly haunts him, and of which he cannot rid himself. Jan Wolkers had started out as a sculptor and painter yet remained relatively unknown to the public until his literary debut in 1961. By 1965, Wolkers had definitely achieved recognition in the literary scene. In a mere four years, he had already produced two volumes of short stories, two novels, and two plays, all of which are situated within or deal with the Christian *milieu*. The critics unanimously praised Wolkers's talent for rendering his past in a direct and visceral manner.

Wolkers's reputation underwent a transition after the publication of the novel *Turks Fruit* ("Turkish Delight") in 1969, the story of a passionate and tragic love affair between an artist (the alter ego of Wolkers himself) and a young girl, Olga. At the time the public was shocked by the explicit and down-to-earth treatment of sexuality, and the publicity surrounding the publication resulted in the expansion of Wolkers's reputation outside of the literary arena and into the public sphere. In the years that followed, Wolkers became a well known media figure, thanks to his presence in a wide range of radio and television programmes as multi-talented artist and champion of the sexual revolution. After his death in 2007, it became clear that this fame had ensured the survival of the orthodox protestant past he himself had experienced and which had figured in his early work. The articles and obituaries appearing in the news media indicated that, although Wolkers had "moved on" from the Christianity of his youth, the traditional religion practiced in the 1930s and 1940s as depicted in his early prose had remained an integral part of his public image.

Jan Wolkers's early prose quite literally represents the orthodox protestant *milieu de mémoire* of the 1930s and 1940s: it gives detailed descriptions of the material surroundings of this environment, its strict rules and taboos, and the appearance and behaviour of those belonging to the religious community. It also incorporates the religious discourse of this community within the literary text. His stories and novels are typical examples of memory conveyed in the "experiential mode", which, as Astrid Erll explains, is characterised by a personal voice, "generated by a first-person narration . . . ; the use of the present tense or of lengthy passages focalised by the 'experiencing I' in order to convey embodied, seemingly immediate experience; and the description of many details of everyday life ...." ("Re-Writing" 166).

Although Jan Wolkers's work represents an actual past, the commemorative mode within Wolkers's texts cannot simply be equated with what Jan and Aleida Assmann would call "communicative memory", that is, the form of collective memory "concerned with making sense in the more limited horizon of social communities (like family, friends or colleagues)" (Erll, "Re-Writing" 181). The reason for this is that the autobiographical experiences related in Jan Wolkers's narratives are explicitly structured upon Biblical stories, imagery, and metaphors. Significant personal experiences—which are told and retold story after story—are almost always based upon (or triggered by) a biblical theme or narrative.

A good illustration of this can be found in Wolkers's autobiographical novel *Terug naar Oegstgeest* ("Oegstgeest Revisited"), which appeared in 1965. *Terug naar Oegstgeest* was received as a narrative that explicitly and quite straightforwardly deals with Wolkers's personal protestant past and *milieu*. It was thought to be the "key" to all his previous work: the original and "true" version of the fictionalized events related in Wolkers's earlier stories and novels. Importantly, many critics stressed the *historical* value of *Terug naar Oegstgeest*, since it revealed life as it was in the 1930s and 1940s. In the novel, all of the childhood memories are dominated by the repressive influence of the author's severely orthodox protestant father and the harsh life of the 1930s and 1940s. The narrator relates the experiences of the boy Jan in a large, poor family of eleven siblings; his fear of his father, God, and death; his sadistic compulsions; and his love for his older brother. The narrator recalls the inevitable deterioration of the family-business, which does not survive the economic crises and the Second World War. The novel is also the story of the *town* Oegstgeest, in which the elementary school of the narrator, the insane asylum and the surrounding luxury villas figure as the décor of the narrator's youth. The childhood memories are alternated with chapters in which we see the narrator, now a grown man, revisiting various places in his home town and registering the slow eradication of his youth, the tragic disappearance of people and buildings. In a paradoxical way *Terug naar Oegstgeest* is both a monument to Wolkers's youth and a chronicle of the decay of this same past.

The following passage illustrates how the novel on the one hand renders a literal personal past, yet at the same time preserves Biblical stories and images for posterity. The narrator relates how his father's slaughtering

of rabbits invested in him the fear that he himself would be sacrificed like
Isaac in the Old Testament:

> Ik dacht weer aan onze konijnen vroeger die mijn vader moest gaan slachten
> omdat dat de enige keren waren dat zijn kroost, talrijk als het zand der zee,
> voldoende vlees te eten kreeg. . . . En de angst dat ik zelf daar omgekeerd in de
> schuur zou komen te hangen als een bloederig gevild konijn. Want mijn vader
> zei, toen hij uit de bijbel voorgelezen had van Abraham die zijn zoon Izaäk moet
> offeren, dat als hij van God het bevel zou krijgen om mij te offeren, hij dat zeker
> zou doen. (172)
> I was reminded of our rabbits in the past which my father had to slaughter be-
> cause those were the only times his offspring, numerous as the sands of the sea,
> would be given enough meat to eat. . . . And the fear that I myself might end up
> hanging up side down in the shed like a skinned and bloody rabbit. Because my
> father had said, after reading aloud from the Bible about Abraham sacrificing his
> son Isaac, that if God would command him to sacrifice me, he would certainly
> do so. (Trans. Jesseka Batteau)

There seem to be two modes of remembrance operating at the level of the
text: on the one hand the Biblical imagery and language are literally "experienced", in the sense that the protagonist is submitted to hours of Bible-reading and suffers under his Bible-quoting father; yet on a different
level these references are part of what Jan and Aleida Assmann would call
"cultural memory", in the sense that the Biblical stories and language are
the product of tradition, passed down from generation to generation.
When one considers the *effects* of the Biblical language and images in
Wolkers's stories on its readers, one could say that they are confronted
with two modes of remembrance: an *experiential mode* which foregrounds
the lived past of the 1930s and 1940s—a past which readers of that generation can identify with—and a *cultural mode* in which the Bible is re-
established as a *kultureller Text* in the collective memory.

From the very beginning the autobiographical nature of Wolkers's
stories was a central theme in the reception of his work and the formation
of his public persona. It is probably for this reason that his stories were
experienced as a window onto the religious past of the 1930s and 1940s.
The fact that personal experiences and events were retold time and again
(in fiction *and* in interviews on television and radio) facilitated the creation
of a familiar Wolkers-"landscape" in the minds of his readers and critics.
Terug naar Oegstgeest, in a way, "sealed the reality deal" in tracing all the
familiar episodes back to the author's youth. The novel was not only the
key to all Wolkers's previous autobiographical fiction, but also started to
function as the prototype of a certain *genre* in the Netherlands, i.e. that of

autobiographical (ex-protestant) prose. This in turn facilitated the novel in becoming iconic for a particular religious past.

It is perhaps for this reason that—of the two modes of remembrance present within his work—it was the experiential mode that captivated his audience for a long time. Yet now, after his death, it seems as if the public focus has shifted to the *cultural* mode within his work, that is, the Bible as the main inspiration behind Wolkers's literary production, thus pushing the actual past of the 1930s and 1940s into the background. Importantly, the obituaries also focus on how Wolkers has been one of the main "promoters" of the Bible in the Netherlands. Many of the articles appearing after his death quoted a relatively long passage from an essay he wrote in 1988 and read to an audience of international authors at the *Buchmesse* in Göteborg: *Op de vleugelen der profeten* ("On the wings of the prophets"). In this essay Wolkers explains (once more—this too is a recurring theme in the Wolkers-reception) how the Bible influenced his work and how his father's Bible-reading acquainted him with all forms of sin, violence, and sexual corruption, as well as with a wide range of literary genres and strategies:

> Hoe had ik kunnen uitleggen dat mijn voorbereiding op het schrijverschap eigenlijk al prenataal een aanvang had genomen. Dat ik tot aan mijn zeventiende jaar, toen ik het ouderlijk huis verliet, niet zozeer gesticht was door een heilsboodschap als wel onderwezen in de wetten van de dramaturgie, poëzie en dialoog. Dat ik dagelijks als het ware gebombardeerd was met een scala aan literaire vormen. Dat de kennis van de mens me met de paplepel ingegoten was. En dat ik, nog voordat mijn eerste baardharen doorkwamen, al alles afwist van incest, sodomie, moedermoord, het gruwelijkste bedrog en het verachtelijkste verraad. Maar dat ik toch door de bijbel, door die godsdienstige opvoeding, geleerd heb om alles zinvol te beleven en te zien. Om te leven alsof ik onsterfelijk ben terwijl ik me terzelfder tijd van bewust ben dat ik ieder moment in de aarde weg kan zakken om voor eeuwig tot stof terug te keren. (Wolkers 1990, 13-14)
>
> How could I have explained that the preparation for my existence as a writer had in fact begun before I was born. That until my seventeenth birthday, when I left my parental home, I had not so much been edified by the gospel as been instructed in the rules of drama, poetry and dialogue. That in a way I had been bombarded daily with a wide range of literary forms. That I had absorbed what I knew about humankind with my mother's milk. And that even before the first hairs appeared on my chin, I knew everything about incest, sodomy, matricide and the most gruesome deceit and the most despicable betrayal. But that despite all this, the Bible and my religious upbringing have taught me to experience and see everything as significant. To live as if I were immortal, but with the realisation that I might sink into the earth at any moment and return to dust forever. (Trans. Jesseka Batteau; based on Adrienne Dixon's translation in Wolkers 1990)

For many a reporter and critic, this passage revealed the essence of Wolk-ers's literary drive and inspiration. The fact that the Dutch Minister of Education, Culture and Science, self-confessed atheist Ronald Plasterk, ended his speech at Wolkers's—nationally broadcast—memorial service with an extensive quote from the Bible-book Ecclesiastes is another indi-cator of how Wolkers's person and work now function (and perhaps will function in the future) as a reminder of the Christian heritage in the Neth-erlands.

(b) Gerard Reve (1923-2006): Practicing and Historicising Religious Tradition

In the case of the second author, Gerard Reve, we are confronted with a very different engagement with the religious past. Unlike Wolkers, Reve came from a non-religious, communist background. He was the first Dutch author to publicly discuss his homosexuality, and his conversion to Catholicism in 1966 was met with great controversy. Reve's work has been described as an ironic combination of extremes: a heterogeneous mix of highly baroque and Biblical rhetoric, mundane language, banal details, and erotic scenes. At the time, Reve's dealings with the Christian religion were thought to be blasphemous, especially since they were com-bined with quite explicit homo-erotic fantasies. Unlike Wolkers, Reve did not depict a Christian community of the past literally, but appropriated the discourse, rituals, and even materials central to the collective remem-brance practiced within the Roman Catholic *milieu de mémoire*, refashioning and refiguring this memory practice within his literary texts and public appearances into his own highly idiosyncratic religion.

Reve is most famous for his debut, the semi-autobiographical novel *De avonden* ("The evenings") of 1947. Yet, despite the fact that Reve was immediately recognised as an important author by the literary scene, it took almost two decades for his breakthrough to the general public to become a reality. This occurred when his first two volumes of autobio-graphical letters appeared: *Op weg naar het einde* ("Towards the End") in 1963 and *Nader tot U* ("Nearer to Thee") in 1966. In these so-called letter-books, the Dutch public was for the first time confronted with the novel incorporation and appropriation of Biblical and liturgical language which would later be considered Reve's trademark. The letters are loosely struc-tured upon the author's memories, fantasies, and daily experiences. The beginnings and endings often follow the style of Paul's letters in the New Testament or are fashioned according to the Biblical psalms.

Importantly, both letter-books were accompanied by extra-literary publicity which foregrounded Reve's idiosyncratic approach to Christianity. The first book appeared in the year of his television debut, in which he gave a frank interview about his homosexuality and religious interests on a well-known and broadly watched literary programme *Literaire ontmoetingen* ("Literary encounters") (Reve, Interview). The second letter-book *Nader tot U* (1966), which I take as my example here, became narrowly associated with the two years (from 1966 to 1968) in which he fought out a lawsuit with the state, after being accused of blasphemous writing. Two similar passages, one published in the literary journal *Dialoog* (Reve, "Brief"), and one included in the second letter-book mentioned above, formed the basis for the trial. The lawsuit—which Reve won in the end—was followed closely by the media at the time. The following passage formed the heart of the controversy and was subjected to extensive interpretation in the court trials. Reve describes how God visits him in the form of a donkey and how, in an upsurge of love and devotion, he takes the incarnated God to bed:

> En God Zelf zou bij mij langs komen in de gedaante van een éénjarige, muisgrijze Ezel en voor de deur staan en aanbellen en zeggen: 'Gerard, dat boek van je—weet je dat Ik bij sommige stukken gehuild heb?' 'Mijn Heer en mijn God! Geloofd weze Uw Naam tot in alle Eeuwigheid! Ik houd zo verschrikkelijk veel van U,' zou ik proberen te zeggen, maar halverwege zou ik al in janken uitbarsten, en Hem beginnen te kussen en naar binnen trekken, en na een geweldige klauterpartij om de trap naar het slaapkamertje op te komen, zou ik Hem drie keer achter elkaar langdurig in Zijn Geheime Opening bezitten, en daarna een presentexemplaar geven . . . met de opdracht: *Voor de Oneindige. Zonder Woorden.* (*Nader* 112-113)
> And God Himself would visit me in the form of a one-year-old, mouse grey Donkey and stand in front of my door and ring the bell and say: 'Gerard, that book of yours—did you know that I wept while reading some of its passages?' 'My Lord and my God! Praised be Your Name to all Eternity! I love You so immensely,' I would try to say, but would burst out crying halfway, and start to kiss Him and pull Him inside, and after a colossal climb up the stairs to the little bedroom, I would possess Him three times in a row and at great length in His Secret Opening, and afterwards give Him a free copy.... of my book with the dedication: *To the Infinite. Without Words* (Trans. Jesseka Batteau)

As is evident from the above, Reve combines the high rhetoric of the Bible with the banal and carnal, using capital letters in an ironic manner.

Another good example of Reve's appropriation and refiguration of Biblical discourse can be found in the beginnings and endings of his letters in *Nader tot U*. In this case, the beginning reminds the reader of the way the psalms are introduced in the Old Testament. We see here how Reve combines the banal—the protagonist's ironic description of his extreme intoxication—with a style which follows the opening of a Psalm as well as the content of the Psalms themselves:[2]

> Greonterp, 17 maart 1965. In de stilte van de nacht. Uit de diepten. Nadat hij 9 dagen aan één stuk door gedronken had, maar je kon niets aan hem zien. Een zang, terwijl hij naar de duisternis ging. Voor de orkestmeester. Een nachtlied. Een lied van overgave, want op U wacht ik, en op U alleen, o Eeuwige. (59)
> Greonterp, 17 March 1965. In the quiet of the night. From the depths. After he had drunk for 9 days straight, but you wouldn't have guessed it. A song, while he went into the dark. For the director of music. A night song. A song of surrender, because for You I wait, and for You alone, o Everlasting One. (Trans. Jesseka Batteau)

The reactions to Reve's letter-books and the lawsuit show that many readers noted the duality of his use of Biblical language. Many critics voiced the idea that, beneath the surface of Reve's ironic appropriation of Biblical discourse, the author was in fact authentic in his search for God and stated that he confessed to a highly personal and individual belief, a belief not found within the existing Christian churches, a typical "Van-het-Reve-belief", which only he understood and had a right to make fun of. Others reflected on the fact that although traditional Christians might suffer under Reve's literary work, he had in fact contributed to the cultural liberalisation of the Netherlands, in which everyone is free to confess to his own religion. A much-heard comparison, also voiced by professional "witnesses" during the trial against Reve, was that the author's view of God is a mystical version (and thus legitimate) of the Christian God. All Reve did, they argued, was adapt the mystical language to twentieth-century imagery and metaphors, as well as to the sexual mores of the 1960s.

Those discussing Reve's work all seemed to agree on the ironic effect, achieved by placing traditional religious discourse in a banal context. Although the operation of displacing religious discourse does and is perhaps intended to have an ironic or defamiliarizing effect, it could also be said that this displacement broaches the boundaries of Christian mnemonic communities. When Reve's work is interpreted as an appropriation of the mnemonic material of a particular religious group—that is, as an appropriation of the language used to preserve a sense of continuity—the issue becomes far more charged than a mere literary interpretation would have it. Reve's engagement with traditional religious discourse and materials found its culmination during a spectacular multi-media event, held in 1969, in honour of his winning a prestigious Dutch literary prize, the P.C. Hooftprijs. The whole celebration took place in a neo-Gothic, Roman Catholic church and was broadcasted on national television, thus making

Reve accessible to an audience unfamiliar with his literary work. The event, which elicited a mass response from Dutch viewers and reminded many a critic of a Medieval carnival, has since been broadcasted many times and become part of the canon of Dutch television. The evening, which started off with an interview with Reve, was filled with playful and camp performances by a variety of artists, including a juggler and a magician. Much time was reserved for a session in which the audience was allowed to address Reve directly and question him about his literary work, his views on religion and the nature of his public persona. Several of Reve's remarks during the interview and in response to the questions from the audience—such as, 'the Catholic Church is a puppet show' and 'the Bible is God's word, except for those passages I dislike and ignore'—have become engrained in the collective memory of the Dutch. The end of the program was filled with the playing of the hymn "Nearer my God to thee" by a local marching band—a clear reference to Reve's second letter-book. The image of the procession slowly leaving the church, while Reve and his partner—hand in hand in front of the altar—wait to fall in line with the music band, had a powerful effect on the audience, since it seemed to sum up the essence of Reve's person and his iconic significance for Dutch culture (*Gerard Kornelis*).

While his literary work merely engaged with traditional religious *discourse*, Reve's presence in the church—seated in front of the altar, surrounded by icons and relics—resulted in the very concrete appropriation of the *material surroundings* of these religious groups. The effects of Reve's use of religious discourse and symbols in his work and public appearances imply that more is at stake here than a mere intertextual play on Christian symbols and narratives. Reve's work seems to have a paradoxical effect. On the one hand his engagement with Christian heritage can be interpreted as a *display* or *performance* of religiosity, while on the other hand he also effectively *historicizes* Christianity. To put it differently, Reve's literary texts and public performances staged the transition of the religious *milieu* into a *lieu de mémoire*.

An indication that Reve indeed fulfils this function as a cultural icon in the Netherlands can be derived from the fact that his dealings with religious tradition are still used in current debates on the place of Islam in the Netherlands. The media used Reve and his "donkey case" as an example of modernity's victory over religious orthodoxy and conservatism after the ritualistic murder of Dutch filmmaker Theo van Gogh by a Muslim extremist in 2003. And even more recently, some have argued that Muslim equivalents of figures like Reve and Wolkers are needed for the liberation from orthodoxy of the Muslim community in the Netherlands (Peters "Zal Reve"; van der Lee).

4. Conclusion

In conclusion, let me recapitulate the various constellations in the dynamics between literature and the collective remembrance of the religious past in the Netherlands. First of all, the authors I have discussed both engage with one *form* of collective memory, namely the remembrance practiced in the religious *milieux de mémoire*. In Wolkers's case this environment is represented as an actual past. Yet, at the same time, the structuring presence of the Bible in his work seems to perpetuate this traditional form of religious remembrance. In contrast, Reve appropriates the material surroundings of the religious *milieux de mémoire*, such as the Bible, the Church, and Christian rituals and places these in a new, often shockingly banal, context. One could say that Reve's work opens up the door for new forms of engagement with the Christian legacy.

Yet another dimension can be added to these observations. While the authors Wolkers and Reve both engage with a form of collective memory, their iconicity implies that they *themselves* (their work *and* person) have become the subjects of collective memory in the Netherlands. Although their engagements with religious memory differ in many ways, they do nevertheless fulfil a similar function in the Dutch perspective on the past: both have become figures of memory for the *pastness* of the religious *milieux de mémoire* (in the case of Jan Wolkers this entails an historical past of the 1930s and 1940s, whereas Reve *historicizes* the rituals and materials sustaining the religious *milieux*), but at the same time represent a *continuation* of religious tradition as cultural heritage. Although Wolkers and Reve might not have been *actors* in the religious and cultural transformations in the Netherlands during the 1960s and 1970s, they have given voice and form to certain values and perspectives on the religious past, providing "images" powerful enough to graft themselves into the collective memory of the Dutch.

References

Assmann, Aleida. "Was sind kulturelle Texte?" *Literaturkanon—Medienereignis—kultureller Text: Formen interkultureller Kommunikation und Übersetzung*. Ed. Andreas Poltermann. Berlin: Schmidt, 1995. 232-44.

Assmann, Jan. *Das kulturelle Gedächtnis: Schrift, Erinnerung und politische Identität in frühen Hochkulturen*. Munich: Beck, 1997.

Becker, J.W., and R. Vink. *Secularisatie in Nederland: 1966-1991: de veranderingen in opvattingen en enkele gedragingen*. Rijswijk: Sociaal en Cultureel Planbureau; 's Gavenhage: VUGA, 1994.

Bouwman, Roelof. "De 10 Wijze Lessen Van Jan Wolkers." *HP/De Tijd* 26 Oct. 2007: 28-34.

Erll, Astrid. *Kollektives Gedächtnis und Erinnerungskulturen: Eine Einführung*. Stuttgart: Metzler, 2005.

---. "Re-Writing as Re-Visioning: Modes of Representing the 'Indian Mutiny' in British Novels: 1857-2000." *Literature and the Production of Cultural Memory*. Eds. Astrid Erll and Ann Rigney. Spec. issue of *European Journal of English Studies* 10.2 (2006): 163-85.

Gerard Kornelis van 't Reve in de Allerheiligste Hartkerk. By Gerard van het Reve, Hans Keller and H.A. Gomperts. Dir. Charles Leeuwenkamp. Public Television. VPRO, Hilversum, 23 Oct. 1969. Television.

Halbwachs, Maurice. *La mémoire collective*. 1950. Paris: PUF, 1968.

---. *On Collective Memory*. Ed. and trans. Lewis A. Coser. Chicago: U of Chigaco P, 1992.

Hervieu-Léger, Danièle. *La religion pour mémoire*. Paris: Cerf, 1993.

---. *Religion as a Chain of Memory*. Trans. Simon Lee. Cambridge: Polity, 2000.

The Holy Bible: New International Version: Containing The Old Testament and the New Testament. 1978. 2nd ed. Grand Rapids: Zondervan, 1983.

Lang, Gladys Engel, and Kurt Lang. *Etched in Memory: The Building and Survival of Artistic Reputation*. Chapel Hill: U of North Carolina P, 1990.

Lee, R. van der. "Gun Moslims de tijd om te wennen aan Nederland." *Brabants Dagblad* 14 Aug. 2007: A14.

Nora, Pierre. "Between Memory and History: 'Les Lieux de Mémoire'." *Memory and Counter-Memory*. Ed. Natalie Zemon Davis and Randolph Starn. Spec. issue of *Representations* 26 (1989): 7-24.

Peters, Arjan. "Rauw en teder: Als er geen dood was kon je driehonderd jaar worden: Postuum Jan Wolkers." *De Volkskrant* 20 Oct. 2007: 22+.

---. "Zal Reve Ook Later Nog Worden Gelezen." *De Volkskrant* 10 Apr. 2006: 3.

Reve, Gerard Kornelis van het. *De avonden.* Amsterdam: De Bezige Bij, 1947.

---. *Op weg naar het einde.* Amsterdam: Van Oorschot, 1963.

---. Interview by H.A. Gomperts. *Literaire ontmoetingen.* Public Television. AVRO, Hilversum, 11 Dec. 1963. Television.

---. "Brief aan mijn bank." *Dialoog: Tijdschrift voor homofilie en maatschappij* 1 (1965): 20-21.

---. *Nader Tot U.* 1966. Amsterdam: Van Oorschot, 1969.

Rigney, Ann. "Portable Monuments: Literature, Cultural Memory, and the Case of Jeanie Deans." *Poetics Today* 25.2 (2004): 361-96.

---. "Plenitude, Scarcity and the Circulation of Cultural Memory." *Journal of European Studies* 35.1 (2005): 209-26.

Vullings, Jeroen. "De gulle reus die met beelden smeet: In Memoriam Jan Wolkers, de schrijver." *Vrij Nederland* 27 Oct. 2007: 62-66.

Wolkers, Jan. *Terug Naar Oegstgeest.* 1965. 3rd. ed. Amsterdam: Meulenhoff, 1965.

---. *Turks Fruit.* Amsterdam: Meulenhoff, 1969.

---. *Op de vleugelen der profeten: On the Wings of the Prophets.* Trans. Adrienne Dixon. Deventer: Ypse Fecit, 1990.

Zerubavel, Eviatar. *Time Maps: Collective Memory and the Social Shape of the Past.* Chicago: U of Chicago P, 2003.

Notes

1 See Zerubavel 4; Hervieu-Léger, *Religion* 125; Halbwachs, *On Collective* 119. Of course, this does not mean that religious memory presents a greater degree of unity or coherence than other mnemonic practices. Halbwachs insists on the highly conflictual nature of religious memory, the main cause lying in the opposition between "a rational, dogmatic type of memory and memory of a mystical nature" (Hervieu-Léger, *Religion* 126). But even so, there is always a deliberate drive to achieve a unified and homogenous memory.

2 See for example the opening of Psalm 18: "For the director of music. Of David the servant of the Lord. He sang to the Lord the words of this song when the Lord delivered him from the hand of all his enemies and from the hand of Saul" (*Holy Bible,* Ps. 18. Introd.).

Index of Names

Notes on Contributors

Laura Basu studied American Literature at the Universities of Sussex and California at Berkeley, obtained her MA in Film Studies from the University of Amsterdam in 2005 and is currently working on a PhD as part of the "The Dynamics of Cultural Remembrance" project at Utrecht University. Her research concerns the development of the memory of nineteenth- century outlaw Ned Kelly, over time and across media, and its role in shaping Australian identity.

Jesseka Batteau obtained an MA in Literary Studies from Utrecht University and is now completing a PhD at the Research Institute for History and Culture at Utrecht University. Her project is entitled *Icons of the Religious Past: Dutch Authors and the Collective Remembrance of the Christian Past in the Netherlands 1945-2005.*

Paulus Bijl studied Dutch Literature at the Free University in Amsterdam and Literary Studies at Utrecht University and UCLA. He is currently working on a PhD as part of the "The Dynamics of Cultural Remembrance" project at Utrecht University. His research brings together memory studies, visual culture and (post)colonial studies; it provides a social biography of a group of photographs from 1904 of atrocities committed in the Dutch East Indies (contemporary Indonesia), examining the way in which they became visible at different moments in their century-long circulation.

Simon Cooke obtained an MA from University College London and is currently a doctoral student at the International PhD Programme in Literary and Cultural Studies at the Justus Liebig University, Giessen. His research is on "Voyages of Recovery and Renewal: Travellers' Tales of Wonder in Contemporary Literature – Chatwin, Naipaul, Sebald". He co-authored, with Ansgar Nünning and Richard Humphrey, *Essential Study Skills for Bachelor / Master in British and American Studies* (Klett, 2007). He has published numerous academic articles and reviews (in a.o. *The Art Newspaper* and *Culture Wars*) relating to travel writing and to modern and contemporary culture.

Richard Crownshaw is a lecturer in the Department of English and Comparative Literature, Goldsmiths, University of London. He has published widely on Holocaust memory in literature, museums and memorials. In particular, he is the co-editor of *The Future of Memory* (forthcoming with Berghahn) and author of *The Afterlife of Holocaust Memory in Contemporary Literature and Culture* (forthcoming with Palgrave Macmillan). Current and future research projects include work towards monographs on transcultural memory and on catastrophe in the American literary imagination from colonialism to the present day.

Astrid Erll is Professor of English Literature and Culture at the University of Wuppertal, Germany. Her many publications include an introduction to cultural memory studies (*Kollektives Gedächtnis und Erinnerungskulturen*, 2005) and a study of the medial representations of the "Indian Mutiny" (*Prämediation—Remediation*, 2007). Together with Ansgar Nünning she is general editor of the series *Media and Cultural Memory/Medien und kulturelle Erinnerung* (MCM, de Gruyter, since 2004) and co-editor of *Cultural Memory Studies: An International and Interdisciplinary Handbook* (2008). She has also published studies on film and cultural memory (*Film und kulturelle Erinnerung*, ed. with Stephanie Wodianka, 2008) and literature and cultural memory (*Literature and the Production of Cultural Memory. European Journal of English Studies* 10.1, ed. with Ann Rigney, 2005).

Meike Hölscher is a graduate in Modern Languages from the Justus-Liebig University, Giessen. Having worked as a research assistant at the Centre for Memory Cultures at Giessen on a collaborative project on memory cultures of the British Empire, she is currently pursuing doctoral research in the International PhD Programme in Literary and Cultural Studies, Giessen. Her research is focused on the thematization of memory and remembrance in the literature of English modernism.

Andrew Hoskins is Associate Professor in Sociology at the University of Warwick, UK, founding Principal Editor of the journal *Memory Studies*, founding Co-Editor of the journal *Media, War & Conflict* and Director of the Warwick Centre for Memory Studies (www.memorystudies.net). He leads the AHRC-funded project "Conflicts of Memory: Mediating and Commemorating the 2005 London Bombings" and is co-editor with John Sutton of the Palgrave book series: *Studies in Memory*. His latest book is co-edited with Joanne Garde-Hansen and Anna Reading: *Save As . . . Digital Memories* (2009); his current work *War and Media: The Emergence of Diffused War,* co-authored with Ben O'Loughlin, will be published in 2010.

Nicole L. Immler took her doctorate at the University of Graz and worked from 2005-2009 at the General Settlement Fund for Victims of National Socialism' in Vienna. She is currently carrying out research at the Austrian Academy of Science (Institute for Culture Studies and History of Theatre), in cooperation with the research programme, "The Dynamics of Cultural Remembrance" at Utrecht University. Her present project is about restitution and its significance for familial and cultural memory. Her book *Das Familiengedächtnis der Wittgensteins* is forthcoming, as is an edited collection on *The making of... Genie: Mozart und Wittgenstein*.

Verena-Susanna Nungesser is a graduate of the University of Constance and currently pursuing a doctorate in the International PhD Programme in Literary and Cultural Studies at the Justus Liebig University, Giessen. Her research is on transformations of the "Bluebeard"-Fairy Tale in Anglo-American fiction and film. She has published several articles, including studies of female gothic fiction, historical metafiction and cultural ecology, and the functions of intercultural literature.

Ann Rigney is Professor of Comparative Literature at Utrecht University, Netherlands, and director of the research programme "The Dynamics of Cultural Remembrance". She is author of *The Rhetoric of Historical Representation: Three Narrative Histories of the French Revolution* (1990; 2002) and *Imperfect Histories:The Elusive Past and the Legacy of Romantic Historicism* (2001). She is co-editor of *Historians and Social Values* (2000; with Joep Leerssen), *Literature and the Production of Cultural Memory. European Journal of English Studies* 10.1 (2005; with Astrid Erll) and *Het leven van teksten* (2006; with Kiene Brillenburg).

Maren Röger is a PhD student in history at the University of Giessen, She has published on the German cultural memory of the national-socialist past, with articles in the *Lexikon der "Vergangenheitsbewältigung" in Deutschland*, ed. by Thorben Fischer and Matthias Lorenz, 2007); on the remembrance in Polish media of the expulsion of Germans after the Second World War, with an article in *Diskurse über Zwangsmigrationen in Zentraleuropa*, ed. by Peter Haslinger, K. Erik Franzen, Martin Schulze Wessel, 2008); and on the widely-read Polish tabloid *Fakt,* with articles in *Inter Finitimos: Jahrbuch zur deutsch-polnischen Beziehungsgeschichte* (4, 2006), and *Studia Medioznawcze* (1, 2009).

David Wertheim is director of the Menasseh ben Israel Institute for Jewish Cultural and Social Studies in Amsterdam. Schooled in intellectual history at the Hebrew University of Jerusalem, the University of Amsterdam and Utrecht University, his research focuses on the cultural and historical significance of the reception of iconic figures. For his PhD, he studied the Jewish reception of Spinoza in Weimar Germany and as a post-doc in the Utrecht project 'The Dynamics of Cultural Remembrance", he worked on the international reception of Anne Frank.